LIGHT RAYS:

JAMES JOYCE AND MODERNISM

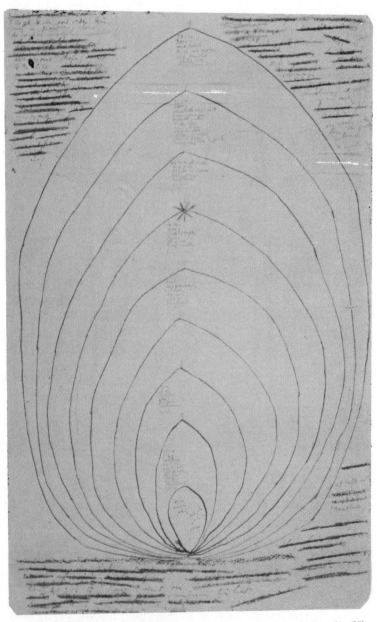

A page of manuscript by James Joyce showing one chapter design for Ulysses. Reprinted by permission of the Society of Authors, literary representative of the Estate of James Joyce.

LIGHT RAYS:

JAMES JOYCE AND MODERNISM

PROLOGUE BY
RICHARD ELLMANN

Morris Beja
Robert Boyle
Zack Bowen

Morton P. Levitt
Fritz Senn
Leslie Fiedler

Hugh Kenner

EDITED BY

HEYWARD EHRLICH

New Horizon Press Publishers
New York

Library of Congress Cataloging in Publication Data
Main entry under title:

Light Rays: James Joyce and Modernism

  1. Joyce, James, 1882-1941—Criticism and interpreta-
tion—Addresses, essays, lectures. 2. Joyce, James,
1882-1941—Influence—Addresses, essays, lectures.
I. Ehrlich, Heyward.
PR6019.09Z7125 1984   823'.912   84-14783
ISBN 0-88282-302-7

Contents

Preface

Heyward Ehrlich

Whether we are Joyce readers, Joyce lovers, Joyce mavens, or Joyce freaks, all of us seem to drift into one of several distinct species: Type One, the academic specialist who teaches, writes about, or gives papers on Joyce; Type Two, the cultural generalist interested in philosophy, psychology, sociology, technology, or aesthetics; Type Three, the practicing writer, musician, painter, or worker in other arts; or Type Four, the amateur fan, collector, or occasional newspaper reviewer. By some unwritten law each Type keeps to itself, well away from the others.

This book, for example, began as a public conference for the 1982 Joyce centennial on the Newark campus of Rutgers University. Most of the participants were professors (only *one* exception), and while it was as impressive a centenary gathering as any in the United States the platform lacked a cultural generalist, a practicing artist, or a spokesman for the amateur. No doubt I exaggerate. But the same gap was visible in some two dozen other centennial symposia, special magazine issues, or other proceedings published to honor Joyce in eighteen countries on five continents. Thus there seemed a ready opportunity for someone to bring the various Joyceans closer together in meaningful dialogue. Accordingly, this book joins the Newark conference not only to several explorations of Joyce in the cultures of philosophy, psychology, music, art but also to a few practical examples of Joycean experimental writing, music, and art.

Coincidence, that noble Joycean organizing principle, seems to have made a few concerns recur in this book. *Ruby: The Pride of the*

Ring, the popular, semi-erotic novel imagined by Joyce, keeps pop-
ping up (we reproduce an illustration from it), reminding us of fun-
damental connections between Joyce's use of popular culture,
sexuality, and creativity. When classicism, modernism, and post-
modernism seem to alternate and rotate in our perception of Joyce,
the effect, like motion within a dynamo, still creates inexhaustible
energy. The sister arts, lately seen in siblinghood that may be half-,
step-, Siamese, or even transsexual, take on vital new meaning in
novements surrounding Joyce cubism to structuralism.

In the Prologue, Richard Ellmann inquires into the degree to
which Joyce's intense, unconventional opinions about the church,
politics, and women are reflected in his writings. In the Introduction, Heyward Ehrlich places Joyce in the context of the various
strands of modernism and gathers lists of poeple interested in and
influenced by him. Joycean light rays next branch forth, a sevenfold
candelabra of Popular Culture, Experimental Literature, the New
Sexuality, Contemporary Philosophy, Neoteric Psychology, Avant
Garde Music, Abstract Art.

Joyce used popular books, music hall songs, and sentimental literature in unexpected ways. Leslie Fiedler points out that Joyce often
began with pornographic and sentimental materials in popular literature relished by a mass audience. Yet Joyce took such stuff, as Zack
Bowen shows, only to transform it into new coalescences of very
different qualities.

As everyone knows, Joyce the modernist re-used Homer the classicist. But much of what we think we know may not be so. As Hugh
Kenner forces us to see, Leopold Bloom in *Ulysses* is many other
characters or people more than he is Ulysses. And when we read
"classicist" Homer with care, as Fritz Senn does, we may discover
some very "modernist" exploitations of both narrative and language. Looking at contemporary literature, along with Ihab Hassan,
Finnegans Wake emerges as the flood gate which released much of
the culture of recent postmodernism.

Sexuality in Joyce takes obscene or sacred forms. Leopold Bloom,
famous cuckold, is often accused of impotence, perversion, and
worse; yet, as Morris Beja argues, an exact reading of the text shows
Bloom's sexuality to be more normal and more human than is often
realized. Matters of gender for Joyce are always closely connected
with creativity, and as Father Robert Boyle suggests, Joyce gradually
moved from associations of the creator as masculine into a view of
the deity as feminine.

Although Joyce was a writer, not a philosopher, his writings place him squarely in the international camp of those modernist novelists who never forgot their essential humanism, as Morton P. Levitt reminds us. At the same time, as Margot Norris shows, Joyce moves in the same direction as much twentieth century philosophy, linguistics, and structuralism. And his explorations of dream life in *Finnegans Wake*, rich in implications for history, myth, and comedy, are synthesized suggestively in the probing psychology of Norman O. Brown.

Four creative artists (among many) who were stimulated by Joyce were Henri Matisse, Ad Reinhardt, John Cage, and Pierre Boulez. The presence and absence of parallels between Matisse's illustrations and Joyce's text are fascinatingly traced for us by Shari Benstock. Finally, Joyce's impact on the painters of the Abstract Expressionist school of New York is surveyed for us by Evan Firestone.

All contributions to this book are published for the first time, except for chapters by Morris Beja, Norman O. Brown, Evan Firestone, Ihab Hassan, and Margot Norris, excerpts from Shari Benstock and John Cage, and the illustrations.

Without the aid of a number of friends and colleagues over many months, this book would not have been possible. I wish especially to thank Alison Armstrong, Murray Beja, Bernard Benstock, Zack Bowen, Judy Brodsky, William Dane, Kathleen Gee, Virginia Hyman, Mort Levitt, Ned Polsky, Charles Russell, Peter Scavuzzo, Jacqueline Shorr, Virginia Tiger, Stuart White, and Hildy York. I am also indebted to Miriam Murphy and the New Jersey Committee for the Humanities for making possible the Joyce conference and exhibit at Newark and to the Rutgers University Research Council for its support of my travel and research. To my editors at Horizon Press, Joan Dunphy and Willian Cowan, I owe more than I will admit here.

Acknowledgments

PAGE 93: Ihab Hassan, "( ): *Finnegans Wake* and the Postmodern Imagination," *Paracriticisms: Seven Speculations of the Times*, Urbana: University of Illinois Press, 1975, pp. 77-94. Reprinted by permission.

PAGE 112: Morris Beja, "The Joyce of Sex," *The Seventh of Joyce*. ed. Bernard Benstock, Bloomington: Indiana University Press, 1982, pp. 255-266. Reprinted by permission.

PAGE 146: Margot Norris, *The Decentered Universe of Finnegans Wake*, Baltimore: Johns Hopkins University Press, 1976, pp. 1-9. Reprinted by permission.

PAGE 158: Norman O. Brown, "An Interlude of Farce," *Closing Time*, New York: Random House, 1973, pp. 41-63. Reprinted by permission.

PAGES 158-170: Selections and a drawing from *Finnegans Wake* by James Joyce. Copyright 1939 by James Joyce. Copyright renewed © 1967 by George Joyce and Lucia Joyce. All rights reserved. Reprinted by permission of Viking Penguin Inc.

PAGE 172: Copyright © 1980 by John Cage. Reprinted from *Empty Words, Writings '73-'78*. By permission of Wesleyan University Press.

PAGES 180-181: Copyright © 1961 by Henmar Press Inc. Reprinted by permission of C. F. Peters Corporation.

Prologue: Two Perspectives on Joyce

Richard Ellmann

I. His Religion and Politics

What were Joyce's attitudes to church and state? To what extent was he shaped by the Catholicism he forswore? How committed was he to the liberation of Ireland? These questions beset us still as we struggle on our own time with concepts of orthodoxy, patriotism, and the revival of religious commitment.

In later life, asked when he had left the Church, Joyce remarked, "That's for the Church to say." By this time he recognized the complexities. In his youth he was not so guarded or ambiguous. He wrote to Nora Barnacle on 29 August 1904, "Six years ago [at sixteen] I left the Catholic Church, hating it most fervently. I found it impossible for me to remain in it on account of the impulses of my nature." The Church's attitude to sexuality was particularly repugnant to him. His letter went on, "I made secret war upon it when I was a student and declined to accept the positions it offered me." These positions, according to his brother Stanislaus, included that of priest. "By doing this I made myself a beggar but I retained my pride," Joyce wrote to Nora. "Now I make open war upon it by what I write and say and do."

His actions accorded with this policy. He neither confessed nor took communion. When his children were born he forbade their being baptized. His grandson was baptized against his wishes and without his knowledge. He preferred to live with Nora Barnacle for twenty-seven years without marrying her. When at last a wedding became necessary for purposes of inheritance, he had it performed in a registry office. At his death, when the possibility of a religious service was mentioned, his wife said, "I couldn't do that to him."

So far all is straightforward. Joyce's rejection of the Church was compatible, however with considerable interest in it and in its procedures. He was often derogatory. Priests, he said, were "barbarians armed with crucifixes." Or he would remark, as on 13 March 1908, "None of the gratifications of the senses are half so odious as their mortifications which the saints practised; also the Church, whilst providing rewards for the senses of the glorified body, has promised none for the sense of taste or of touch." Some of his devout friends took comfort in the way that Joyce regularly attended the services of Holy Week, and had particular pleasure in *Tenebrae*. He did so, however, like a tourist of another persuasion, standing at the back of the church. Another remnant of his early piety survived as a superstitious fear of thunderstorms, which he would do anything to avoid. Once, when thunder crashed and Joyce quailed, Thomas McGreevy admonished him, "Look at your children. They aren't frightened at all." "They have no religion," said Joyce with contempt. The marrow in his bones was at variance with his brain.

Critics have sometimes contended that his books should not be taken as opposed to the Church. Of course, no frontal attack is made in them. Joyce spoke in an early autobiographical essay of having adopted "urbanity in warfare" as his strategy. He was anxious that his books should not commit propaganda, even against institutions of which he disapproved. In his brother's diary for April 1908 it is recorded that Joyce said of the novel, *A Portrait of the Artist as a Young Man*, on which he was then working, "it would not be aimed at Catholicism in Ireland; he didn't care a rap if Ireland continued in Catholicism for the next two thousand years. Some Hottentot religion would be too good for the people. At any rate, with the Catholic doctrine of grace—which he considered the main doctrine of the Church—the priests could well defend these lenten banalities if they kept the faithful with the Church, the accumulator of grace. Their hell, too, they could defend in a similar manner, and it was a logical belief if one admitted their theory of sin and punishment."

Stephen's apostasy is accordingly presented as a choice for himself, and not necessarily one for others. On the other hand, he is an exemplum, not only in his capacity as artist, but in his character of emancipated man. His initial submission, in fear and remorse, to the terrifying sermons about death, judgment, and punishment, changes to revulsion at their cruelty. Yet Joyce is careful not to overstate his case. If Father Dolan, who in Chapter I pandies Stephen unjustly, is sadistic, the priest who hears the boy's confession after the retreat in Chapter III is kind and gentle.

Apart from such sporadic concessions, the Church in Joyce's works is regularly presented in terms of darkness, constriction, and thwart. Stephen finds that its emphasis on the soul is as lopsided as the prostitute's emphasis on the body. His most adroit maneuver is taking over its vocabulary for his own secular purposes. He receives a *call*, hears "a voice from beyond the world," but what it summons him to is not the priesthood but life, including sexual love, and an art that would content body and soul alike. The word *sin* is modified to error, to *fall* is only to experience: Stephen ecstatically contemplates: "To live, to err, to fall, to triumph, to recreate life out of life." He himself achieves *resurrection*: "His soul had risen from the grave of boyhood, spurning her graveclothes." He is ordained into a new *priestcraft* of his own devising: he imagines himself "a priest of eternal imagination, transmuting the daily bread of experience into the radiant body of everliving life." At the book's end he even takes over from the Church the care of *conscience*; it is he and not the Church who will forge a conscience for his race.

Just what this new conscience was to be Joyce would clarify in *Ulysses*. Neither Bloom nor Stephen could be described as pagan, though neither acknowledges any institutional belief. Bloom, in offering his conception of love as against the Citizen's hatred and violence, is voicing a humanistic ethic (though Joyce would have disliked the term). He also fulfils the role of the Good Samaritan when Stephen is knocked down. So far as Catholicism is concerned, he ruminates humorously about confession, communion, resurrection, marvelling at the hold these strange conceptions have. Stephen, reared among them, but unwilling to accept Catholic limitations of his independence, is in active rebellion. His climactic moment comes as his mother's ghost, like that of the Commendatore in *Don Giovanni*, thrice summons him to repent. His anguished retort is "Shite!", when the true pagan would neither see the ghost nor recognize any inclination to repent. Stephen is never insouciant. When he points to his head and quotes William Blake, who in his turn was alluding to Dante, "But in here it is I must kill the priest and the king," Joyce at once sanctions his "mental fight" and acknowledges the responsibility of this rebellion.

In *Finnegans Wake* Joyce seems more relaxed about the Church and about rebellion. Shaun, as a hypocritical do-gooder, with a claim to piety, is steadily mocked, but so is his errant and agnostic brother.

Catholicism has its place in the book, a pervasive one that involves
Saint Patrick, countless popes, church history and theological squab-
bles. In terms of universal history, which the *Wake* presents, the
Church's punctilio about forgotten issues adds to the joyful polyphony. In the night world of this novel shot through with dreams,
religion appears no better and no worse than other human obsessions.

To be opposed to the Church as an institution is one thing; to be
opposed to all religious feeling is another. At moments Joyce surprised his atheistical brother Stanislaus by unexpected concessions.
Stanislaus noted in his diary on 7 August 1908 that James said "he
believed that in his heart every man was religious. He spoke from
his knowledge of himself. I asked him did he mean that everyone
had in his heart some faith in a Diety, by which he could be influenced. He said, 'Yes.'" That this was not just a passing fancy appears to be borne out in *Ulysses*, less in Stephen and Bloom, who
disclaim faith, than in Molly. She, while contemptuous of piety, is
also contemptuous of impiety, and approves a vague theism: "as for
them saying there's no God I wouldn't give a snap of my two fingers for all their learning why dont they go and create something I
often asked him atheists or whatever they call themselves . . ." Although Joyce in May 1905 pronounced himself to be incapable of
belief of any kind, he evidently had more than a few grains left. But
any approach to orthodoxy repelled him. When a priest in Zurich
pointed out on a starry night the order of the stars and used it to
prove the existence of God, Joyce replied acidly, "What a pity that it
is all based on mutual interdestruction!"

He had much the same feelings of intransigence towards the British state, as the occupying power in Ireland, that he had towards
the Catholic Church. "Political awareness" was a quality he valued
in writers. Joyce was politically aware without being political. That
is, day to day politics did not interest him, but he thought of his
writing as subsuming politics within it. His earliest recorded work
was his lost poem about the man who had tried to lead Ireland to
independence, Parnell. Flagwaving nationalism was not to his taste,
but he regarded political independence as an aspect of the larger
independence he was seeking. His brother records a conversation
they had in April 1907. Stanislaus urged that an independent Ireland would be intolerable. "What the devil are your politics?" asked
James. "Do you not think Ireland has a right to govern itself and is
capable of doing so?" During his ten years in Trieste Joyce wrote
nine articles setting forth the Irish "problem" for a local newspaper,

and in 1914 he offered them as a book to an Italian publisher. They were not accepted: a pity, because they would have demonstrated that Joyce was altogether aware of and concerned about the political situation of his country.

Joyce is sometimes said to have been a lifelong Parnellite, but he was opposed to turning great dead men into stone effigies. In *Ulysses* he mocks the idea that Parnell is still alive and will return. The one post-Parnellite politician whom Joyce felt he could endorse was Arthur Griffith, who pleased him by being "unassuming" and "not indulging in flights." He liked Griffith's policy for two reasons especially, its non-violence (at that time) and its economic boycott of Britain. About the boycott he remarked on 16 May 1907, "The Sinn Féin policy comes to fighting England with knife and fork," and said it was "the highest form of political warfare I have heard of." In 1912 he asked Griffith's advice in connection with his troubles over publishing *Dubliners*, and was pleased to be treated as a man having a common cause though working in a less obviously political medium. For he had remained faithful to his goal of creating new Irishmen and Irishwomen through the honesty and scorching candor of his writing. In *Ulysses* he acknowledged Griffith's political importance by making many references to him, alone among politicians of the day. And he called attention to the ultimately political direction of his own work by having Irish Stephen, at the end of the brothel scene, beaten up by a *British* soldier, whom he defies as "the uninvited." Joyce was gratified when, just before *Ulysses* was published in 1922, Arthur Griffith was elected the first president of Ireland. The cultural emancipation of the country, with which Joyce had charged himself, seemed to be succeeding at the same time as the more limited but almost equally necessary political emancipation, which he associated with Griffith.

But Griffith died within a few months, and then the Civil War broke out. When Nora Joyce with their two children was fired on while visiting Galway during that war, Joyce grew more sceptical. He had called himself a socialist in his early twenties, then said he was an anarchist, though not a "practical anarchist in the modern sense." During the First World War, when he was committed to neutrality, he began to describe himself as apolitical, though he considered his litigation against a British consular official named Henry Carr to be a nationalistic action. The creation of the Free State had satisfied his political ambitions, always secondary to his cultural ones, but subsequent events made him feel that his immediate reaction could not be sustained. In 1932 he was invited to a St. Patrick's

Day party in Paris; he declined to attend it because the Irish Ambassador to France, Count O'Kelly, was also to be present, and Joyce did not wish to imply that he in any way endorsed the present Irish state. "I do not mind 'larking' with [High Commissioner] Dulanty in London but I care nothing about politics," he wrote. "Ireland, with Ulster in, will probably be a separate republic in ten or fifty years and I do not suppose anyone in England will really care two hoots whether it is or not. They are doing many things more efficiently, I am told, than was possible under the old regime but any semblance of liberty they had when under England seems to have gone—and goodness knows that was not much."

Yet indifference was not a characteristic of a man who made a point of reading Irish newspapers every day, and who took a passionate interest in every detail of his native land. However sceptical of political progress he became, he endeavored in all his books to achieve something superpolitical, by disclosing sharply what life in Ireland was, and dimly what it might be. This was his higher politics.

II. His Women

The marriage bed, which is supposed to open the curtain, may well draw it. Writers who shunned marriage, Proust and James for example, have given us some of the best portraits of wives that we have. James Joyce felt more at ease in portraying men; his Leopold Bloom is as variegated and complete as could be. But he resolutely continued to portray women, even if in lesser numbers. Perhaps he was acting on the principle he suggested for dramaturgy, "When things get slow, bring a woman on the stage." Not everyone has felt that Molly Bloom is an achieved totality. Still, the psychologist Jung thought so, and wrote to Joyce, "I suppose the devil's grandmother knows so much about the real psychology of a woman. I didn't." Molly Bloom herself pays her husband a compliment which must be one of the rarest that men hear from women: "I saw he understood or felt what a woman is." But Nora Joyce said of Molly Bloom's creator, "He knows nothing at all about women." She was thinking of Joyce the man. Joyce the writer was closer to Bloom.

From early in his career Joyce recognized women as a problem both for his life and for his art. He was only in his early teens when he defied the tenets of his church by consorting with prostitutes, and equally young when he veered in the other direction by prostrating himself before the Virgin Mary. Debasement and abasement were the prevailing modes of his adolescence. He had the classic mixture of social fear and hostility. Towards girls of his own circle he was shy, and perhaps in defence regarded them as hypocritically coy. He met the woman who was to become his wife in a casual encounter, more conducive to further acquaintance with him than a conventional introduction would have been. Living with her did not release him from his earlier attitudes, for letters he wrote to her when he was twenty-seven continue to seesaw between feelings of lust and adoration, between a desire to desecrate and a loathing of himself as desecrator. Though he wanted her to give herself "freely and wholly," he did not find it easy to resolve his own contrarieties. Nor, perhaps, did he want to. Joyce could not hope to be insouciantly pagan.

The women whom he knew well in childhood and early youth were not of the sort that Joyce could disparage or lust after. His mother was stable, devoted, and intelligent. After her death, his Aunt Josephine took her place as his confidant, and served also as a sounding-board for his early writings. But when he spoke of women, it was not of these but of younger ones. "To tell you the truth," he admitted to his brother in 1907, "I have an Irish way of looking at women. I can't take them seriously in anything they do." As he grew older, his remarks became more splenetic. "La femme c'est rien," he informed Stuart Gilbert. To the forthright Mary Colum he said, "I hate intellectual women." She dared to respond, "No, Joyce, you don't." He did, though. He liked women who were not intellectual but intelligent, especially if their minds were directed towards helping along his career. He was lucky enough to find them. Then his unconscious sense of how dependent he was upon not only his mother and aunt, but upon his patrons Edith McCormick and Harriet Weaver, his publishers Sylvia Beach and Adrienne Monnier, and his wife, may have paradoxically encouraged misogyny.

Living with women was one thing, writing about them another. Joyce conceived of his art as the overcoming of difficulties, and creating women characters was one of these. In print he does not belittle them. The example of his master Ibsen may have helped. He told his brother that Ibsen was the first writer who had led him to believe that women had a soul. But he had never met, he said, "a woman capable of doing what Nora Helmer did." His first book, *Chamber Music*, consisted of love poems addressed to someone largely imaginary in a tone of diffidence or feigned assurance. Nora Barnacle was too untutored, too unliterary, to fit them, though in tenderness and guilt over having suspected her of infidelity he wrote them all out for her on parchment.

In *Dubliners* the women who appear are mostly mothers, some good and some bad. The capstone of the book, however, is "The Dead," and in it Joyce makes a powerful defence of a woman much like Nora. The heroine Gretta Conroy confounds her sophisticated husband by the depth of her feelings for a boy she knew when she was young in the west of Ireland. Of all the characters in *Dubliners* Gretta is probably the most admirable. Joyce was struggling to impart to the world the intensity he saw in his own wife.

When he came to write *A Portrait of the Artist as a Young Man*, he again came up against the problem of women. Stephen's mother and fanatical governess were easy enough, but how to deal with the girl by whom young Stephen is attracted? In an early version, *Stephen Hero*, Joyce dreamed up a scene in which Stephen suddenly catches up with Emma Clery as she is walking and asks her to spend one night with him and then part forever. Understandably she is not won by this approach. On reconsideration, Joyce discarded it, presumably as a male fantasy. In *A Portrait* Emma has for most of the book only a shadowy existence. Not even a name, only the initials E——C——. She serves to focus Stephen's emotions, without appearing to have any of her own. So she can serve him as model for his poem, the villanelle of the temptress, where he foists upon her something of the Virgin, something of the prostitute:

> Are you not weary of ardent ways,
> Lure of the fallen seraphim? . . .
> Your eyes have set man's hearts ablase,
> And you have had your will of him.

The poem, written before the poems of *Chamber Music*, embodied Joyce's two urges to abase and debase. But here, in *A Portrait*, it is a way station to a more mature attitude. The girl who inspires it is allowed, in the very last pages, to take on a reality she had not had hitherto. Suddenly she is both fleshed and souled, neither debauched nor worshippable. Stephen's ability to conceive of her at last as a real person is a mark of his having grown up. He cannot leave Ireland until he can see her without preconception.

In his next two books Joyce presented contrasting women. Bertha, the wife of Richard Rowan in *Exiles*, is again based upon Nora. She cannot read her husband's books or understand half of what he says. She is contraposed with Beatrice Justice, in whom Joyce attempts to present a woman of more obvious culture. Richard has been sharing his intellectual life with her by letter for years. Beatrice is little more than a foil for Bertha, and the main theme is Richard's effort to allow his wife to behave freely and independently while at the same time he is racked by jealousy and the desire to bind her to him. What Bertha does with her body is never defined, but her feelings are all directed to her husband. It is the brain that counts.

In *Ulysses* also two female characters are developed, Gerty Mac-Dowell, who is virginal, coy, adoring, and Molly Bloom, who is married, bold, and critical. Yet Joyce betrays an unexpected sympathy for both. Gerty proves to be lame, and hobbles off as Bloom, and the reader, re-estimate her erotic fantasies. Molly, though she has committed adultery that day, proves unexpectedly innocent. Her amorous career has been limited. Though Joyce said jocularly of her that she is the flesh that always affirms, she is cerebral too. The tenor of her monologue is to acknowledge grudgingly that her husband, who recognizes her wit and talent and inner nature, is a better man than her lover Blazes Boylan. Although she dislikes her husband's opinions, especially when they differ from her own, she is not to be identified with unconsciousness, or mother nature, or fertility. Sometimes women used to say to Joyce, "Yes, those women are like that," upon which he said he would raise his eyes and stare at a corner of the ceiling. For if Molly does not seem capable of impersonal thought, as Bloom is, she is not therefore a caricature. She is always interesting, always clever. She does not stand for her sex, she stands for herself.

In *Finnegans Wake*, as in *Dubliners*, the most sympathetic character is a woman. This time it is a woman vaguely like Joyce's mother and aunt. Anna Livia is a mother and a wife (though she had had her adventures); she holds the family together. By the time he wrote this book, Joyce had been obliged to submit his leisure-hour misogyny to a bitter test. His fatherly love for his daughter Lucia took him off in a different direction. He identified so closely with her, feeling that the fire in his brain had somehow kindled one in hers, that gender was irrelevant. Men and women might be more alike than they were different.

But in a way he had always known this. When he describes Bloom as "a womanly man," he was thinking also of himself. He conceived of the artist as androgynous, of his writings as enwombed in the brain. His works were intended to touch the hearts of women as well as of men, for out of both would come the new race which he heralded. When he sat down to write, Joyce put out of his head antifeminine epithets; his talent took over and raised him in fiction above his fact. In his life he inveighed against women like Falstaff; in his writing he was absolved of hostility, and could not but offer them their due.

Introduction: James Joyce's Light Rays

Heyward Ehrlich

James Joyce—who usually pretended not to notice his contemporaries in the arts—made a memorable exception one day in Zurich during the First World War. In questioning his friend, the painter Frank Budgen, about *Ulysses*, Joyce wanted to know whether the structure of the double storyteller in the *Cyclops* chapter seemed like modern Italian art: "Does this episode strike you as being futuristic?"

In reply, Budgen turned away from Italy and towards France: "Rather cubist than futurist." Neither Joyce nor Budgen thought it odd to discuss literature as though it were painting or to compare the arts of different nations.

Supported by Joyce's tacit approval, Budgen went on to compare the writing of *Ulysses* to the composition of a cubist painting:

> Every event is a many-sided subject. You first state one view of it and then draw it from another angle to another scale, and both aspects lie side by side in the same picture.

Simultaneity and interpenetration, the two principles of modernist theory alluded to by Budgen, provide clues we might well apply to the entire body of Joyce's work over the first four decades of the twentieth century. Joyce's materials—his characters and their situations—are generally quite simple and ordinary. But his writing becomes "many-sided" by the continual addition of views from different angles or to different scales. Often Joyce took actual events from the Dublin of his youth and wrote about them in the styles and structures of the modernist movements of the other cities in which he lived, Trieste, Zurich, and Paris, during the successive eras of Futurism, Dada, and Surrealism.

To exaggerate only slightly, it might be said that Joyce wrote four different modernist materpieces—*Dubliners, A Portrait of the Artist as a Young Man, Ulysses,* and *Finnegans Wake*—because he lived through four different manifestations of modernism.

Irish modernism in Joyce's youth was caught between the lure of the Aran Islands on one hand and London or Paris on the other— precisely the choice confronting Gabriel Conroy in "The Dead." It resembled a belated outpouring of cultural nationalism, the discovery in the twentieth century of the same regional folklore, archaic language, antiquarianism, mysticism, anti-industrialism, and aesthetic occultism that many continental writers had absorbed in the nineteenth century.

Had he wished, Joyce surely could have become another successful poetic figure after the mold of W. B. Yeats, Sean O'Casey, or J. M. Synge. But what already existed always repelled Joyce. At the end of *Portrait*, Stephen Dedalus leaves Ireland to be become in exile "the uncreated conscience of my race," just as in 1904 Joyce himself left Ireland, rejecting the models of Irish moral sentimentalism to go in quest of the consciousness of a still uninvented aesthetic.

The youthful Joyce knew instinctively that there was no place for him in the Irish Literary Revival even though no doubt he was challenged and stimulated by its activities and alliances. Rarely a joiner, Joyce gave himself instead to the rival continental naturalists, especially the social critic and playwright Henrik Ibsen. Deciding to support himself through medicine, Joyce went to Paris in 1902 to study and to enjoy for the first time the European mainstream, then teeming with the artistic forms of the new century. The older symbolism, naturalism, and impressionism were supplanted by a new expressionism that pushed the representation of objects to its limits by focusing interest on the inner meaning of physical things or the artist's use of overall structures.

In 1904, the decisive year of Joyce's life, he heard his several callings: to become a writer of everyday Irish life, to write from exile on the continetnt, and to elope there with Nora Barnacle. All of *Ulysses* takes place on June 16, 1904; the action in *Portrait* ends only a year or two earlier; and the stories in *Dubliners* are set in the period just before. Yet prior to leaving Ireland, Joyce had already published the first few tales of *Dubliners*, had written an unpublished projection of a novel in an essay entitled "Portrait of the Artist," and had begun to write his eventually abandoned autobiographical novel, *Stephen Hero*.

When these writings are compared to each other and especially to the early lyric poems which Joyce wrote at about the same time, they acutely impress the reader with their extraordinary stylistic and formal variety, even their inconsistency. Evidently Joyce was deeply into artistic multiplicity and complexity only a year after attaining his majority.

The three stages of the novel we know as *Portrait of the Artist*—essay, draft version, and final published form—show Joyce's rapid development as he shuttled among the cities of Dublin, Paris, and Trieste, in the years prior to the First World War. The three versions of *Portrait* ran the gamut of styles—in its essay-plan a prose poem, in its first draft an example of photographic naturalism, and in its final, published state a careful expressionist structure in which its objects and events were not in traditionally fixed representational perspective but in an organic design of flowing images and motifs.

Joyce's first novel is at once autobiographical and confessional, a painterly self-portrait, and, as the conclusion of the title—*As a Young Man*—warns us, a work of personal irony and distance. The multiple layers of the work also reflect the multiple layers of culture in the city in which it was completed. Politically, Trieste was part of Austria and thus nourished by the older Viennese modernism of the 1890s that had flowered with Freud, Mahler, Strauss, and Schoenberg. At the same time by language Trieste was tied to Italy and the new modernism of the Futurists Balla, Boccioni, Marinetti, and Severini.

The traditions of Vienna and the revolutions of Milan collided in Joyce's Trieste. Vienna, with its quest for unity in psychology, philosophy, and music was in retard, while Milan, presenting the new visual art of mechanization and discontinuous motion, was in spasmodic acceleration. An even more important product of the collision of styles was Joyce's plan for *Ulysses*, one chapter of which Joyce and Budgen had likened to a Futurist or Cubist painting. The novel is justly famous for its dynamic structure, its reversal and mixture of temporal and spatial clues and perspectives, and its technical brilliance.

In his letters Joyce confessed his pleasure not at the story of *Ulysses* but at his inventon of different narrative styles and structures for each of its eighteen chapters. The artist was no longer a god imposing a single simple order at the conclusion of a complex plot but rather the opposite, a creator who imposed a complex order of styles and narratives on a simple situation.

Although it contains only indirect evidence of it, *Ulysses* is very much a product of wartime. Serialized from neutral Zurich and completed in post-war Paris, *Ulysses* parallels the tumult of Dada, that other product of wartime Zurich. Both undermine the authority of known conventions of representation until all schemes become equally plausible and possible, and art is reduced to a spontaneous outpouring of the uncensored unconscious—a flagrant banging together of anachronisms and nihilisms. Needless to say, neither the world after the Great War nor the novel after *Ulysses* were ever the same again.

Until Joyce arrived in Paris in 1920 he had lived on the fringe as an exile, but from now on he could surround himself with supporters, patrons, and even a cult of followers. *Portrait* and *Ulysses* had been serialized in *The Egoist* and the *Little Review* via mail order, so to speak, since Joyce lived across Europe. But the serialization of *Finnegans Wake* took place virtually in Joyce's own Paris neighborhood, often in magazines whose aesthetic radicalism was proclaimed by their eschewal of capital letters—the *transatlantic review* and *transition*. After two decades of the indifference and hostility of publishers, Joyce suddenly found himself supported and provoked to go onward.

In *Finnegans Wake*—serialized as *Work in Progress*—Joyce departed from the political, mechanical, and spontaneous elements which characterized both Dada and *Ulysses;* he arrived at a different scale which had much in common with Surrealism in its use of dream language to pursue the quest for universal history and myth. In Joyce's words substance and style were inseparable, and the transfiguration and metamorphosis of language through punning, compression, and polyphony became both the subject and the purpose of writing.

As a consequence of his endless personal and creative odyssey, Joyce emerged as one of the prototype modernists, along with Pablo Picasso and Igor Stravinsky. Each became a political exile, rejected the church, never attained a single final style but always grew through new styles, mixed the ancient and the contemporary in astonishing ways, never flinched from what audiences might find shocking, and, by the example of creative life and work, served to define the modern era. And the three were almost exact contemporaries, born within a few months of each other.

Indeed, in the 1980s centenary celebrations are marking the births in the 1880s of an unusual number of artists who attained greatness as modernists: in addition to Joyce, Picasso, and Stravinsky, we find the writers Sean O'Casey, Virginia Woolf, D. H. Lawrence, Joyce Cary, Katherine Mansfield, H. L. Mencken, William Carlos Williams, Sinclair Lewis, Ezra Pound, Robinson Jeffers, Marianne Moore, T. S. Eliot, John Crowe Ransom, Eugene O'Neill; the musicians Bela Bartok, Alban Berg, Ernest Bloch, Anton Webern, Heitor Villa-Lobos; the painters Braque, Chagall, Derain, Franz Marc, Beckmann, Kokoschka, Utrillo, Lehmbruck, Modigliani, Joan Gris, Leger, Delaunay, Duchamp, Boccioni, Severini, Marinetti, Diego Rivera, Hopper, Arp, Schwitters; the architect Le Corbusier; and the photographers Weston, Salomon, Coburn, Sheeler.

One mark of the new modernism was its reliance on the physical and social sciences rather than on traditional arts and humanities as sources and sanctions for creativity. Truth—once the beacon of fixity and the absolute—now seemed comparative, relative, and pluralistic in the light of the new anthropology, psychology, and physics. Even space and time, once represented in the arts from static perspectives, changed in everyday life because of the new practical technology of the motion picture, the airplane, and the telephone. The old and socially oriented aesthetic order, inherited, shared, and harmonious, suddenly succumbed to a new artistic anarchy, to the craving for fresh, direct, and primitive portrayals of unrefined experience.

If we believe a famous remark of Virginia Woolf, human nature changed in the year 1910. Models of proper Victorian and Edwardian behavior suddenly became ridiculous. The idea of proper art for a proper public became old-fashioned; the new art sanctified the private processes of creativity: what happened in the studio, an entry in the notebook, changes in a working draft. Art came more and more to a tentative tracing of its own making. The thickly upholstered texture of late nineteenth century art, so full of harmonized gradiosity, gloom, and guilt, gave way to an ironic new art that was angular, audacious.

One unexplained fact about the creative generation of the 1880s is that its painters and musicians matured before its writers did, so that modern literature, when it came of age, had a ready inheritance from modern painting and modern music. Picasso's *Demoiselles d'Avignon* was painted in 1907, and Stravinsky's *Sacre du Printemps* was performed in 1913, while the comparable monuments of modernism in literature were not produced until after the World War in Joyce's *Ulysses* and Eliot's *Waste Land*—both published in 1922—together the most influential works in the literature of the twentieth century.

But when Eliot read *Ulysses* in serialization, it became an important influence on *The Waste Land* and thus on twentieth century poetry as well. Yet the effect of *Ulysses* is much more obvious than its cause. Where did Joyce himself turn for example and encouragement?

According to Joyce's own explanation, he took the idea of the interior monologue from Eduoard Dujardin and a concern for everyday life from Italo Svevo. But these acknowledgements hardly seem adequate. Even if we add to them Joyce's known interests in Homer, Aristotle, Shakespeare, Defoe, Swift, Stern, Blake, Whitman, Flaubert, the French Symbolists, Ibsen, Yeats, and the philosphers Vico and Bruno, we still do not encounter an "explanation" of Joyce's modernism.

Nor can we readily find a simple explanation in Joyce's own statements. He stopped writing aesthetic manifestoes at the age of 22—a feat of considerable self-restraint in a manifesto-writing age—and left only technical hints in his letters. Joyce encouraged fellow writers, such as Ezra Pound and T. S. Eliot, to explain him in reviews, or left authorized biographers, including Stuart Gilbert, Herbert Gorman, and Frank Budgen, to say things about him. Moreover, the study in recent years of Joyce's drafts and notebooks only seems to make his writing more magical and mysterious than ever.

After sixty years of study of *Ulysses* and forty years of the scrutiny of *Finnegans Wake* no agreement seems to emerge among Joyce readers, scholars, and critics as to his unequivocal "purpose"—in the sense in which preface-writing contemporaries such as James, Conrad, Shaw, Pound, Eliot, and Yeats stated clearly expressible literary intentions.

Perhaps this is so because Joyce was emphatically a writer of practical and creative temperament rather than of theoretical and aesthetic intention. In a sense, he worked more the way composers and painters work than the way writers do. If Joyce never fully explained his purposes, perhaps it was because he did not have language to describe his practice or his ideas. It is said that Joyce drew upon his superb musicianship. Whether or not he might have become a professional tenor, the world of Dublin parlor song *is* the social world of *Ulysses*. But Joyce's tastes in music were for such things as traditional tenors, the opera, and sentimental favorites—not for the daring new work of Stravinsky, Bartok, or Schoenberg. Nevertheless, he was much more interested in modern visual arts—

painting, photography, sculpture, and architecture—than is usually recognized.

There is no doubt that Joyce was superbly equipped with all the endowments of more traditional writers—an absolute ear for dialogue, a sharpshooter's eye for visual detail, and an extraordinary feeling for the voice and tone of narrative. In his early works he plays a definite author—the celebrant in *Chamber Music*, the observer in *Dubliners*, the participant in *Portrait*.

But if Joyce early became different authors, he never became one author, the single familiar voice of the kind we find throughout Fielding, Austen, Dickens, Thackeray, Hardy, and even in such contemporaries as James, Conrad, D. H. Lawrence, Virginia Woolf, and E. M. Forster. To some extent such writers formed a bond with the reader by agreeing to render the unfamiliar familiar. To a large extent Joyce deliberately reversed the process, taking the familiar and making it unfamiliar. To read Joyce properly one should read all that he wrote, yet the experience of reading any one book by Joyce is certainly no preparation for what to expect in any other book from his pen.

The notion of making the familiar seem strange, complex, or obscure was hardly original with Joyce; indeed it was inherent in the naturalistic renderings of perception and other mental processes that was essential to impressionism. It can be found playfully in Richard Strauss's *Domestic Symphony* (1903), shockingly in Picasso's *Demoiselles d'Avignon* (1907), analytically in Gertrude Stein's *Three Lives* (1908), and hauntingly in Boccioni's triptych, *States of Mind* (1911-12).

Yet each of these works is accompanied by a sense that there is some coherent code to be discovered which will unlock all its secrets. The reader of *Ulysses* and *FInnegans Wake* has no such assurance. The familiar "author" in early Joyce—celebrant, observer, participant—is different from the sublime "author" in middle and late Joyce—the entity who can tell a story eighteen ways in *Ulysses* or dream while reinventing language in *Finnegans Wake*.

The absence of the author as guide may be the reason why a visual reading of Joyce on the page often seems incomplete, just as a auditory reading of Joyce in performance or recording also seems inadequate—until the separate readings of eye and ear are brought together in glorious union. Thus it may be helpful to think of Joyce not as a painter or musician imposing spatial design or temporal variations on his material, but rather as a painter and musician doing both such things simultaneously.

Surely Joyce's resistance to facile classification remains one reason for his enduring influence on modern literature, painting, and music. Although many Joyce specialists have attempted to prove Joyce's adherence to some hitherto undiscovered single principle of philosophy or aesthetics, Joyce's multiplicity, playfulness, and energy endure. Perhaps Joyce's modernism resides in his unusual ability to validate and leave unresolved plural cosmologies or structures that achieve separate creative validity in the same work.

An incident representative of Joyce's way of thinking about his work took place after Eliot's laudatory review of *Ulysses*. Joyce was worried that the well-worn critical term *interior monologue* had become a cant phrase which had outlived its usefulness. He got an idea from something Eliot had said in conversation and sent a message to be delivered to Eliot to ask him to take up his pen to "use or coin some short phrase, two or three words, such as the one he used in speaking to me, 'two plane.'"

What Eliot meant was the parallel in literature between the mythologial and the contemporary. Even though Eliot never used the phrase "two plane" in print, it nevertheless reveals Joyce's preference for the practical, the spontaneous, the unfamiliar over the theoretical, the formulated, the traditional. Furthermore, the prhase "two plane" provides an unexpected benefit: it might be applied with equal validity not only to Joyce's *Ulysses* but also to painting by Picasso or music by Stravinsky, an additional clue to the essential interconnections between art, literature, and music in twentieth century modernism.

How did Joyce become the modernists' modernist? His epic wanderings—from Ireland in the time of the Irish Literary Revival, to Trieste in the era of Viennese modernism and Italian Futurism, to Zurich at the outbreak of Dada, to paris at the flood of surrealism and the semi-permanent avant-garde—made his career an epitome of the literature of Europe in the four decades from the turn of the century to the eve of the Second World War.

Like Odysseus, who once wandered the Mediterranean in quest of treasure, Joyce plundered languages—English, Italian, German, French, and more—until he amassed a treasure for twentieth century literature nearly as monumental as the Homeric epics. *Ulysses* in 1922 marked the beginning of the modernist novel, stamping everything with its specific structures and techniques—stream of consciousness, mythological parallels, language motifs, and imitative form—while also illuminating contemporary literature with its paradigm of transformative and revolutionary renewal. Joyce ended the old novel; Joyce began the new novel.

After *Ulysses* traditional fiction with common sense social, moral, and commercial values seemed outdated. Novelists returned to a zero-point in order to create anew in a ceaseless process of revitalization. Joyce himself had done no less. Each of the eighteen chapters of *Ulysses* creates its own technique: thus seventeen times within its pages, a new style arrives to erase or revise the standing structure of the whole book. Almost every writer of the day felt the lure to follow. Innovation in style, structure, and technique became the order of the day in Britain, on the continent, in North America, in Latin America, in the Third World. The modernist novel became the cause of the party of the future. Virginia Woolf, Samuel Beckett, William Faulkner, John Dos Passos, and Thomas Wolfe—joined by other key poets and playwrights—participated in an unprecedented blaze of innovation and exploration that gave the fiction of the 1920s and 1930s much of its distinctive character.

It was as though a Joycean law of transformation had been created, and, of course, not even Joyce himself was exempt from it. After *Ulysses*, Joyce too had to make a new structure and technique for *Finnegans Wake* (1939). And that book, which ended modernism and began most-modernism, represented another evolutionary stage for the new generation of novelists of the 1940s and 1950s—a newly discovered underground earthquake, as it were, upstaging the still half-explored volcano of *Ulysses*. Delayed by the Second World War and by Joyce's death in 1941, the response to *Finnegans Wake* produced a second Joycean swirl which transformed itself into an even larger galaxy than the first.

Now Joyce's impact left the confines of fiction and extended further and further afield—to drama, media studies, psychology, philosophy, music, and art. One of the first labors by a disciple was Thornton Wilder's *The Skin of Our Teeth* (1942), which developed Joyce's notion of a language community of plural speakers. Soon the mythologist Joseph Campbell became a collaborator on *A Skeleton Key to "Finnegan's Wake"* (1944), and the critic Northrop Frye began to explore cycle and quest motifs in late Joyce. Then the ripples began to reach outside the bounds of literature. In 1942 John Cage used a closed piano for a musical setting of a passage from *Finnegans Wake*. En route to fame for his theories of media, Marshall McLuhan in the 1950s studied Joyce as a writer of the typographic era who, while fully understanding the printed languages of the newspaper and the encyclopedia, also explored the unprinted languages of speech and the unconscious. By the end of the 1950s the composer Pierre Boulez was writing music and publishing new theories based on distinctively Joycean notions of aleatory or chance organization. The same late works of Joyce inspired the psychologist and generalist Norman O. Brown, and he conveyed that interest to several students who achieved distinction. McLuhan and Brown encouraged Cage, and they in turn spurred on Boulez, and all of them were soon joined by the novelist Anthony Burgess. By the 1960s, such followers of Joyce had armed themselves for an avant-garde crusade of conquest.

In France, in the influential pages of *Tel Quel,* Joyce begame a name to conjure with for theorists and practitioners of the New Novel, for structuralists, for semioticians, for cinéasts. What was more, Joycean conceptions were indepently taken up by painters of the New York Abstact Expressionist school, including Jackson Pollack, Robert Motherwell, Ad Reinhardt, and Tony Smith, all of whom were working right at the cutting edge of experimentation. Thus Joyce seemed to sanction not only aleatory music based on literature but also literature as a ground for action painting. All this Joycean creative activity had the effect of joining philosophy, psychology, literature, linguistics, painting, and music in one single rainbow right across the humanities.

Three times in recent decades—for the twenties, the fifties, and the seventies—Joyce emerged as a main force behind international literary, musical, artistic, philosophical, and cultural developments. No wonder some historians borrowed his name as an epithet for the century: "The Age of Joyce." But to support such a claim demands weighty and persuasive evidence. Here are some names of writers who have written significantly about him: AE (George Russell), Margaret Anderson, Djuna Barnes, Robert Benchley, Arnold Bennett, Louise Bogan, Elizabeth Bowen, Morley Callaghan, G. K. Chesterton, Paul Claudel, Cyril Connolly, Peter Costello, Hart Crane, Caresse Crosby, Harry Crosby, Edward Dahlberg, Edouard Dujardin, T. S. Eliot, James T. Farrell, F. Scott Fiztgerald, Janet Flanner, E. M. Forester, William Gass, Andre Gide, Ellen Glasgow, Gerhardt Hauptmann, D. H. Lawrence, Wyndham Lewis, Sinclair Lewis, H. L. Mencken, Laszlo Moholy-Nagy, Vladimir Nabokov, Sean O'Casey, Joyce Carol Oates, Frank O'Connor, George Orwell, S. J. Perelman, Ezra Pound, John Crowe Ransom, Dorothy Richardson, George Bernard Shaw, Edith Sitwell, Stephen Spender, James Stephens, Alan Tate, Robert Penn Warren, H. G. Wells, Rebecca West,

Thornton Wilder, William Carlos Williams, Virginia Woolf, W. B. Yeats, and Stefan Zweig.

Add to this rollcall another just to represent studies that trace Joyce's influences upon Sherwood Anderson, James Baldwin, John Barth, Donald Barthelme, Brendan Behan, Saul Bellow, Bertolt Brecht, Hermann Broch, William Burroughs, James Baldwin, Albert Camus, Hart Crane, Broch Döblin, John Dos Passos, Sergei Eisenstein, Ilya Ehrenbourg, Ralph Ellison, William Faulkner, Dudley Fitts, Ford Madox Ford, E. M. Forster, Carlos Fuentes, William Gaddis, Henry Green, Julien Green, Ernest Hemingway, Aldous Huxley, David Jones, Franz Kafka, Jack Kerouac, Arthur Koestler, Seymour Krim, Doris Lessing, Malcolm Lowry, Archibald MacLeish, Norman Mailer, André Maurois, Alberto Moravia, Howard Nemerov, Flann O'Brien, Flannery O'Connor, Thomas Pynchon, V. S. Pritchett, Sylvia Plath, Herbert Read, Alain Robbe-Grillet, Nathalie Sarraute, Upton Sinclair, Alan Sillitoe, Gertrude Stein, Dylan Thomas, John Updike, Kurt Vonnegut, Jr., Thomas Wolfe, and Richard Wright.

Not surprisingly, almost every man and woman of letters of mid-century (not bothering to count Joyce specialists) has written some appreciation of Joyce: Joseph Warren Beach, John Peale Bishop, R. P. Blackmur, Wayne C. Booth, Kenneth Burke, Cleanth Brooks, Van Wyck Brooks, Malcolm Cowley, Leon Edel, Francis Ferguson, Northrop Frye, Ihab Hassan, Gilbert Highet, Stanley Edgar Hyman, Wolfgang Iser, Alfred Kazin, Frank Kermode, G. Wilson Knight, F. R. Leavis, Dwight MacDonald, Robert McAlmon, Marshall McLuhan, Vivian Mercier, Edwin Muir, Malcolm Muggeridge, C. K. Ogden, Henri Peyre, Richard Poirier, Paul Rosenfeld, Gilbert Seldes, Robert Scholes, Mark Schorer, Frances Steloff, Arthur Symons, Lionel Trilling, William Troy.

But the most astonishing testimony to Joyce comes from those who normally do not write about literature at all. Long ago the psychologist and philosopher Carl Jung offered several interpretations of Joyce, and Judge John M. Woolsey wrote a legal opinion of unusual literature discernment to lift the ban against *Ulysses*. The composer and conductor Pierre Boulez credited Joyce as the source of the new principles of construction of aleatory music. Marshall McLuhan championed Joyce as an early discoverer of the possibilities of media as media: form as content. By the 1970s the short articles began to grow into full length books such as *Closing Time* by Norman O. Brown; Anthony Burgess' *Re Joyce* and other books; John Cage's typographic poems, *Writing Through Finnegans Wake*, his oratorios, and other unorthodox works; the collection *Trois Jours avec Joyce* by the photographer Gisèle Freund; and the ongoing series of Celtic heads by the portrait artist Louis LeBrocquy.

In this manner musicians, artists, photographers, and filmmakers have taken up Joyce in unexpected ways. Some years ago Henri Matisse illustrated a limited edition of *Ulysses;* Sergei Eisenstein developed a film theory of montage that owes something to a Joycean collision of images; and over the decades composers as different as George Antheil, Arnold Bax, Luciano Berio, Andre Hodeir, and Virgil Thompson became interested in Joyce. Musical settings of Joyce ranged from simple songs for piano or orchestra to electronic music, jazz cantatas, and oratorios freely based on his texts.

The year of Joyce's centenary, 1982—also the sixtieth anniversary of *Ulysses* and almost the fortieth of *Finnegans Wake*—was noted by more than two dozen celebrations, symposia, and collections. Yet well before 1970, when the revaluation began of the major modernists of the 1920s and 1930s—Proust, Mann, Eliot, Kafka, Pound and Joyce—the stock of most individual modernists was already in decline. Joyce was the outstanding exception.

Only in the 1970s did literary historians full confirm *Ulysses* and *FInnegans Wake* as the landmarks of twentieth century fiction. First, Vivien Mercier in *The New Novel* (1971) traced the impact of Joyce upon the writers of fiction in France during the 1960s. Then Robert M. Adams in *Afterjoyce* (1977) established a canon of post-*Ulysses* Europe: Virginia Woolf, Samuel Beckett, Carlo Emilio Gadda, Alfred Döblin, Hermann Broch, Vladimir Nabokov, Lawrence Durell, Anthony Burgess, José Lezama Lima, Flann O'Brien, Jorge Luis Borges. David Hayman edited the pioneering study of the impact of *Finnegans Wake,* entitled *In the Wake of the Wake,* which appeared in *TriQuartlery* magazine in 1977. Finally, Craig Hansen Werner in *Paradoxical Resolutions* (1982) traced Joycean influences upon such American writers of fiction and poetry as William Faulkner, Richard Wright, Flannery O'Connor, Sylvia Plath, Jack Kerouac, James Baldwin, John Updike, Roland Sukenick, Donald Barthelme, William Burroughs, Saul Bellow, Ralph Ellison, John Barth, Norman Mailer, William Gaddis, and Thomas Pynchon. But a full account of Joyce's impact on modern poetry, both directly and through T. S. Eliot, is a book still unwritten.

In any event, Joyce's central position in Modernism, Post-Modernism, and whatever follows—Joyce past, Joyce present, Joyce future—is more than a matter of accident or luck. Joyce positioned himself with all deliberateness: he followed theories sacred equally to Romantics and Moderns that made the artist not only the most godlike of men but also in the very act of creation a god onto himself. The universe was, as Edgar Allan Poe said, a plot of God. Overturning the classical dicta of Lessing, Joyce played with space and time, the supposedly separate provinces of the eye and ear. In *Ulysses* Leopold Bloom first trains his binoculars on a neighborhood clock, thereby making time visual. Then Bloom turns to a more important clock:

> He faced about and, standing between the awnings, held out his right hand at arm's length towards the sun. Wanted to try than often. Yes: completely. The tip of his little finger blotted out the sun's disc. Must be the focus where the rays cross. If I had black glasses . . . There will be a total eclipse this year . . .

In June, before the summer solstice, Bloom performs a Druidic act of divination: Stonehenge sits in his hand. Control the sun and become king. With this tiny, detached, ironic gesture, Bloom extinguishes the universe—and then, playing the game of Genesis, brings it back again amist the birth upheavals of sunspots. Guard of the sun: god of the sun.

In depicting Bloom bringing the sun to a focus in his little finger, Joyce apparently had some Renaissance engraving in mind. Yet if Bloom had black glasses, the light would come to a focus within his eyes in all safety. Or is the other way around? Is it the light emanating from the eyes of Bloom/Joyce that illuminates the universe—as some philosophers of perception and optics once believed? For Joyce these light rays—knowledge, sexuality, identity, creativity—originate not in the physical world but rather within the darkening eyes of the artist in the act of divination. To see: to perceive: to understand: to believe. Joyce is at one center of our century. We orbit elliptically around his art, his sun, his light rays.

POPULAR CULTURE

To Whom Does Joyce Belong? Ulysses as Parody, Pop and Porn

Leslie A. Fiedler

Several years ago I swore to whatever gods preside over literary criticism that I would never again speak in public about James Joyce—being convinced that I had long since said what I have to say about his work, and weary, in any case, of the ritual occasions on which his memory is piously evoked and his books tediously analyzed. But here I am on the point of breaking my oath of silence; in part, surely, because the gathering to which you have invited me occurs in 1982: the year not only of the hundreth anniversary of his birth, but also the fiftieth of my first encounter with his fiction. It is being held, moreover, in Newark, New Jersey, where in 1932 at age fifteen, I persuaded a reluctant librarian to let me check out a copy of *Portrait of the Artist as a Young Man*, at that point still hidden away in the "Locked Room," to keep it from the eyes of the profane, particularly the young.

I was, however, already well on my way to a career as an *enfant terrible*; and so I kept insisting on my rights at the top of my voice, until the guardians of decorum decided it would be less of a scandal to let me have the "dirty book" than to prolong the scene. At any rate, encouraged by my initial success, I managed next to talk an

unsuspecting maiden aunt into giving me as a High School gradua-
tion present *Ulysses,* which had just then won its long battle in the
courts and could be legally purchased in the United States.

It is a novel which ever since has been so intertwined with my life
as a reader and a writer that I feel it not merely permissible but
obligatory to speak of it autobiographically. I have, indeed, read
Ulysses more often than any other work of fiction, except perhaps
for *Huckleberry Finn,* which I came upon at age ten and *Uncle Tom's
Cabin,* the first book I ever bought for myself, when I was only
seven or eight. I do not mean to imply, by putting *Ulysses* in the
context of those works, that like them it totally subverts the distinction between Pop and Art Novels, High Literature and Low. Certainly, not in quite the same way.

I am, however, insisting that it *is* different from the fiction of the
kind of modernist novelist with whom Joyce is usually associated,
Marcel Proust, for example, or Thomas Mann. Ponder for a moment
the fact that Leopold and Molly Bloom have passed—via stage versions, movies and word of mouth—into the public domain of Mass
Culture; which is to say, are likely to be known by people who have
never read Joyce or, indeed, except on school assignment, any fiction at all. In this respect, those two characters are more like Huck
and Uncle Tom (or, for that matter, Superman and Little Orphan
Annie) than Proust's Baron de Charlus or Mann's Settembrini. Yet
they are, in another and quite as important sense, different from the
former as well. I was, indeed, aware of the difference long before I
had come to perceive the similarity; conscious that I was considered
by my elders and betters a "good boy" when, however precociously,
I began reading Twain and Stowe, whose books, after all, were
stocked in the Children's Departments of Public Libraries. But to be
caught reading Joyce, even at fifteen, meant being regarded as a
"bad boy," since his forbidden works had not yet made it on to the
open stacks in the Adult Department.

I would have denied, of course, that the "dirty words" and the
"sex scenes" in *Ulysses* thrilled my lubricious teenybopper's heart
quite as they thrilled other kids of my own age, who riffed through
the novel solely in quest of Molly Bloom's soliloquy. But, of course,
they did; and I must therefore grant in retrospect that if hypocrisy
and self-deceit are sins, I was indeed "bad"—worse than my parents and teachers deemed me, though for different reasons. I was,
moreover, a snob, despising those parents and teachers, not merely
for their fear of sex and advocacy of censorship; but even more because they had not, like me, slogged their way through the scarcely

comprehensible chunks already published in *transition* of what was then still called *Work in Progress* and would finally be entitled *Finnegan's Wake*. It was consequently inevitable that (unaware of how blessed I was *not* to have first read *Ulysses* in class and on assignment) I would end up myself assigning it to undergraduates: becoming thus a willing accomplice in the unfortunate process which has turned Joyce's books from the underground reading of young rebels into a part of required academic culture.

But the real damage was not done, until I (who had escaped that final indignity on my way to a PhD in English Literature) was re-introduced to *Ulysses* in the classroom. Immediately after World War II, I went on a Rockefeller Fellowship to Harvard to be, as they said, "renewed and refreshed"—meaning, academically reborn after a four years interruption of my academic career. To be sure, I had managed to read during an interminable sixty days at sea, most of it under fire, the whole of *Finnegans Wake*. That experience was given a little extra zest by the fact that once more I had to hide a book by Joyce from the scrutiny of those around me. This time, however, I was obliged to conceal it not because it was too "dirty", but because it was too highfalutin'—which should have taught me something. But it was a lesson I was still not ready to learn; and it was therefore with a sense of relief that I enrolled in Harry Levin's celebrated course in "Proust, Mann and Joyce."

In his classroom, the troubled and troublesome Irish parodist was presented to Harvard students and their visiting relatives as a High Priest of Modernism: one of the heroic pioneers who had redeemed the Novel, most stubbornly popular of all literary genres, for High Art: capturing it from the poor slobs who could not tell a master-work from a best-seller, and thus making the former as *kosher* as the Epic itself for writers of PhD dissertations. I must confess that in 1946, though old enough to know better, I unequivocally rejoiced that *Ulysses* no longer had to be smuggled through Customs or wheedled out of the "Locked Rooms" of libraries; that it and I had simultaneously made it out of our respective ghettoes to academic respectability. But in my rejoicing I forgot what I had intuitively be-gun to perceive on the banks of the Passaic River (much closer spir-itually to the banks of the Liffey than those of the Charles, or, for that matter, the Seine): that *Ulysses* is not respectable literature, and that it never was at home in the canon of the Arnoldian Culture Religion. It is, in fact, a dirty book with ambivalent cultural preten-sions, the work of a writer who at his deepest level of consciousness felt himself in as peripheral a relationship to European culture as any Jewish schoolboy in Newark, New Jersey.

For such a schoolboy, encountering Joyce between the two World Wars, at a point when he was trying to suppress his own hostility to the culture of the West as somehow unworthy, it seemed easy to grant that *Ulysses* was an attack on Christ and Caesar, Church and State. But I found it impossible back then to grant that it might also be an even more ferocious assault on the third bastion of the elitist civilization of Europe—High Culture. Besides, I had been confused by the well-intentioned lies contained in Judge Woolsey's famous courtroom decision of 1933, which had finally made *Ulysses* available to ordinary readers like me. That momentous decision came to us in the first Random House edition, attached to the text itself as a kind of inseparable preface: a piece of criticism really, aimed at convincing would-be censors that the novel "did not tend to excite sexual impulses or lustful thoughts": and that though perhaps "somewhat emetic," it was "nowhere an aphrodisiac."

The Judge's opinion, however legally useful to the publishers, is palpably false as criticism. More dangerous in the long run, though, than his exculpation of Joyce from the charge of obscenity was Judge Woolsey's further observation (added, he tells us, at the suggestion of the "two friends . . . whose opinions on literature and life I value highly"): "In writing '*Ulysses*', Joyce sought to make a serious experiment in a new . . . literary genre." The assumptions behind that statement reflect a key dogma of Literary Modernism: that whatever is truly literature (and especially "new" or "experimental" or "serious" literature) cannot be pornography, and conversely, whatever is porn cannot be "serious" literature.

But such an assumption holds only as long as we understand literature in terms of Arnoldian "High Seriousness", and thus continue to endure the division of the books we read into two kinds, High and Low, the first providing self-satisfaction to the few, and the second pleasure to the many. Pornography is, indeed, essentially trash: the absolute pole of Popular Art; tending, as Plato condescendingly observed, to "water the emotions," instead of giving rational instruction or even proper delight, much less the pseudo-religious consolation which Arnold attributed to "the best that has been thought or written."

To read *Ulysses*, however, without being titillated represents as inadequate a response as reading it without laughing or weeping. Moreover, like all pornography, it titillates us without the presence of real flesh; just as like comic or sentimental trash, it impels us to laugh or weep at absurdities and calamities which exist only in fantasy. In short, it permits us to go vicariously and temporarily mad, i.e., to respond to the hallucinations of another as if they were real. That *Ulysses* is essentially a comic work most critics (though, indeed, they seem to forget the fact in their too solemn analyses) are prepared finally to grant; and rather more reluctantly, some of them at least will concede that it is on occasion sentimental. But the pornographic dimension of Joyce's work they find it difficult to confess.

Yet of all the popular modes porn is most central to *Ulysses*. We must therefore read that novel not only in the Modernist context of Proust and Mann, Eliot and Pound—along with those mythographic source books from which Joyce drew the references and allusions he tabulated for Linati; but also side by side with the volumes we find Bloom turning over at a bookstall in the episode of the "Wandering Rocks": *The Awful Disclosures of Maria Monk, Aristotle's Masterpiece, Tales of the Ghetto* by Leopold von Sacher-Masoch, *Fair Tyrants* by James Lovebirch, *Ruby, the Pride of the Ring*, and especially *Sweets of Sin* by Paul de Kock, whose name in a world of Hibernian punsters evokes much hilarity. "I suppose," Molly muses, "people gave him that nickname going about with his tube from one woman to another."

But, of course, Paul de Kock was the actual name of a popular French Novelist of the 19th century, whose vogue survived in England as well as in France into the twentieth. It is his book of all those on our list which wins Bloom's approval ("I'll take this one. . . .that's a good one"), and apparently Joyce's as well; since he not only quotes some of its choicer phrases ("opulent curves . . . heavy embonpoint. . . "), but tells us the name of its hero, Raoul, a name which echoes and re-echoes up to the very end of the book. It is worth noticing that what especially intrigues Bloom (and presumably Joyce) is not hard-core porn, but softer stuff, more suggestive than explicit.

And even this Joyce asks us not so much to imagine Bloom reading, as to imagine Bloom imagining Molly reading; for both Bloom and his author are readers of porn at a second remove: meta-porn savored over the shoulder, as it were, of a female reader. But Bloom's taste proved to be a little too kinky, too obsessed with tortured animals, beaten butts and monstrous babies to please Molly as much in fact as in his fantasy. At one point, we overhear her thinking back on *Aristotle's Masterpiece*, whose title she perhaps innocently mangles, though in the service of Joyce's self hatred: "some

Joyce's imaginary circus novel, Ruby: the Pride of the Ring, *used the actual* Ruby (1889) *by Amye Reade, here illustrated by Talbot Hughes. (From Mary Power, "The Discovery of* Ruby," *James Joyce Quarterly, 18 [1981], p. 119.)*

old Aristocrat or whatever his name is, disgusting you with those rotten pictures children with two heads and no legs." Her comment not merely characterizes her, but reflects an effort of the author (in a final involution of irony) to mock the kind of book which the Leopold in him relishes by showing us the negative reaction to their perversity of a normally sexy woman.

But he also ironically travesties the sort of "dirty books" which the Molly-side of him prefers, sentimental rather than sado-masochistic—like *Sweets of Sin* or *Ruby, Pride of the Ring*. *Ruby*, Joyce places with almost too obvious intent, under the Blooms' soiled conjugal bed: "The book fallen, sprawled against the bulge of the orange-keyed chamber pot." The point is made painfully clear: such works are shit. But reflecting on the Blooms' chamberpot is likely to remind us of the title which Joyce gave to a collection of his own poetry—poems still written in the uncontaminated popular mode, as was then possible in Ireland, where Modernism never quite succeeded in convincing poets they must "break the iamb" and eschew all clichés of phrase or feeling.

Chamber Music, he called the poems; and the pun in the title is, as he himself confessed later, intentional: a warning to the reader perceptive enough to catch it that this, too, if not quite shit is a kind of musical tinkling in a pisspot. It would seem, then, that for Joyce—in some moods at least—the whole world of literature seemed bounded by the walls of a thundermug: not just pornographic or sentimental pop, but his own most "serious" work, as well as that of the writers he most admired. And in this Molly would certainly concur, having been invented in fact to project precisely such anti-literary doubts. Her famous final soliloquy, therefore, demands to be read not just as an equivocal celebration of the flesh but as a no less equivocal piece of literary criticism.

To begin with, she is permitted to put down (as we have already noticed) Joyce's favorite philosopher with the apparently inadvertent change of name which turns "Aristotle" into "Aristocrat." But she is also allowed to dismiss his beloved Rabelais and Defoe (whose portrayal of women, Joyce had declared elsewhere, "reduces contemporary literature to stupified impotence") in a pair of contemptuous phrases: ". . . the works of Master Francois somebody supposed to be a priest about a child born out of her ear because her bung just fell out . . .": and "books with a Molly in them like the one he bought me about the one from Flanders who's always shoplifting anything she could. . . "

Obviously, it could be Molly herself who is being mocked in these passages, rather than the books she rejects. But Joyce, we remember, gave her (in contempt of the Greek poem which served as his model) the final word; and we should be aware, especially those of us who are tempted to take her final affirmation unequivocally, that Molly's "yes" to the impulses of the flesh implies a "no" to everything we call Great Literature. But, of course, almost nothing in Joyce can be taken unequivocally. Consequently, I remind you that if he did on one level share with Molly the conviction that much High Literary Art was crap, on another, he shared with Leopold a certain fondness for crap.

As dearly as Joyce would have loved to sustain the elitist image of the Artist as an unacknowledged Legislator of Mankind, a Secular Priest, a Holy Oracle leaving messages to be deciphered by exegetes through the centuries, he realized he was also a coprophile and a voyeur—a sniffer of bicycle seats, a fingerer of the miniature drawers he liked to carry about in his pocket. Even worse, he seems sometimes to have suspected himself of being the peddler of his own most shameful erotic fantasies, a writer of dirty letters to the world, in short, once more a pornographer. Of this charge, Judge Woolsey may have acquitted him in a New York courtroom; but at the continuing trial in the depths of his inner mind (the trial recorded in the text of *Ulysses* itself, at its Nighttown center), he was constantly being found guilty by an inexorable horde of Women, simultaneously his accusers and his judges, mythological Furies. And what they found him guilty of was offending womanhood simply by writing a novel.

But this seems fair enough in light of the fact that the novel historically represented an attempt (think, for instance of Daniel Defoe and Samuel Richardson) to give a voice to the long voiceless female majority—as well as to certain suppressed elements in the male psyche suppressed as being too "girlish" or "womanly." To put it another way, the novel begins with an act of female impersonation—with male authors speaking in the first person as if they were females, or at least knowing what it is like to be *one of them*. More precisely, what certain male writers purport to have revealed is precisely what they know they cannot ever really know: how (and at this point they cross the line into pornography) it feels to be screwed by us; or even more intimately, to menstruate, to piss sitting down. In this sense, the most flagrant pornographers from Jon Cleland and the Marquis de Sade to Paul de Kock are the true heirs

of Richardson and Defoe. In them it becomes clear that from the first
the novel was guilty of the crime of Julius Caesar and Leopold
Bloom: the impious intrusion into the female mysteries.

No wonder, then, that the majority of women readers have until
very recently remained immune to the appeal of pornography, preferring works produced in an alternate line of descent from Richardson: the distaff line which reaches a climax in the middle of the
nineteenth century with what Nathaniel Hawthorne described as "a
horde of female scribblers." The names of the Anglo-Saxon lady
novelists who dominated the literary marketplace from the 1850s to
the 1870s are likely to be unknown to most readers of Joyce, particularly the academics: Mrs. E.D.E.N. Southworth, Maria S. Cummins,
Susan Warner. But Joyce himself was quite familiar with them; so
that fully to understand his novel, one needs to have some sense of
what *St. Elmo* is really about (or *The Wide, Wide World* or *The
Lamplighter*). They are all of them tantalizingly expurgated erotic
tales, in which ribbon clerks are oppressed by cruel aunts and
guards or especially shown in bed dying ecstatically for many pages.

Joyce most clearly shows the influence of such Pop Novelists in
the Gertie MacDowell episode of *Ulysses*, which simultaneously
mocks and imitates Miss Cummins' *The Lamplighter*, whose under-
age heroine is also called Gertie. This strategy permits him to in-
dulge shamelessly but safely (i.e., without running the risk of
making himself seem ridiculous) the sentimentality which everywhere threatens to break through the experimental surfaces of his
text, especially when he deals with unappreciated young artists,
dead children or mothers on their deathbeds. It is a virtuoso performance, the Nausicaa episode—shifting in a single brief scene between the male point of view, i.e., that of pornography, to the
female, i.e., that of sentimentality; and leaving us finally with a
sense of the mingled pathos and comedy of unconsummated love,
sex-in-the-head. We begin with an awareness of the pathos of poor
lame Gertie: a pathos not quite lost even in the comic anticlimax of
Bloom's detumescence: "Up like a rocket, down like a stick."

Meanwhile, we have had foisted on us the theory, devised by
Joyce from Bérard and Samuel Butler, that Homer's *Odyssey* was a
poem about a Semite written by a woman, the Wandering Jew re-
imagined by a kind of proto-Maria S. Cummins. Though we are
never quite sure how seriously Joyce took that theory or wanted us
to, we are reminded of what we may have momentarily forgotten:
that *Ulysses* is not merely parody in general (and in that sense Pop,
parody being Pop's way of coming to terms with High Art); more

particularly, it is a parody of the poem with which the Literature of the West began. In his own Irish way, then, Joyce is saying, like the American Walt Whitman before him, "Cancel out please those long overdue accounts to Greece and Rome!" It is possible to understand, of course, the transformation of the sublimated love of Odysseus for Nausicaa into Bloom's voyeuristic masturbation as an assertion that the latter represents all of the heroic and erotic which has survived into our pitiful times. Yet it can also be read as a suggestion that perhaps Bloom represents all of the heroic and erotic there ever really was; that indeed there never was anything like what Arnold meant by Hellenic culture—only a deceptive fiction created by Romantic poets and scholars, which it is high time to blow away.

In light of all this, it is tempting to believe Stanislaus Joyce, who, however uncharitably, argued that if his big brother, James, is to be considered an "artist" at all, it is in the colloquial Irish sense of the word, meaning a joker, a mocker; and that *Ulysses* is therefore properly read as a gigantic "put-on" or "send-up"—a joke on the joke of Western High Culture. Certainly this irreverent approach helps us to make sense of two otherwise quite baffling pieces of literary criticism, or perhaps better, anti-literary anti-criticism in *Ulysses*: the first of which is set in the National Library, and the second in a Lying-in Hospital. In the former, Stephen Dedalus develops a rather implausible theory about *Hamlet*, based on Shakespeare's presumed relationship to his wife, his brother and especially his father and his only son, Hamnet, both of whom died just before he wrote the play. In the end, however, Stephen disavows his own theory; and Bloom who—like almost every other male in the book—turns out to be an amateur Shakespearian critic, suggests that Hamlet-Shakespeare is not so much his own grandfather as a secret androgyne, most appropriately played by an actress.

Bloom, moreover, is given the final word on the subject, saying—after he has come in his pants at the sight of Gertie's drawers—"For this relief much thanks." It is, of course, an ironically misapplied quotation from *Hamlet*; and I must confess that after all the solemnities of the Library, I welcome the comic implications of the phrase. For me at least (and I suspect many other readers as well) *Hamlet* has become the hardest of Shakespeare's plays to take quite seriously, since generations of scholarly exegesis and popular adulation have made it seem less a Garden of Dainty Delights than an anthology of weary clichés. I am consequently moved to echo Bloom, responding to his parodic send-up of the play, "For *this* relief much thanks."

But Joyce's climactic onslaught against literature, including the book he has written, the reader foolish enough to be holding it gravely in hand, and especially the critic unwary enough to be attempting (like me) one more exegesis is, of course, the "Oxen of the Sun" episode. What else except hostility to the whole of "Eng. Lit." could have motivated that deliberately boring series of pastiche-travesties of English Prose Style through the ages, as pointlessly sterile finally as the most unimaginative PhD examination, unless its point be the pointlessness of *all* style, of the very notion of style, and certainly the study of it. A real baby is being born of a woman even as this male parody of procreation moves toward its abortive close, suggesting that the proper translation of *le style c'est l'homme* is "Every Man his own wife, a honeymoon in the hand . . ."

Those words are, of course, Buck Mulligan's; and clearly Joyce's satire is throughout *Ulysses* directed *against* that mocker and his crew: the wild gaggle of Medical School cynics, who find motherhood and conception, like love and God, occasions for the display of condescending wit. Joyce may have intended to mock their mockery; but precisely in his mocking he is more like them than he would have cared to admit. Certainly, the ironic analogy he implies between the nine hundred year long development of English prose and the nine months of gestation is one they would have greeted with appreciative laughter.

Yet Mrs. Purefoy bears a manchild when her labors are done; while the Fathers of English Style apparently labored only to bring forth a miscarriage of rhetoric in the Sermon of "Alexander J. Christ Dowie"—the Elijah of Bloomsday, as Billy Sunday was to be of the next generation and Billy Graham is of ours. With Dowie, English (not, of course, the native tongue of Joyce's own homeland as the opening quotation in Irish reminds us), which had begun in bondage to Latin, involuted, polysyllabic, pedantic, has become a truly demotic tongue, which is to say, American.

It is, at any rate, American which Joyce puts into the mouth of Dowie—or at least the closest thing to it he could manage:

> Come on, you winefizzling ginsizzling booseguzzling existences! Come on, you doggone, bullnecked, beetlebrowed, hogjowled, peanutbrained, weaseleyed fourflushers, false alarms and excess baggage! . . .The Deity aint no nickel dime bumshow. I put it to you that he's on the square and a corking fine business proposition. He's the grandest thing yet and don't you forget it . . .You'll need to rise precious early, you sinner there, if you want to diddle the Almighty God. Pflaaaap! . . .He's got a coughmixture with a punch in it for you, my friend, in his backpocket. Just you try it . . .

And American he was aware is also the language toward which all late Gutenberg English aspires, especially journalism and advertising, the other favorite reading matter of porno-loving Bloom, and presumably of Joyce as well—who, we are told, entered the famous contest for a slogan to sell more Guiness eventually won by "Guiness is good for you."

That he read the daily newspapers well is attested by the skill with which he composed the quite convincing, though to be sure ironic, headlines in the *Aeolus* episode. One in especial I prize as as Joyce's final thumbing of the nose (and in what other language could he have written it except journalese) at the Epic tradition:

SOPHIST WALLOPS HAUGHTY HELEN

SQUARE ON THE PROBOSCIS. SPARTANS

GNASH MOLARS. ITHACANS VOW

PEN IS CHAMP.

It is possible that "PEN" means only, or chiefly—as the context suggests—Penelope; and the whole phrase therefore signifies that final victory belongs to the real wife waiting at home (which in this case is literature-hating Molly), rather than to the legendary Helen, whose beauty launched not only a thousand ships but the High Literature of Europe. It is tempting, however, to read "PEN IS" as the single word "penis," which would translate the sentence into a phallic boast appropriate enough in a pornographic work. But perhaps finally we should take "PEN" in the simplest sense of all: as the name of the humble tool of the writer's trade which writers themselves have long boasted is mightier than the sword—though no one else has ever believed them. That meaning, at any rate, evokes the figure who in *Finnegans Wake* represents his author: SHEM/SHAM/SHAME THE PEN MAN: parodic caricature of the real Seamus alias James Joyce, who alone might have told us his true intent. But of course did not.

Joyce and the Modern Coalescence

Zack Bowen

The idea of the unity of all things has been central to our civilization at least as far back as antiquity. The continual process of transformation taking place in events, people, and their environment is merely the affirmation of unity over time. Artists have always represented this universal commonality directly or indirectly, as each generation recapitulated its predecessors, making new variations on the theme, and becoming in the process the latest in a succession of "modern" ages. Twentieth century literature, while addressing itself to questions about man's relationship to his cosmos, has increasingly come to see all facets of that relationship as partly explainable by archetypal analysis as structured by the processes of amalgamation and synthesis.

James Joyce's chief contribution to the age was his recognition of such transformational processes and his ability to synthesize characters, events, literature, even language itself. Joyce transforms the common, the mundane, by means of the philosopher's stone of his art into the sublime. The more the reader begins to piece together the interconnections in Joyce's work and to understand the complexity of its structures, the more he is led to the idea that everything is interrelated. Joyce's art is transformation, the endless combining of theme, event, and character. His transformation reaffirms the basic proposition that everything is ultimately the same. It is his representation of the common identity of people and their environment, and of the transformation process which is the basis of that unity, which paradoxically makes Joyce "modern" at the same time that it welds him to the past.

Finnegans Wake has been the most blatant statement of Joyce's intent, but it is not so obvious—though nonetheless true—that the theme of commonality is central to Joyce's earlier work as well as the *Wake*. For purposes of this paper, then, I am going to explore three examples of Joyce's ingenious combining of seemingly disparate sources into one unified pattern, providing a common identity for the whole. The first example, involving widely divergent musical allusions in *Ulysses*, is typical of how Joyce uses transformation in structure. The second example, also from *Ulysses*, involves character and unlikely literary source allusions mixed in the pot of contemporary events and scenes. Finally, I would like to demonstrate how Joyce uses his own work as a source of his basic concept of unity, the idea that everything is ultimately the same. While each of his fictive works uses the same techniques, I have chosen my last example primarily from *A Portrait of the Artist* because Joyce's technique of recapitulation is less obvious here. In my conclusion I will try to show how all of his work is drawn together at the end of the *Wake* into one great amalgamation which testifies not only to the common identity of the Joyce canon, but by extension to the common identity of all human experience which is his subject matter.

. . . .

In a way Joyce was ideally equipped to deal with the unity and common identity of things, since his own tastes and experiences were so catholic. In the Dublin circles in which he grew up, the cheap, the bawdy, and the popular coexisted side by side with the classical, the cultured, and the refined. Similarly, the cerebral, the essential, the mystical, and the religious coexisted with the excremental, the debased, the vulgar, and the gross. All were important aspects of urban Irish life. For example, Joyce was a singer in a time and place where tenors were not merely operatic or popular, but included in their repertoires the whole spectrum of music from common street ballads to Grand Opera, and it is not surprising that their harmony should be blended into his works. My example interweaves strains of a popular music hall song with Wagner's Ring Cycle.

The Music Hall song, "My Girl's a Yorkshire Girl," occurs in two sections of *Ulysses*. It is introduced in the Wandering Rocks section and later performed in its entirety in Circe. In the original section the song is intimately linked with Blazes Boylan:

> By the provost's wall came jauntily Blazes Boylan, stepping in tan shoes and socks with skyblue clocks to the refrain of *My girl's a Yorkshire girl.*
>
> Blazes Boylan presented to the leaders' skyblue frontlets and high action a skyblue tie, a widebrimmed straw hat at a rakish angle and a suit of indigo serge. His hands in his jacket pockets forgot to salute but he offered to the three ladies the bold admiration of his eyes and the red flower between his lips. As they drove along Nassau street His Excellency drew the attention of his bowing consort to the programme of music which was being discoursed in College park. Unseen brazen highland laddies blared and drumthumped after the *cortège*:
>
> *But though she's a factory lass*
> *And wears no fancy clothes.*
> *Baraabum.*
> *Yet I've a sort of a*
> *Yorkshire relish for*
> *My little Yorkshire rose.*
> *Baraabum. (253:41-254:18)*[1]

The unseen brazen Highland laddies who are playing the song behind the wall of Trinity College are the Second Seaforth Highlanders, who performed during the afternoon at the Half-Mile Bicycle Handicap, which was run on June 16, 1904, in College Park, and the "Baraabum" is a roll of the Highlanders' drums. The association between Boylan and the song is not difficult to grasp, since it carries overtones of the Blazes-Molly assignation. In the song two young men discuss their sweethearts, both named Rose, and both Yorkshire girls, who look alike and work in a factory. Deciding that they are one and the same, the men go to her house to find out which lover she prefers. They are met by her husband, who eventually runs them off, clearly another Homeric parallel to the usurpation of the suitor, Boylan, and perhaps an indication that Bloom will emerge triumphant from the battle over Molly's favors. Boylan will after all be on his way in a few minutes to Molly's house for an assignation, and the song acts as one of his courting leitmotifs. Of more immediate interest here is that the Yorkshire Girl, who seems different to three separate men, turns out to be only a single individual.

When we hear the song again in Circe, however, the situation is a great deal more complicated. Initially the symbolism is straighhtforward enough with Privates Carr and Compton together with Cissy

Caffrey singing the words as they pass the window of Bella Cohen's. Carr, Compton, and Caffrey might easily fit the roles of the two British youths in search of their not unwilling Yorkshire girl. Zoe, who has informed us (U 550:5-6) that she is also "Yorkshire born," responds to their melody drifting in through the window, and puts tuppence in the pianola, which begins to play the song, while Zoe invites everyone to dance. As the dancing, under the direction of Professor Maginni, begins, the pianola echoes the baraabums of the earlier Highland drummers overheard by Blazes Boylan. The concluding lines of the stage directions of this rendition of the song carry with them direct references of earlier situations, words, and characters from Wandering Rocks and Stephen's Parable of Plums in Aeolus.

STEPHEN

Dance of death.

(Bang fresh barang bang of lacquey's bell, horse, nag, steer, piglings, Conmee on Christass lame crutch and leg sailor in cockboat armfolded ropepulling hitching stamp hornpipe through and through, Baraabum! On nags, hogs, bellhorses, Gadarene swine, Corny in coffin. Steel shark stone onehandled Nelson, two trickies Frauenzimmer plumstained from pram falling bawling. Gum, he's a champion. Fuseblue peer from barrel rev. evensong Love on hackney jaunt Blazes blind coddoubled bicyclers Dilly with snowcake no fancy clothes. Then in last wiswitchback lumbering up and down bump mashtub sort of viceroy and reine relish for tublumber bumpshire rose. Baraabum! (U 579:5-18)

The outcome of this dance of death is Stephen's ghoulish vision of his mother, the once beautiful May Goulding, and in keeping with the rivalry motif of the song, the object of Stephen's oedipal rivalry with his father. She reminds Stephen, "You sang that song to me. *Love's bitter mystery*" (U 581:2-3). The latter line, from Fergus's song in *The Countess Cathleen*, has already occurred to Stephen in Telemachus (U 9:37-8) as a sort of love motif between Stephen and his mother. Now, in the light of rivalry of the young men with the Yorkshire girl's husband and each other, the appearance of May Goulding may be another manifestation of deep-level oedipal desire on Stephen's part. To rid himself of her image and her linkage with the Blessed Virgin Mary, Stephen lifts his ashplant, breaking the chandelier as he refers to Siegfried's sword in Wagner's opera from the Ring Cycle. The sword is the one Siegfried used to break Wotan's ash spear and bring an end to the old order of Gods. We have been prepared for this image some pages earlier by a reference Stephen made to the blood oath in *Gotterdammerung*, the opera immediately after *Siegfried* in the Ring Cycle. The oath, chanted by Stephen in answer to Zoe's innocuous question "Is he hungry," is translated roughly "Intense desire/questioning wife/destroys us all." Clearly such a preamble to his attempt to rid himself of his mother's image by taking up Siegfried's sword is an effort to dispel the mental state brought on by "The Yorkshire Girl." Thus "The Yorkshire Girl," originally linked with Boylan's rivalry for Molly's hand, now is associated with Siegfried's attempt to bring to an end the old world which is doomed to extinction, an old world not unlike May's Christianity and the matriarchal Ireland.

The Ring Cycle has, of course, been viewed by generations of Germans as a political allegory, a myth about the creation of the new Germany. Stephen in invoking the mythic image transforms German nationalistic hopes into Ireland's with himself the Siegfried-like liberating force.

A few moments later, Stephen, out on the street again, begins an altercation with Privates Carr and Compton over a supposed insult to Cissy Caffrey. All of them have mistaken Stephen's cryptic remarks as overtures to Cissy and insults to the Crown. In fact, Stephen's quotation from a 16th Century Canting song, "The Rogue's Delight in Praise of His Stroling Mort," does identify Cissy as a prostitute. At any rate, Cissy protests Stephen's alleged advances, saying to Private Carr, "Amn't I with you? Amn't I your girl? Cissy's your girl" (*U* 598:2-3). In the ensuing fanciful conflagration we return again to echoes of *"The Yorkshire Girl," "Factory lasses with fancy clothes toss redhot Yorkshire baraabombs"* (*U* 598:29-30). Thus Stephen, now suitor for Cissy's hand, and in his own political allegory a suitor for Ireland, participates in a miniburlesque of the perpetual hostilities between England and Ireland. Cissy, as a figure of her country, is possessed by the British, while Stephen, the suitor, is vanquished by a superior military force. Lest there be any question of Cissy, the female figure, being identified with Ireland, Joyce has Old Gummy Granny, that Shan Van Vocht image from Telemachus, urge, like Yeats' Kathleen ni Hoolihan, that Stephen take up arms against the British, "(*Thrusts a dagger toward Stephen's hand.*) Remove him, acushla. At 8:35 A.M. you will be in heaven and Ireland will be free. (*She prays.*) O good God, take him!" (*U* 600:16-18).

Thus, "The Yorkshire Girl" becomes the center of an elaborate and delicately interwoven tapestry of music based on the rivalry and usurpation themes beginning with Bloom's rivalry, continuing through Stephen's oedipal complex and the representation of the Holy Mother Church, and ending in a political allegory. The range of music from 16th Century canting music through Wagnerian opera to musical hall song is symptomatic of the spectrum of sources that Joyce used as strands for this tapestry. In *Gotterdammerung* Siegfried is finally conquered by the mistaken love and betrayal of a woman who thinks she herself has been betrayed, but who in the divine form of Valkyrie has wed herself to her perishable hero. Brunnhilde, like the Yorkshire Girl and Stephen's perennial symbolic images of women, is larger than life, though at the same time mortal. Joyce combines here the common and the sublime, a Yorkshire Girl-Brunnhilde, yet another aspect of Molly Bloom, sitting in bed waiting for her hero.

What Joyce does with music and theme he also does with character. Drawing from a number of unlikely origins, he again effects combinations of the high and low, the comic and sublime. It bears repeating that while this technique is readily apparent in the *Wake*, in *Ulysses* it is not always so clear. Nevertheless it is a principal feature. The very incongruity of such disparate literary sources, while helping to establish the theme of universal unity, provides much of the novel's comedy. For instance, that the title of the novel overtly links one of the least effectual of protagonists in literature, Leopold Bloom, with the greatest epic hero of the western world seems a wholly comic proposition until one is several hundred pages into *Ulysses*, when the inherent truth of the comic juxtaposition, with all of its implications of marital faithfulness, ingenuity, resourcefulness, etc., leads us to a far broader and truer definition of heroism, in which the common man (who is not common at all) is, in fact, the hero of the *Odyssey*, and Ulysses the hero of Joyce's novel. Supporting this major conjunction of characters are a series of character-theme identifications which give substance to the major premise that at the core, everything is interrelated. My second example, W. B. Murphy, is typical.

Murphy is at the center of a complex web of allusion, linking a number of characters in Joyce's last two novels. One of the main threads in this web is Murphy's relation to Sinbad the Sailor. Murphy is directly referred to as Sinbad (*U* 636:33), a name not unexpected in the series of nautical pseudonyms the narrator bestows on Murphy. But later Murphy does tell us that the *Arabian Nights' Entertainment* was his favorite book (*U* 659:28). As a wanderer, a voyager, and a teller of fantastic stories, Murphy has much in common with Sinbad the Sailor, whose tales of his seven voyages comprise the five hundred and thirty-seventh night through the five hundred and sixty-sixth of *The Thousand and One Nights*. On his voyages Sinbad's general *modus operandi* is to lose all the goods and wealth that he has brought with him to trade, either through shipwreck or other natural calamity, undergo some fabulous adventure, and then come upon his goods again toward the end of the story, whereupon he relates his tale to those who hold his goods for him, supposing him dead. Invariably his tale is so farfetched that the merchants or captain, whoever has his goods in escrow, do not believe him. But, someone comes forward either to corroborate part of his testimony or to recognize him so that the goods are generally recovered. And, of course, in the main tale Sinbad the Sailor relates to Sinbad the Porter a story of how he related the story to the custodians of his property as well as underwent the vicissitudes of plot and action himself.

The tale within a tale is common to the *Odyssey*. Further, in reading the tales, one is struck by the similarity of Sinbad's voyages to parts of Odysseus's travels. For instance, the third voyage is a great deal like Odysseus's blinding of Polyphemus. There are echoes of Lestrygonians, cannibalism, and the casting of rocks by giants, as well as other hints of the *Odyssey*. The fourth voyage closely resembles Circe, and the fifth, Oxen of the Sun. The tales themselves go back to antiquity in Indian folklore with early references to its present form with the frame tale appearing as late as 956 A.D. Sinbad's voyages were based on a collection of Arabic travel romances, in part from the experiences of Oriental navigators especially in the 8th to 10th century, and in part from ancient poetry, particularly Homeric poetry. Scholars have long known the *Odyssey* to be an integral part of Sinbad's stories. But there is no such thing as a standard text of the *Arabian Nights*, and stories in the oral tradition have drifted in and out of the collection over the centuries. But, clearly the strongest links between the stories and sources are with the *Odyssey* and Sinbad's voyages, thus bringing about the linkage among Murphy, Sinbad, Odysseus, and Joyce's modern Odysseus, Leopold Bloom. These links appear in both Eumaeus and the rest of the book.

Bloom the wanderer, the traveler, the Ulysses figure, produces for Stephen a postcard photo of his wife, a piece of advertising literature associated with the song "In Old Madrid," itself a source of Eastern enchantment for Bloom. With this ocular proof Bloom proceeds to document his own personal history, just as Murphy exhibits his Chilean postcard picture of savage women in striped loin cloths to authenticate his own adventures. Like Odysseus, Murphy claims he has waiting at home a wife who has not seen her husband for seven years, just as Bloom's own Penelope waits less expectantly at home for his return. Murphy's stories, like Sinbad's stories and the masquerading Odysseus' stories, all suffer from a credibility gap in the ears of their listeners in this chapter full of half-truths, unexplained meanings, and fuzzy correspondences. Bloom too is a wanderer and in the passage which most clearly deals with his Sinbad side he discusses a Persian scene:

> Somewhere in the east: early morning: set off at dawn, travel round in front of the sun, steal a day's march on him. Keep it up for ever never grow a day older technically. Walk along a strand, strange land, come to a city gate, sentry there, old ranker too, old Tweedy's big moustaches leaning on a long kind of a spear. Wander through awned streets. Turbaned faces going by. Dark caves of carpet shops, big man, Turko the terrible, seated crosslegged smoking a coiled pipe. Cries of sellers in the streets. Drink water scented with fennel, sherbet. Wander along all day. Might meet a robber or two. Well, meet him. Getting on to sundown. The shadows of the mosques along the pillars: priest with a scroll rolled up. A shiver of the trees, signal, the evening wind. I pass on. Fading gold sky. A mother watches from her doorway. She calls her children home in their dark language. High wall: beyond strings twanged. Night sky moon, violet, colour of Molly's new garters. Strings. Listen. A girl playing one of these instruments what do you call them: dulcimers. I pass.

> (*Ulysses*, 57:15-32)

The affinity to Sinbad in this passage is more than merely the spirit of Eastern wandering. The allusion to Turko the terrible is intimately linked with Sinbad, Murphy, and Bloom. The pantomime of Turko the terrible was put on at the Gaiety first in 1873 and ran with great popularity during the closing decades of the 19th century, later evolving into another popular pantomime called "Sinbad the Sailor," the first edition of which appeared in December 26, 1892. The pantomime, like Turko and like the *Arabian Nights*, was widely popular and returned year after year, revised with new material added and other sequences deleted. Because of the popularity of the earlier Turko, the character of King Turko was inserted in the Sinbad pantomime. Robert Adams has suggested that Joyce in Stephen's earlier reference to Turko the terrible (*U* 10:2) really referred to the character Turko in the later "Sinbad the Sailor," since Joyce had in his possession typed copies of the reviews from December 1892 to January 1893.[2] They are now in the Buffalo Joyce collection. Nevertheless, Turko and Sinbad were inextricably intertwined. In addition, "Sinbad" ran at the Gaiety theatre, and the narrator's reference to Murphy as Sinbad contains an allusion to the Gaiety theatre: "However, reverting to friend Sinbad and his horrifying adventures (who reminded him a bit of Ludwig, *alias* Ledwidge, when he occupied the boards of the Gaiety" (*U* 636:31-33). The quotation continues with reference to the *Flying Dutchman*, which, like the Turko-Sinbad references, is also confused, because Wagner's opera and the musical by the same name, popular on the Dublin stage at the time, were often confused. Joyce is creating, of course, all through Eumaeus a pattern of obfuscation and confusion, but with enough hints to keep us sniffing after the scent. The point is that the reference to Sinbad links Bloom, both indirectly and directly, with the sailor. As Bloom drops off to sleep that night he has traveled with Sinbad the Sailor and Tinbad the Tailor and Jinbad the Jailor and Winbad the Whaler, etc. Both Tinbad and Winbad were characters in the first edition of "Sinbad the Sailor" in 1892-3. So beside being fanciful, the passage ties in the pantomime with Sinbad, and the last answer in Ithaca is a reference to Sinbad's fifth voyage—a voyage which, like the Oxen episode, involves eggs, fertility, and the new word.

Incidental but interrelated to this investigation of *Ulysses*, Bloom's dream might turn out to be *Finnegans Wake*. Part of this seemingly outrageous assumption is based again on *The Arabian Nights*, in which there are two Sinbads, the Sinbad of the sea and Sinbad of the land. The Sinbad we have been discussing here is, of course, the first of this pair, who tells his story to another Sinbad. Sinbad the Sailor is a fabulously rich merchant prince, a man of adventure and enthusiasm, of courage and daring, while his land-locked counterpart is Sinbad the porter, who is invited day after day to come and hear the adventures of Sinbad the Sailor and is given one hundred gold coins each day. They eventually spend their lives together in happy companionship. Now the *porter* Sinbad (what's in a name) is the mundane counterpart of the sailor. While the porter stays at home and profits mildly, his namesake engages in fabulous voyages, just as Porter keeps the mundane pub in Chapelizod while his counterpart, Here Comes Everybody, goes everywhere and does everything.

Once we involve HCE and his multiple identities, the links among Sinbad, the Norwegian Captain and the Ship's Husband expand the metaphor into a galaxy of associations, which comprise the subject matter as well as the method of Joyce's final ultimate blend of mundane and sublime, of the disparate and the similar into one gigantic monomyth. The point to be made here is that the principle of the interconnectedness between people and things operates in *Ulysses* and even earlier in the Joyce canon. For purposes of our present discussion of *Ulysses*, however, it suffices to draw the conclusion that Porter and HCE may in fact be Sinbad the porter and Sinbad the sailor as combined in the rocks of Darkinbad the Brightdayler, the dreamer Leopold Bloom.

Bruno Bettleheim in *The Uses of Enchantment* has drawn a Freudian inference between the two Sinbad figures. The porter Sinbad, a poverty stricken merchant, is the superego, stay-at-home-Penelope of the story, while the fabulous Sinbad, the rich merchant, engages in libidinous adventures, bringing fabulous wealth. The two Sinbads operate as alter egos in *Finnegans Wake* in precisely the same manner, just as the Sinbad figure of Murphy with his fabulous tales of adventure, his aggrandizing of the Phoenix Park murders, makes his alter ego, Bloom, more understandable and lovable in mundane everyday terms. Perhaps both are realized in Bloom's night dream. There is a touch of the superego even in Murphy, for Sinbad the porter is carrying around men's clothing to sell, while Murphy's son works in a draper's shop and he himself wishes that he might stay home to be a "gentleman's valet at six quid a month" (*U* 630:40). If Murphy is the sailor Sinbad, and Bloom the porter, it is fitting that Bloom's last thoughts of Murphy deal with the ambiguity of his and Murphy's joint identity, and "the usual blarney about himself for as to who he in reality was let XX equal my right name and address, as Mr Algebra remarks *passim*. At the same time he inwardly chuckled over his repartee to the blood and ouns champion about his God being a jew" (658:16-20). The reference to XX in roman numerals corresponds to the chapter II of *The Arabian Nights*, which encompasses the story of Sinbad the Sailor, Bloom's encounter with the citizen being one of the direct accounts of Sinbad's voyages.

If Murphy is Bloom, and father and son are one and same in this trinitarian manifestation called *Ulysses*, it stands to reason that there might be some relation between Murphy and Stephen. John Henry Raleigh, in his pioneer essay "On the Way Home to Ithaca" has already speculated that Joyce and Stephen are also reflected in W. B. Murphy. One of Raleigh's principal proofs is the tatoo on Murphy's chest made by one Antonio in the form of a self-portrait of the artist, [3] not unlike Stephen Dedalus's portrait in *Portrait* of James Joyce-Shem writing with his own excrement his own life on his skin.

I have a footnote to add to Raleigh's portrait of the portrait of *A Portrait of the Artist as a Young Man*: that involves the song that Murphy is inspired to sing by the mention of Antonio's name and his own perhaps narcissistic or unnatural love for the young artist. The song is one we heard echoed from Hades, "Has Anybody Here Seen Kelly?" or "Oh, Oh, Antonio." The first time Bloom hears this song in Hades, it is being played on a street organ. It occurs as Bloom thinks of his father's suicide and in the midst of a series of references to fathers and sons, particularly Simon and Stephen, Bloom and his father, and Bloom and Rudy. Now we hear W. B. Murphy's gravelly voice growling out part of the chorus, *"As bad as old Antonio'/For he left me on my ownio"* (*U* 632:10-11). The song has three different versions, "Oh, Oh, Antonio," "Has Anybody Here Seen Kelly?" and "Kelly From the Isle of Man." It is the same music with the same chorus. The composer kept altering the words, but they all fit the tune. And who was the composer you might ask—C. W. Murphy, the artist making up the work of art about his namesake Antonio, who was drawing a work of art on the chest of his maker, W. B. Murphy, the Shem-Shawn-Stephen Dedalus figure and mirror image of James Joyce himself, both as Sinbad the porter—Leopold Bloom, with his life of domestic scratching and meager subsistence in Dublin—and Sinbad the sailor—*Ulysses's* Odysseus, W. B. Murphy—the voyager of fabulous wealth and dreams, the Here Comes Everybody-Finnegan, the counterpart to the dreaming porter, every man's journeyer.

. . . .

If sources, themes, characters are all interconnected, and if the process of transformation establishes those connections in an imitation of human existence, it stands to reason that the self-conscious artist, in presenting the transformation process in his art form, will also seek to explain how his work is in itself a part of the subject matter. No one will deny the unity inherent in Joyce's four major fictional works, but their commonality of purpose, lest it be lost to the reader, is set forth in the conclusion to each work.

These endings each take the form of a recorso, which in part recapitulates major themes, often with specific scenes or allusions from the rest of the book, putting those into a new perspective, to blend the old or what has already been said with the future. In *Portrait* the diary entries provide just such a recorso. In Joyce's first two books, *Dubliners* and *Portrait*, the perspectives are those of two men, Gabriel Conroy and Stephen Dedalus, while in Joyce's last two works, *Ulysses* and *Finnegans Wake*, the perspective is feminine. The second hypothesis I would like to propose is an extension of the recorso theory: while at the end of *Finnegans Wake* the perspective is

Anna Livia's, the narrator also takes on overtones of an androgynous figure, both male and female, as the final passages bring together not only the novel which they conclude, but all of Joyce's fiction in a recorso that is both recapitulatory of Joyce's earlier works and a conclusion to his last great novel.

Because it has the least obvious recorso pattern, the conclusion of *A Portrait* is an interesting example. The five and a half pages of the diary which cover five and a half weeks of Stephen's young life begin with immediate links to the previous scene and at the same time put the diary in a considerably different prospective from the scene we have just read, belying either the diary view, or the previous account of Stephen's conversation with Cranly. Like the situation in the beginning of the novel, Stephen is initially concerned in the diary entries with fathers and mothers, with beards, with uncertainty about parental age, and with references to beds. These are followed by recapitulatory allusions to John the Baptist, the precursor of Christ, to *BVM*, and to Stephen's Green (reminiscent of the novel's opening, not only because of the color, but also because it is associated with St. Stephen the martyr). The diary entries continue through a dream vision (taken from Joyce's own epiphanies) of a long curving gallery "peopled by the images of fabulous kings," reminiscent of the jesuit founders whose portraits hung on the halls leading to Father Conmee's study. The crocodile entry of March 30th becomes the muck of Ireland in which Stephen is reared, suggesting Stephen's disgust with Stradbrook, "with its foul green puddles in clots of liquid dung and steaming brantroughs," and his own eventual self-conceived roles as a Moses figure leading Ireland out of her bondage. Throughout the whole of the diary pages there runs the contemporary vision of EC which succeeds the discussions of Stephen's mother and later blends with her just as they are combined in the composite female image throughout *Portrait*. In this respect, the first entry of April 6th forms a structural crux of the diary section, just as the end of Chapter 4 forms a climax to the novel as a whole.

> Certainly she remembers the past. Lynch says all women do. Then she remembers the time of her childhood—and mine if I was ever a child. The past is consumed in the present and the present is living only because it brings forth the future. Statues of women, if Lynch be right, should always be fully draped, one hand of the woman feeling regretfully her own hinder parts. (P 251)[4]

Thus, women represent the heritage of the past and the pregnant promise of the future. Stephen's life and work will be linked to a composite female image, "as a type of her race and his own, a batlike soul waking to the consciousness of itself in darkness and secrecy and loneliness and, through the eyes and voice and gesture of a woman without guile, calling the stranger to her bed" (*P* 183). Thus they are the temptresses of his future and the symbols of his past. In a second diary entry later on April 6, Stephen alludes to Yeats' poem "Michael Robartes Remembers Forgotten Beauty," "when his arms wrap her round, he presses in his arms the loveliness which has long faded from the world" (*P* 251). Unlike Yeats, Stephen will not let the feminine temptress lure him back into the past and Ireland's history: "Not this. Not at all. I desire to press in my arms the loveliness which has not yet come into the world" (*P* 251). It will not be as a spokesman for Ireland or his heritage but as the creator of a new beauty that Stephen will emerge. The nationalistic speculation leads us into John Alphonsus Mulrennan's account of a conversation with the quintessential old Irishman and Stephen's attempt to come to terms with his heritage. This will be examined in more detail presently. The entry is followed by another meeting with EC, in which for the first time Stephen sees her not as a symbolic Dantesque inspiration figure but as a real person, one to be liked rather than worshipped. It is a dangerous diversion into reality, and Stephen restrains himself, preferring kinship with both past and future in the company of Dedalean figures, resplendent with bird imagery and Irish exiles, those "wild geese (who) spread the grey wing upon every tide."

In the entry of April 16, when "the spell of arms and voices" assails Stephen, "They are held out to say: We are alone. Come." The statement recalls two triumphful scenes, the first when Stephen has triumphed over Father Dolan and is in the Clongowes yard: "He was alone. He was happy and free" (*P* 59), and the second, at the beginning of the climatic scene on the beach concluding Chapter 4: "He was alone. He was unheeded, happy and near to the wild heart of life. He was alone and young and wilful and wildhearted" (*P* 171). Now in Stephen's diary, the voices bid him to take off on another Dedalean excursion like the one that concluded Chapter 4: "Come. And the voices say with them: We are your kinsmen. And the air is thick with their company as they call to me, their kinsman, making ready to go, shaking the wings of their exultant and terrible youth" (*P* 252). So the dramatic climax of the book and the call to the future are recapitulated now near the end of the diary entries, before returning, recorso-like, in this cycle within cycles, to Stephens' mother in the entry of April 26: "Mother is putting my new secondhand clothes in order. She prays now, she says, that I may learn in my own life and away from home and friends what the heart is and what it feels. Amen. So be it. Welcome, O life! I go to encounter for the millionth time the reality of experience and to forge in the smithy of my soul the uncreated conscience of my race" (*P* 252-53). Like the recorso, the last entry returns from mother to son, from past to present, from the beginning of the book to the end, con-cluding with the diary entry of April 27th: "Old father, old artificer, stand me now and ever in good stead" (*P* 253).

It is easy to see, as countless critics have, how "The Dead" fits the recorso pattern. References, both direct and indirect, to the rest of *Dubliners* appear in the concluding story. Some are obvious, like the relationship of the coin given by Gabriel to Lily, the Morkans' slavey, and the coin taken from the slavey in "Two Gallants." The general themes of paralysis, death, simony and the like are all there, represented in other circumstances. But it is Greta's memory of the past and the dead Furey which brings life to the conclusion of the story and the collection.

While women's voices prevail in the conclusions of only the later two novels, both Gabriel's and Stephen's closing lines are strongly influenced by the women which are prominent in their minds. Gabriel—the artist, the writer—influenced by his wife's memories of an early love, broadens his vision into the Christ-like sacrifice of a young singer whose song inspires a Christian vision of the intermin-gling of life and death. The white snow falls,

> upon every part of the lonely churchyard on the hill where Michael Furey lay buried. It lay thickly drifted on the crooked crosses and head-stones, on the spears of the little gate, on the barren thorns. His soul swooned slowly as he heard the snow falling faintly through the uni-verse and faintly falling, like the descent of their last end, upon all the living and the dead.[5]

In this encomium to universal unity, Gabriel's loathing for his country and its citizens is combined with Furey's loneliness, as he longs to slip away to the continent but is overtaken by the over-powering vision of the West and death. The same things conclude the diary entries of *A Portrait of the Artist as a Young Man*:

> John Alphonsus Mulrennan has just returned from the west of Ireland. (European and Asiatic papers please copy.) He told us he met an old man there in a mountain cabin. Old man had red eyes and short pipe. Old man spoke Irish. Mulrennan spoke Irish. Then old man and Mulrennan spoke English. Mulrennan spoke to him about universe and stars. Old man sat, listened, smoked, spat. Then said:

—Ah, there must be terrible queer creatures at the latter end of the world.

I fear him. I fear his redrimmed horny eyes. It is with him I must struggle all through this night till day come, till he or I lie dead, gripping him by the sinewy throat till. . . Till what? Till he yield to me? No. I mean him no harm (*P* 251-52).

The old man is not only Irish; he is a symbol of death. The parenthesis following the beginning of the first sentence of this April 14 diary entry, "(European and Asiatic papers please copy)," was traditional exhortation following obituary notices in the Irish papers. Mulrennan has not only come from the west of Ireland, the country's source, like Furey he has also come back from the dead. Stephen will wrestle through the night with the old man, whose name he does not know, a representative of the peasant roots of Ireland, or as Mary Reynolds put it in her Yale lecture, "Joyce, Yeats and the Irish Renaissance," a symbol of Ireland, which was to give Stephen the subject matter of his art, a new life, a forward look at the same time it represented the past and death. Compare the concluding lines from *Dubliners* and *Portrait* above to others in the conclusion of *Finnegans Wake*:

But I'm loothing them that's here and all I lothe. Loonely in me loneness. For all their faults. I am passing out. O bitter ending! I'll slip away before they're up. They'll never see. Nor know. Nor miss me. And it's old and old it's sad and old it's sad and weary I go back to you, my cold father, my cold mad father, my cold mad feary father, till the near sight of the mere size of him, the moyles and moyles of it, moananoaning, makes me seasilt saltsick and I rush, my only, into your arms. I see them rising! Save me from those therrble prongs! Two more. Onetwo moremens more (*FW* 627-28).

The passage combines Stephen's and Gabriel's loathing, loneliness, and escape; father images (Stephen's feary father, Mulrennan's old man, and Furey's Christ-like association with the spears of the little gate and the barren thorns, not unlike ALP's beseeching the father to save her from *the rising* (both phallic and resurrectional) and to save her from those 'therrble prongs!" She further beseeches her father, "Yes. Carry me along, taddy, like you done through the toy fair! If I seen him bearing down on me now under whitespread wings like he'd come from Arkangels, I sink I'd die down over his feet, humbly dumbly, only to washup" (*FW* 628). The passage of "whitespread wings" links the Arkangels Michael and Gabriel, Furey's snow, Stephen's conclusion "Old father, old artificer, stand me now and ever in good stead," and Molly's last lines, "and first I put my arms around him yes and drew him down to me so he could feel my breasts all perfume yes and his heart was going like mad and yes I said yes I will Yes" (*U* 783) in one great Leda and the Swan image. In *Dubliners* we have the falling snow, in *Portrait* the plunging Icarus, and in *Ulysses* Molly's descent into coital embrace. Indeed the leaves of Joyce's earlier works are not unlike Anna's leaves: "My leaves have drifted from me. All. But one clings still. I'll bear it on me. To remind me of" (*FW* 628). The parallels among the endings go on and on: The conclusion of Molly's soliloquy and Anna Livia's rush into her father's arms, the blend of Bloom and Mulvey into an indistinguishable everyman figure, the merging of characters and motivations, the father's and son's searches are all too apparent.

The conclusion of *Portrait* has an equally compelling resemblance to the *Wake* recorso. Like Anna, mother and father are blended in a past, full of future. Like Christ, Stephen's father is essential, inspirational and spiritual, the holy ghost, while like Christ's own mother, May Dedalus is real and temporal. If the old father, the sea, at the end of *Finnegans Wake* provides a way, alone, for the artist, a last ending to his travels, a loved vision as it flows along, it also provides a new beginning to the endless cycle. The recorso of *Finnegans Wake* is a recapitulation not only of the novel, but of all Joyce's works, just as the *Wake* itself is both new and recapitulatory, a new direction to the old which will ever flow in the minds and hearts of Joyce readers, just as the *Portrait* has circled back on itself and flowed into the great androgynous amorphous mass of the cold mad Furey father, Ulysses the Finn again.

Thus is Joyce's modern answer to the age-old problem of man's identity in relation to the rest of the universe. If the answers of the past were ultimately different, Joyce has subsumed them into his equation. His particular formations of the mundane and the extraordinary, the dross and the gold are the substance of his art—enormous as human experience, microscopic as the seedcake on Howth. Making the modern world on one day in Dublin into a paradigm of all of everything is Joyce's unique gift, the source of his modernity, and the greatness of his art.

Notes

1. All references to *Ulysses* are taken from the Random House 1961 edition.

2. Robert Adams, *Surface and Symbol: The Consistency of James Joyce's ULYSSES* (New York: Oxford University Press, 1962), pp. 76-82.

3. John Henry Raleigh, "On the Way Home to Ithaca: The Functions of the "Eumaeus' Section in *Ulysses*," *Irish Renaissance Annual II*, (East Brunswick, NJ: Associated University Presses for University of Delaware Press, 1981), pp. 105-6.

4. All references to *A Portrait of the Artist as a Young Man* are taken from the Viking Press 1968 edition.

5. James Joyce, *Dubliners* (New York: The Viking Press, 1967), pp. 223-24.

6. All references to *Finnegans Wake* are taken from the Viking Press 1957 edition.

EXPERIMENTAL LITERATURE

Who's He When He's At Home?

Hugh Kenner

"**M**et him what?" might be an alternative title. Molly Bloom has put a mark in a book ("There's a word I wanted to ask you"). The book is *Ruby: the Pride of the Ring*, and by the way is that a book about gemstones and their settings, or about circuses? We can never be sure with words. Joyce's passage bristles with other curiosities. Molly holds her cup "by nothandle" (how does anyone do that?) and searches "the text" with "the hairpin" till she reaches "the word." The Word.

> —Met him what? he asked.
> —Here, she said. What does that mean?
> He leaned downwards and read near her polished thumbnail.
> —Metempsychosis?
> —Yes. Who's he when he's at home?

Who indeed? Who's Poldy when he's at home? He has been learning that for one thing he's teamaker and letter-carrier to someone addressed by a correspondent as "Mrs Marion Bloom." Also it's only when he's at home that he's "Poldy"; elsewhere he's "Mr Leopold Bloom," more often just "Bloom" as when someone urges him to jump into a cab ("Come along, Bloom"), but occasionally even "the jew" or even "that bloody jewman." In print (not Joyce's print though recorded by Joyce's print) he becomes "L. Boom," the

"Boom" by typographic inadvertence, the "L." because he'd responded to a tactless question with "L." (The question had been, "What is your christian name?") What he'd said in full was "L. Leopold," but most of the phonemes weren't heard.

Who he is when not at home is something commentaries have taught us: he is Ulysses. Just *how* he is Ulysses is something seldom gone into. True, the book is called *Ulysses* but that need not be decisive; merely an enigma. Back in 1930, when the book had been eight years published, a mythographic analyst, since renowned, claimed jauntily in the *Westminster Review* that *Ulysses* wasn't difficult at all; you just had to understand that Stephen Dedalus was Ulysses. . . . That article—I withhold its author's name—would have been in press at the same time as a book which both demonstrated that Leopold Bloom was Ulysses and also killed off interest in the topic.

That, of course, was the book by Stuart Gilbert: *James Joyce's Ulysses*, thought to be the authorized guide. It was authorized, in the sense that its author read it aloud to the author of *Ulysses*: that makes two authors, which seems authorization enough. It was also a solemn deadly lead-footed schematization, from which the world learned that Mr Bloom was Ulysses thanks to an algebra of correspondences that turned the Cyclops' fiery club for instance into Bloom's "knockmedown cigar." (It knocks nobody down; an uncivil narrator is merely claiming that Bloom smokes vile tobacco. Is the word "knockmedown" enough of a link to the Cyclops' club? That's the order of question we'll be looking at.)

After 1930 there was a long hush, and subsequent commentaries had little to say about Homer. As for Bloom being anyone but Bloom, the subject seemed as dull as a telephone book. Recent studies of *Ulysses* have been concentrating, fruitfully, on narrative strategies, also on the space-time witticisms we can recover with the aid of Thom's and other guides to the Dublin of 1904. But lately Intertextuality has been rearing its heads and subheads; the question how anything is readable at all has been agitated; and it seems feasible to canvass anew the identity of "The Canvasser at Work".

So I'll start from something Fritz Senn pointed out long ago, that the narrator commences his day's work by calling Mulligan "Buck," which is not his name, and having Mulligan call his roommate both "Kinch" and "you fearful jesuit," the former not Stephen's name and the latter not his calling. This can mean only that people's names are what they will answer to at the moment, not a fact to get excited about. But in the closed world where a new reader confronts a new book it also means that characters have names only as the text bestows them; also that there may be fewer people for us to imagine than there are names in the text. (If you've struggled with a Russian novel you'll know what I mean.) "Poldy," "Mr. Leopold Bloom," "Henry Flower," "Senhor Enrique Flor," these are four names but one person, two names being bestowed by the narrator (in a moment of formality and a moment of playfulness, respectively), one by Molly (whose real name by the way is "Marion"), while one is adopted by Mr. Bloom himself, part of his disguise as clandestine correspondent, the writer who affects Greek *e*'s.

Except for "Senhor Enrique Flor," none of these need surprise a frequenter of the 19th century novelists; assumed names are the familiar stuff of their plots, nicknames and petnames of their dialogue. And when the likes of Dostoyevsky were being moved into English, readers were getting used to the number of ungainly syllabifications a text could use in referring to the same person. It was probably in Russian fiction, notably in its bewildering habits of nomenclature, that Anglo-Saxons first felt the icy douche of Textuality.

Things get more interesting when Stephen, for a time unnamed, walks Sandymount strand.

> Ineluctable modality of the visible: at least that if no more, thought through my eyes. Signatures of all things I am here to read, seaspawn and seawrack, the nearing tide, that rusty boot. Snotgreen, bluesilver, rust: coloured signs. Limits of the diaphane. But he adds: in bodies. Then he was aware of them bodies before of them coloured. How? By knocking his sconce against them, sure. Go easy. Bald he was and a millionaire, *maestro di color che sanno.* . . .

"He," who is he? Why, Aristotle, as we know, though he is not named, from *maestro di color che sanno,* "master of those who know," a phrase Stephen borrows from a well-known passage in Dante. . . . In which, to our surprise it may be, Aristotle is not named either. Commentators have simply known that it must have been Aristotle the Divine Comic had in mind. As Stephen next advises, "Shut your eyes and see." Commentators have done that, and who shall doubt them?

Move forward now several hundred pages into the text, and contemplate Leopold Bloom becoming aware of them bodies before of them coloured. At about 1:45 A.M. on 17 June 1904 he "reapproached the door of the front room, hallfloor, and reentered."

> What suddenly arrested his ingress?
> The right temporal lobe of the hollow sphere of his cranium came into contact with a solid timber angle where, an infinitesimal but sensi-

ble fraction of a second later, a painful sensation was located in consequence of antecedent sensations transmitted and registered.

Sure enough, our new Aristotle has knocked his sconce against a
relocated sideboard. Colors impress him next—blue, white,
brown—and soon he is reading the signatures of such things as
present themselves, notably two chairs.

> What significances attached to these two chairs?
> Significances of similitude, of posture, of symbolism, of
> circumstantial evidence, of testimonial supermanence.

He's at home. Who's he when he's at home? Why, Aristotle, a
second Aristotle. (By the way, the first Aristotle had a wife,
Hypatia, who if we're to trust tradition used him worse than Molly
ever used Poldy.)

But who else is he when he's at home? Why Shakespeare, as is
easily demonstrated. "What's in a name?" Stephen had asked, not
surprisingly, apropos of Shakespeare. "He has hidden his own
name, a fair name, William, in the plays, a super here, a clown
there, as a painter of old Italy set his face in a dark corner of his
canvas. He has revealed it in the sonnets where there is Will in
overplus. . . . " As there is; there is not only Will in overplus, there
is, in Sonnet 135, the very phrase, "Will in overplus."

> Whoever hath her wish, thou hast thy Will,
> And Will to boot, and Will in overplus. . . .

That sonnet exhibits the word "Will" 13 times.

And Bloom? His plays, if any, are lost; his libretto, commissioned
by the impressario Michael Gunn 11 years ago for the Gaiety Theatre the way young Shakespeare got commissions from the Lord
Chamberlain's men, was never written; but he has hidden his name,
a fair name, in the lyric he wrote Miss Marion Tweedy when he was
22, the name "POLDY" running in acrostic down the lines' initials;
and in the poem he wrote at 11, the one which ends,

> . . . If you'll so condescend
> Then please place at the end
> The name of yours truly, L. Bloom,

we may safely say that there is Bloom, in evidence if not in overplus. It seems that tropes in the earlier parts of *Ulysses* are creating
identities for Bloom in the later.

And identities are being created for other people than Bloom. At
one point in the day he has installed himself in *Don Giovanni*, as the
Commandante, the Stone Guest who came to confront the Don and
haul him off to Hell. He has hummed,

Don Giovanni, a cenar teco
M'invitasti . . .

How conscious Bloom is of this role is unclear; but if he plays the Comandante, then Blazes Boylan plays Don Giovanni. (Blazes will sing the Don's part with Molly a little after 4 P.M.) Don Giovanni's conquests are famous for sheer quantity. His servant Leporello has kept a list, which gets sung in the opera *con brio*; and sure enough, when Bloom's at home, the anonymous polymorphic narrating voice, at this point feigning Leporello, recites a list: the famous list of those by whom Bloom has felt cuckolded. ". . . Penrose, Bartell d'Arcy, professor Goodwin, Julius Mastiansky, John Henry Menton, Father Bernard Corrigan, a farmer at the Royal Dublin Society's Horse Show . . .". . . . .On and on.

This is a list we have been learning not to trust, mainly because (1) lists don't tell you what they are lists of, (2) person after person on it can be dismissed, on textual evidence, as a conceivable occupant of Molly's bed. It is possible to say that by 1984 critical consensus on number of her violators before Boylan was hovering between zero and one. But before Richard Ellmann first cast doubt on that list in 1959, critics concurred in a number equal to the number of non-Boylan names on the list: 24, as many as the books in the *Odyssey*.

Now the list affects something essential to the way we conceive the human triangle *Ulysses* presents. If Molly has been promiscuous on the old scale, then Poldy has spent all his married life with a whore. That was the way it once seemed. But if this list is, as is now thought, no more than a list of Poldy's jealousies, then today, Bloomsday, marks her first venture into adultery, and the pathos of the day is marked, and so is his trauma, and hers. It is not too much to say that in differently reading this one list we read two different novels.

So let us draw back, take a deep breath, and consider what this may mean. Are we to say that for 35 years everybody was simply wrong, was reading a *Ulysses* Joyce didn't write? Yes, we can say that; but we should also note that when Stuart Gilbert read to Joyce conclusions about Molly's whorishness based on the list, Joyce seemingly did not raise a finger to correct him. Nor did similar judgments of Frank Budgen's elicit Joyce's protest, though Joyce had Budgen's book in typescript and did not glance perfunctorily but suggested inclusions. A reading at least plausibly compatible with the text, that seems to have sufficed for Joyce's passing grade. He withheld whatever knowledge he may have had of what was "really" so. What he had written he had written. Ineluctable modalities of the readable would shake it all down in time.

For what was "really" so was after all so only in Joyce's mind, a mind increasingly occupied with the reality of constellated words, and only those. That was, after all, the sole reality that he could fix on paper. You cannot put characters on paper, or places on paper: only words on paper. And Homer, or whoever it was wrote Homer down, had done nothing more, absolutely nothing more. It was only in 1870, the year of Molly Bloom's birth, that Heinrich Schliemann had proven with his spade that there had even been a Troy. For centuries men had believed that Troy existed solely in Homer's words. "Troy" was a city built by Homer's readers. Even after Schliemann, Homer's Troy still was.

There's a nice analogy in a late novel by Samuel Beckett, *Comment C'est: How It Is.* The book is filled with personages whose three-letter names end in -m: Pim, Bom, Bim, Pam. Its narrator, though, is nameless. Are we not forced to conclude that the name of the narrator must be Sam? But what does it mean, to say that we can deduce the name of someone fictional, when the text does not specify his name? How can we know we are right? And the minute we ask *that* question we are conceding that the only reality past appeal is the reality of marks on paper, which may be more than we'll want to concede.

That Bloom is Aristotle is likewise our deduction; likewise that Bloom is Shakespeare. Like the text's Aristotle, he bangs his head and reads signatures; like the text's Shakespeare, he embedded his name in poems. It may be protested that there was an Aristotle who did much more, and a Shakespeare who did much more. Any Dublin pub contains an Irishman who would argue you off the face of the Erse to this effect, that—

(a) the "much more" of Shakespeare or Aristotle is ascribed by sheer convention, the same sort of convention that builds Troy: windy, with ringing plains. ("Far on the ringing plains of windy Troy": that's a Troy Tennyson built, not Homer.)
(b) the Aristotle who bangs his head is a Joycean Aristotle, there being no shred of classical evidence whatsoever; thus Joyce's Bloom has only Joyce's Aristotle to correspond to, as correspond he does. The Aristotle who wrote the *Metaphysics* was someone else of the same name.

This latter argument acquires some force from the fact that *Ulysses* contains an Aristotle, unknown to classical curricula, who wrote something called *Aristotle's Masterpiece*. Bloom turns it over in the stall where he finds *Sweets of Sin*. It is a book of untidy blotched print, embellished with plates that depict "infants cuddled in a ball in bloodred wombs like liver of slaughtered cows." That, we may think, is such a masterpiece as Bloom/Aristotle might be responsible for, especially after a nicely-placed blow on the head. What it illustrates is one more order of uncertainty: that "Aristotle," like "Shakespeare," is the sum of the works that have been attributed to him, a fluctuating attribution even when we ignore vulgarities like the *Masterpiece*. If so, then the "Aristotle" we have in our heads has been the creation of library cataloguers, rearranging their cards. And so is "Shakespeare," who may have written a page of *Sir Thomas More*, or not. We'd like to think he did, since if so, we possess a whole page of his handwriting, but if not, no. "Weave, weavers of the wind."

Here, as when we noticed a while ago that Aristotle's much-advertised presence in the text of Dante depends solely on critical convention, we are walking the very brink of deconstruction, and had best be wary of how we plant our feet. Should we slip over that brink our fall through infinite space will be recompensed by a no more than fleeting glimpse of a disintegrating *Ulysses*, the one-time coherence of which, back in the glory days before Derrida, rested solely on the agreement of its readers.

Joyce, not surprisingly, has anticipated our vertigo. When Stephen, talking of Shakespeare, compares authorship to fatherhood, he also calls fatherhood a mystical estate; "on that mystery . . . the church is founded and founded irremoveably because founded, like the world, macro- and microcosm, upon the void. Upon incertitude, upon unlikelihood." (He also says to himself, "What the hell are you driving at?")

It is not long after that passage that *Ulysses* commences to taunt us with the unwelcome awareness that we are responsible for as many certainties as the text is. Crevices will flaw the once-solid narrative ground. Within a few pages we shall be hearing for instance of "Mr Bloom's dental windows" (which belonged to a different Bloom entirely, Marcus Bloom the dentist) and commentators will be throwing ropes to unwary readers. For there *was* a dentist Bloom in 1904 Dublin, at least according to Thom's Directory (a book by the way peppered with errors), so it is hard to say why a novel about that city in that year should not mention him. Yet it does seem irresponsible that two Blooms, one "real" but unheralded, should trouble the economy of a text that seems centered on just one. We seem installed in something else Shakespearean, a comedy of errors. It is on a nearby page that Bloom—this time, *our* Bloom, scans *Aristotle's Masterpiece*; right Bloom, wrong Aristotle.

So who's Bloom when Bloom's at home? One answer has to be, he's a fictional character, existing, like all fictional characters, in the minds of readers, at the prompting of a text. From time to time he pretends to be other people, such as Henry Flower, much as Stephen, more complexly, pretends to be Hamlet (perversely wearing black, donning what he himself calls "my Hamlet hat"). And here we come upon a central and saving distinction. If you told Bloom he was masquerading as Henry Flower he would have to agree; if you told Stephen he was playing Hamlet he would agree too. Blazes Boylan likewise would acknowledge without dismay that for the duration of the duet with Molly he was impersonating Don Giovanni; when you sing opera you're always impersonating somebody. But if you told Bloom he was Ulysses he'd not know what you were talking about; likewise if you mentioned Telemachus to Stephen.

Yet Bloom is Ulysses as much as he is anything, since if you can exist in a sentence you can equally well exist in a myth, and you needn't know you are playing a classical part. One entire episode, the longest in the book, is devoted to role-playings of which the characters are totally unaware. That is "Circe," where words like "fantasy" and "hallucination"—words used by commentators, not by Joyce—have bedevilled understanding for many decades. Here let me be quite explicit. When Bloom in "Circe" rises to public eminence—Lord Mayor, Pope, King, Messiah—only to be burned at the stake, there is no indication whatsoever that any of this goes through his head: that it's right to say he has "fantasies of power." He simply talks a bit heatedly to a girl in the street. It is the text that seizes a comic opportunity, prolonged for twenty pages. Just as only readers ever see Bloom as Ulysses, so only readers see him as Lord Mayor; and the sole difference between these two roles for Mr. Bloom is that the text is a good deal more explicit about Lord Mayor than it is about Ulysses. If anyone has fantasies in "Circe" it is the reader, solely the reader, moreover responding exactly as the text bids.

Yet the text is only doing, on a large and explicit scale, what language can never help doing: putting one thing in the guise of another. In the early morning, when the narrative seemed to be proceeding quite normally, we were treated to an incident of some vigor. We were in the Blooms' bedroom. Metempsychosis, Bloom was in the midst of saying, was what the ancient Greeks called it. "They used to believe you could be changed into an animal or a tree, for instance" . . . when suddenly:

> Her spoon ceased to stir up the sugar. She gazed straight before her, inhaling through her arched nostrils.
> —There's a smell of burn, she said. Did you leave anything on the fire?
> —The kidney, he cried suddenly.
> He fitted the book roughly into his inner pocket and, stubbing his toes against the broken commode, hurried out towards the smell, stepping hastily down the stairs with a flurried stork's legs. ["A flurried stork's legs"! There's metamorphosis for you.] Pungent smoke shot up in an angry jet from the side of the pan. By prodding a prong of the fork under the kidney he detached it and turned it turtle on its back. [Kidney to turtle: a second metamorphosis.]

We have just seen the hero take heroic action, his trusty weapon in hand. If there was no second Troy for him to burn, there was a burning kidney anyhow to assault. (We can imagine, if we like, how it would have gratified him to plunge that fork into the vitals of Boylan, something his Homeric prototype would not have thought twice about doing.) And we can note the sudden violence of language: a gesture effected "roughly"; then smoke that shoots up, its angry jet, his prodding prong, the capsizing of the kidney. The whole climate of things is suddenly, crazily physical: we are in the domain where men no longer talk but resolutely, rapidly *act*. That's the single most aggressive thing our hero does all day: the hero of a book which by the pages in question we're still just getting into, a book, moreover, mystifyingly entitled *Ulysses*.

What has happened here is that Joyce has slyly demonstrated the premise of his whole book. He has introduced the theme of metempsychosis, has let Bloom himself explain it (and muddle it, incidentally, with "metamorphosis"); has postulated the mind of ancient Greece; finally has effected the transformation of a man of talk first into a bird, then into a man of action with a weapon; and seen to it apparently that no commentator shall notice, since so far as I know none has. And no one can deny that the language by which Joyce narrates the descent into the kitchen holocaust is perfectly straightforward. Which is the point.

The most straightforward language conjures up what it does amid contexts which we supply. *Ruby: the Pride of the Ring* is a handy example in this very scene, within a few lines of the word "trapese." For though Ring-and-Trapeze says circus, Ruby-and-Ring says jewellery, or would say jewellery if some habit of ours did not screen that possibility out. When we know that we are reading a novel, experience with novels prompts us, page by page, chapter by chapter, to screen out a great deal, else the pages would generate a mental chaos.

To reduce the amount of possibility our habits screen out is the business of the whole second half of *Ulysses*, explicitly undertaken for instance when prose style after prose style sponsors, in the lying-in hospital, a wholesale renaming of characters every couple of pages. In chivalric contexts, created by a pastiche of Malory, we deal with Sir Leopold; in Bunyanesque sentences Stephen and Bloom become Boasthard and Calmer; the cadences of Pater transform Molly Bloom into Our Lady of the Cherries, "a comely brace of them pendant from an ear, bringing out the foreign warmth of the skin so daintily against the cool ardent fruit." Struggling to retain our focus on a 1904 scene, we acknowledge the authority of stylistic context to effect these renamings. This same book, written in some other time with other conventions, would be a quite different book. Written long enough ago, moreover in Greek hexameters, it might be the *Odyssey*.

"Tell me, Muse," translations of the *Odyssey* commence. "Tell me, Mulligan," says Stephen on our book's second page. Anyone might say a thing like that in any novel without our thinking of Homer; save in reading translations of Homer, we screen Homer out. But not in this book. "The most beautiful book that has come out of our country in my time," mocks Buck Mulligan elsewhere; "One thinks of Homer." And of Aristotle, and of Shakespeare, and of, Lord help us, Oliver St. John Gogarty. Joyce is pretending that Gogarty's name is Mulligan, while Mulligan at that moment was pretending to be W.B. Yeats; one thinks of him too. It was he who made us think of Troy and Maud Gonne in the same thought.

That was a natural extension of language, since whenever we read we are thinking of something else. Otherwise we could only read what we'd read before. Every bit of the language we carry in our heads had been installed there by thoughts of something else. The act of reading brings a little of it to life. The intent of the seven years' preparation of the text of *Ulysses* was to bring as much of it to life, simultaneously, as possible, this side of something then unglimpsed: *Finnegans Wake*.

I can't think of any alternative save this: that if Bloom "has been" (by metempsychosis) Ulysses, then he's also "been" Shakespeare; also Mozart; also Aristotle; also other Greeks, including someone who wrestled with a value for *pi*; also Moses; also—Lord, the mind boggles. Jesus? And never mind "symbolism."

For by what criteria can we withhold from these past lives of Bloom any of the reality we accord to his past life as Ulysses, for that matter his present life as Leopold? What's in a name? Exactly everything.

Am I suggesting that Joyce foresaw these possibilities? Yes, I am. Why else, save by vestigial memories of having been Shakespeare, does Bloom know "How poets write, the similar sounds?" Why else, save by remembering having been Aristotle, does he read signatures after receiving a bang on the head? Why else, save by having been a disciple of Euclid's, has he wrestled with *pi*? And as Moses brought down from Sinai "the tables of the law, graven in the language of the outlaw," so Bloom bore about Dublin "the secret of the race, graven in the language of prediction." That's not coincidence either. "He is all in all," says Stephen of Shakespeare. "Everyman," our text says of Bloom. Yes, Everyman: many men: in *Ulysses*, an enumerable list. (The text, in the same breath, also says "Noman.")

Thus when they're discussing Shakespeare in the library, a man who was once Shakespeare himself is elsewhere in the building, hunting a back issue of *The Kilkenny People*. And when they're discussing Moses in the *Freeman* office, a man who has been Moses is elsewhere in the building, telephoning. (The telephone! What a wondrous analogue for the Bible's mysterious transactions between Moses and God!) And why does the editor say to Bloom, "Kiss my royal Irish arse"? Because God told Moses (Exodus 33:23) how he'd gaze not on the divine face but only on the divine hinderparts. And who else is divine, at the *Freeman*, save the editor?

"Search the scriptures," say the scriptures, "for in them you think that you have eternal life." Search, says *Ulysses* rather, "the text" for "the word," if necessary aided by a hairpin, and if necessary too follow Molly's example further in consulting a commentator, who'll tell us in plain words about ancient Greeks. That's Bloom's first Greek role: grammarian. Grammarian Bloom got "metempsychosis" mostly right, but talked too much and mixed metamorphosis in. Most commentators are mostly right about *Ulysses* too, so the tradition persists.

Meanwhile there's no escaping the ancient Greeks. Downstairs in Bloom's library every single book descends from a Greek prototype: *The Useful Ready Reckoner* from Archimedes, Lockhart's *Life of Napoleon* from Thucydides, *Physical Strength and How to Obtain It* from the gymnasts, *Short Yet Plain Elements of Geometry* from Euclid,

In the Track of the Sun for that matter from the *Odyssey.* As for Hozier's *History of the Russo-Turkish War,* it describes battles fought on the ringing plains of the *Iliad.* Bloom has a Shakespeare too; it descends from Aeschylus and Aristophanes. But Dublin's Ulysses, oddly, has no Homer, and Dublin's Moses no Bible. No matter. In 1904 he is still a relatively young man: just 38. He has only to wait till 1922. Then, aged 56 and full of mature wisdom, with Blazes Boylan no doubt long since burnt out, "Henry Flower" will be able to set upon his shelves the book he has been waiting for all his life: the one that tells him who's he when he's at home.

Remodeling Homer

Fritz Senn

The topic is Modernism. I begin, a true pedestrian, with a footnote in *Finnegans Wake*, one that can be conveniently misappropriated.

This is modeln times (*FW* 289.n6)

Modern times is what the spelling seems to aim at. The footnote is attached to "the reptile's age." *Finnegans Wake* spans such periods, from prehistory to modernity, with nonchalant ease. "Modern" is a strange word, by its very nature something relative and mobile, by grace of literary fashion the portion of twentieth century conventions for which Joyce has been selected as prototype. "Modern times" is continually possible as a boast, a program, or a lament, at *any* time; but "Modernism" can become outdated. Joyce's phrase, added to his work in progress during the heyday of that movement, may antedate the title of a famous movie by one of the outstanding leaders of that up and coming medium, Chaplin's *Modern Times* (1936). It is a matter of manuscript evidence whether this reference would be within the author's intended range; but we have learned that texts, especially accomodating ones like the *Wake*, are not bound by their creator's legislation. Nowadays it would take a conscious effort to *diss*ociate Joyce's "modeln times" from a cinematic fiction, a pictorial evocation of the hazards of survival and the rhythms imposed by modern mechanisation. Chaplin's Bloomian resilience among the wheels within reels of the movie are now integrated in the *Wake's* clockwork. A Wakean consciousness permits the past to be affected by the future.

So far I have been so concerned with the temporal setting of the phrase that I overlooked the mechanics of the graphic actuality of "modeln," and the models they suggest. Maybe someone—an exiled foreigner?—is having trouble with the liquids and takes an *r* for an *l*. A German foreigner would be using a native verb, *modeln*, and changing the syntax. *Modeln* means to "change the shape of," "modulate"; it is of course derived from Latin *modus* (measure or manner), and related to "modern," an offshoot of the same family. Family members quibble and quarrel, have different manners or moods (another cognate of "mode"), want to form the world according to their own divergent views. *Finnegans Wake* is energy that modulates itself, that modulates times and reshapes words. It was written, at a time of vigorous disruptions and new starts, by a man whose works were considered novel, progressive, revolutionary, but who had steadily been reshaping classical models. They also modeled new types of readers—or revived obsolete reading skills.

At this point I should fulfill my cultural obligations and casually work in Bergson, Einstein, Husserl, Heidegger, Russell, Proust and, certainly, Wyndham Lewis. Instead, I had rather stick to Joyce's pliable "modeln times" to lead gradually to my subject, the modernist reformation of the past. New movements have always affected old ones. The Middle Ages exploited Antiquity within their own frames, and they were succeeded by a new departure which rediscovered more of Antiquity differently, and was aptly named Renaissance. Ultramodernist Joyce always turned back to the classics, Aristotle, Homer, Ovid; to medieval figures like Augustine, Aquinas, Dante; and later to Giordano Bruno, Nicolas of Cusa, Pico della Mirandola, or Shakespeare. History, Vico, and *Finnegans Wake* all say that each impulse of new life is a *revival*. Some such revivals, like the Irish Renaissance, appeared to Joyce too narrow-mindedly nostalgic. His backward looks were far more radical. If anyone, Joyce was always altering, remodeling times, including his own past. *A Portrait* puts this into words and style. *Dubliners* went into *Finnegans Wake* and *Finnegans Wake* changed *Dubliners* for us.

In this essay I will look back to Homer's metamorphoses, not to find out, once again, how Joyce adapted them for himself, but to figure out (or to feign) how Joyce influenced *them*, the classics. Such retrospection may unearth old chestnuts, or make tiresome rediscoveries, or it may resurrect dormant ghosts. I am confident that this will happen to some degree. The classics may not be quite as staid as they have appeared; they may be more dynamic and full of "Modern" tensions. So the result may produce necessary adjustments but also, just as likely, falsification. Since no one knows how the Greeks (which Greeks? Homer's audience, 5th century Athenians, Alexandrians?) responded to the epics, we may simply add one more specious reading to the conventional ones. A lay reader conditioned by Joyce, deformed by *Finnegans Wake*, will naturally project features that historical philologists may disprove.

Joyce could intentionally imitate stilted recreations of heroic styles ("A many comely nymphs drew nigh . . ." *U* 341). He even set out to fake the more recent past of English literature in a series of blantantly flawed forgeries, fashioning, in the wake of Daidalos, the sacred cows of Helios. By artificially fathering the fathers of English prose, he meddled in their ancestry and perverted it, so that Carlyle or Bunyan may never be quite the same again in the eyes of the corrupted beholder. Irrespective of intention, Joyce also agitates the *Odyssey* (as did the Grimm brothers, Schliemann, Frazer, Jung). The title "Ulysses" is here used as a signpost—not to go and re-explain the new by the old, but to look at the old as though it were modernist. The title gently advises us to do what Homeric agents do: *peirāein*—test, try out, inquire, experience. Such backward glances at an epic are not to be trusted, all the less so since that author left behind no eyewitnesses like Stanislaus or Frank Budgen for corrective common sense.

The areas touched will be Functionality, Semiotics, Ambivalence, Self-Reference, and Listener Response or, to put it plainly, a few samples will be inspected *as though* they had been composed by James Joyce.

Each adventure . . . should not only condition but even create its own technique (*Letters*, 1, 147)

There are no conspicious similarities in the *Odyssey* to the narrative variation of *Ulysses*, certainly not those highly idiosyncratic chapter modes and the stylistic orchestration. Joyce could have found his models in the past, but he hardly needed any. His devices appear to have evolved in the workshop, almost naturally. What could be more naturally conformant than a chapter about music that should contain songs, have a vocabulary in tune with it, with appropriate metaphors, and be made, more and more, to comport itself *like* music? Such increased styling in fact moved the novel away

from the Greek groundplan. Homer's poem cannot have corresponding scope. An epic diction had shaped itself out of centuries of
a bardic tradition we can only guess at. The language is generally
elevated, "noble," artistic, with a great store of ready-made, but still
flexible, formulaic supports. That would not allow for too much
variation, though there is a lot more of it than some translations
would have us believe.

In *Ulysses*, to move from the end of Nausicaa into the next chapter
and then into Circe, is quite a jolt, with instant changes of scenery,
idiom, atmosphere, arrangement.* Not so in a classical epic. One
vague impression we often get is of an extended uniformity, accen-
tuated by metre. But there are considerable shifts. The transition
from omniscient narrative (*here* the epithet makes sense) to personal
tale is the best known variation. Beyond that, the disparity between
the time actually passing and the narrative expenditure for it may be
very effective. Many lines may be lavished on an exact movement,
or a well-wrought object; then again time can be crowded—one
whole year's stay on Kirke's island takes up slightly more than a
single line (10:469). Another long detention, on Kalypso's Ogygia, is
handled quite differently. We first hear, through several sources, of
Odysseus pining there; then we ourselves watch him leave; later on,
on two separate occasions, he tells of his arriving there: so the seven
long years are suggested by a circumfluent vacuum. Not even
Ulysses can boast of such a model of splitting time; the *Wake* seems
to make the time potentially passing from the final "the   " to the
initial "   riverrun" somehow meaningful. So the adventure part
of the *Odyssey* doubles back from the end of Book Twelve to its
opening at 1:14.

I will now briefly compare two adjacent episodes. The escape
from the Laistrygonians is told rapidly, succinctly. In the preceding
disasters (the Kyklopes, Aiolos) we were sharing the thinking and
wavering of Odysseus and his emotions: he was terrified, coura-
geous, cool, crafty, miserable, considering suicide. Of such feelings
the Laistrygonians episode is stripped; there are hardly any super-
fluities, no glimpses into the psyche. There is the habitual geograph-
ical outline, one remark about the closeness of day and night (and a
very Bloomian reflection on someone who could do without sleep
being able to earn double wages). The description of an excellent
harbour remains factual, but Odysseus, contrary to epical practice,

---

*Homeric names are closely transliterated here so that figures or places (Kirke, Eu-
maios, Ithaka) are easy to distinguish from the Latinized forms Joyce used in his
schema to refer to *Ulysses* chapters (Circe, Eumaeus, Ithaca).

fails to reveal why he alone did not moore his ship in the harbour, but stayed outside. As usual some companions are sent out to reconnoitre, and the story takes its quick course. Not a single spoken word is quoted. One Greek messenger is seized and eaten; the other two escape, followed by the natives who hurl down rocks and spear the men like fishes from their boats. Odysseus, with his ship and his crew, can flee. The whole episode, containing the largest massacre in the whole poem, takes up less than sixty lines (10:76-132); the report is so objective, almost neutral, that the loss of eleven ships and of several hundred men is tucked into less than one full line, one austere sentence. But we can feel a powerful undercurrent not stated, in the sound as well as the shape of the words, even in transliteration:

autar   *hai*   *allai*   *aollees*   *autoth'*   *olonto* (10:132)

[but   these   others   altogether   there   perished]

We need not know Greek in order to get some impression. The adjective *aollees* (in a body, a mass, close together), of four syllables, seems to add assonant reinforcement to an implicit warning against being herded together.

After this the remaining Greeks came to Aiaia, where they lay for two days, and everything (although nothing very exciting for a while) is told in far greater detail. There is much talk. As though in compensation, the pent-up grief and shock finds belated expression: now we hear of weariness, grief, despair, encouragement—and hunger. We share the doubts and fears of Odysseus, and also his deliberations. There is perhaps even subliminal psychology in a straightforward epithet for the harbour: it is *naulochos*, which means safe or "ship-sheltering," where, literally, ships (*nau-*) can lie (*lochos*, from *lechō*, 10:141). As it happens, *lochos* alone would mean a special kind of lying-down place, in concealment for an attack, an ambush. Odysseus has learned his lesson about ambushes in caves or in harbours surrounded by cliffs; he may be cautious of even an echoing word[1].

Exploring the new territory, Odysseus comes upon a magnificent stag, a welcome prey, which he kills and carries back to the camp. It looks as though the compassion withheld from the hundreds of Ithacans who had been harpooned and eaten by the cannibals in the previous episode is now transferred onto the hunted animal as it is turned into food for humans. The individual's plight is brought out. The stag has been drawn to a spring by the heat of the sun, the spear strikes him, he falls into the dust with a moan; it is all vivid, like the death of an Iliadic hero, full of empathy. We even learn how the animal is carried, and what Odysseus does with the spear at each moment. All is told with the loving care that is so patently absent from the previous episode (10:156-72). Throughout, much attention is devoted to eating and its effect on human beings. We have another focus: close-ups in a different narrative "style."

Parallax stalks behind (*U* 414)

It is difficult to talk about *Ulysses* without posing the question of narrative trust. There is a lot that we know merely through associations or memory, highly unreliable sources. Much information also comes through hearsay, in a city which is particularly given to gossip, rumor, and the production of what Hugh Kenner has termed "Irish facts." One safeguard is the multiple reference from different sources or places. Joyce has Bloom introduce the scientific term for the analogous method in astronomy, *parallax*, the key principles of stereoscopic vision based on at least two different reports. If an improbable claim—like Bloom giving "the idea for Sinn Fein to Griffith" (*U* 335)—is not supplemented elsewhere, we tend to disbelieve it. On the other hand we can fairly trace Bob Doran's meteoric progress through a Dublin afternoon by matching displaced observations, and we can form some conclusions about his domestic situation. What we learn in the novel also parenthetically serves as parallactic external confirmation of what we might have surmised from a set of reports in an earlier short story, "The Boarding House" (which in itself consists of three sequential views grouped around a narrative void—a past event and a present decision). If all we knew about Doran only derived from the unknown narrator of Cyclops, we would have our doubts as to what to make of it.

The Homer of the *Odyssey* knew too that reports do not automatically deserve credence. We can mistake appearances, we have devious motives, a lie is as easily phrased as a truth, and it is ever impossible to tell a whole truth. Distrust in words is built into the poem, with great emphasis on something being told *kata moiran* (in a proper way, accurately), *kata kosmon* (truly, in order), or *atrekeōs* (truly, exactly); some statements are labeled *nēmertea* (unerring, infallible, in accordance with reality). That such expressions have become stereotypes (compare "as true as I'm telling you, "I'm told for a fact," or "declare to God," etc., especially in the Cyclops chapter), does not make them less functional as signals or reminders.

Odysseus's return is set in motion by benevolent dissemblance. The gods decree it at a meeting, at a moment when Poseidon's back is turned, and Athene has set off for Ithaka. She takes on the appearance of Menthes. When asked her name and origin ("declare it truly"—*atrekeōs*, 1:169), she "truthfully" (*atrekeōs*, 1:179) makes up the first fictional biography, to urge Telemachos on. Some time later when Penelope is visited and advised by her sister in a dream, it is a phantom sent by Athene. Hermes, dispatched to Kalypso to proclaim the will of Zeus, pretends he does not know the name of the man she keeps on her island. Kalypso in turn says nothing of a divine threat, but tells Odysseus of his release as though it were due to her own generous nature. He does not believe her, doubting not so much her motivation as her intention, rightly, though misdirectedly, suspecting her of not meaning what she says.

The *Odyssey* is full of deceit. Without it Penelope or the kingdom of Ithaka could not have been won back (nor Troy captured). It is fitting and significant that the final reconciliation with Poseidon should be contingent upon future misrepresentation. When an oar that Odysseus will have to carry inland shall be mistaken for a "winnowing fan," then he can make his peace. This harmless deception will be the "manifest sign" (*sēma. . .ariphrades*, 11:126-9). Practically all translations render the landlubber's misinterpretation as "winnowing fan" (Butcher & Lang, Murray, etc.). A reader of *Ulysses* and its chapter of illusions might mistake Bella Cohen's "large fan winnows wind" (*U* 527), and dislocute two words into a sign of something—Kirke's magic wand, perhaps.[2] The last person we hear of in the poem is Mentor, and he once again is an impersonation of Pallas Athene's; the last words we read are *demas* and *audēn*—a (spurious) shape and (an assumed) voice. In *Ulysses* the first shape is stately Buck Mulligan, masquerading as a priest; the first sound heard is his dissembling voice. He proceeds to mentor Stephen, not too seriously, to go with him to Athens.

As listeners, or readers, we have to be circumspect like Odysseus, alert for verification. What about that famous web that Penelope reputedly wove by day and unwove at night? Did it happen? We might not believe the suitors, for they want to brand her in public for treachery; nor would we necessarily (having been warned that her mind may be set "on other things," *passim*) trust her own telling to the stranger, since her motive is to show herself as loyal in adversity. But together the two equivalent reports bear each other out from different points of view (2:92f, 19:137f; see also 24:128f).

At times there is intriguing parallactic doubt. At the palace of Menelaos and Helen, Telemachos is treated to reminiscences of Troy. Helen recalls Odysseus, how he once sneaked into the besieged city, disguised as a beggar. We know that he will do this again later, and since Helen cannot know that, the story sounds very plausible. She then recognized him and he, binding her by an oath, "told her all the purposes of the Achaeans." If *that* is true, Odysseus may have forgotten his proverbial caution and endangered the Greek cause; or it may prove how greatly he trusted the one woman whose elopement started the whole war; or it may show she was simply too charming to resist—in any case, the anecdote which is offered to demonstrate Odysseus' cunning shows her in a favorable light, and at the centre of attention. There were, naturally, no witnesses (4:240-66).

Her husband (who had been in the other camp when all this occurred) immediately remarks that Helen has spoken "aright" (*kata moiran*), and goes on to tell another war story, perhaps the most decisive moment of all. When the Greek leaders were in ambush (*lochos*) inside the wooden horse, she came along with the Trojans and walked round it, three times. She tempted the Greeks. "You must have been urged by some *daimon*"—he surmises, speaking no doubt with utter courtesy—"who made you call the Greek chieftains by their names, imitating the voices of their wives." Odysseus, not taken in, handled the dangerous situation with customary aplomb, so that the invaders did not give themselves away. And Athene took care of Helen (4:265-89).

This illustrates the resourcefulness of Odysseus, but also a different Helen. Both stories fill us in on incidents of the siege that are not otherwise reported. They are also comments on Helen's character and her adaptive skills that seem to match those of Odysseus. The two anecdotes do not quite tally, but need not contradict each other. They are full of domestic decorum and connubial tensions. And there is enough for us to wonder at and to interpret. If we are modernist interpreters we may puzzle whether this staging of several Helen *personae* (sophisticated hostess in the present; confidante of Odysseus, artful temptress, in the past; perhaps also clever inventor of fictions) should systematically be aligned with the sequel, a story which Menelaos introduces with the words "I will not deceive you" (4:348). It is the story of changeable, wily, adaptable Proteus, master of many roles and appearances.

This is a story that we hear twice. First, in a more general way, his daughter predicts what will happen and gives advice. This advice is put into practice, and Menelaos' own account, much more comprehensive, then also includes what Proteus, once caught, reveals. This is a frequent doubling device. Often a goddess foretells what we will ourselves witness later on. Kirke carefully instructs Odysseus about the Sirens, and he follows her counsels. We get both her description and his own chronicle. There is some overlapping as well as complementation. Odysseus quotes what the Sirens sang to him (which Kirke did not anticipate), but Kirke tells him (and us) some facts from her divine and multiscient perspective that were not within the range of his vision (the mouldering bodies of former victims). The seduction of course was vocal, so he only reports what he heard. So we have a perfectly stereoscopic-stereoacoustic impression.

Almost everything important outside of our range is either parallactically confirmed, or implictly questioned. All of the adventures of Odysseus are listed once more, in due order, when he tells them to Penelope in a brief summary (23:310-41). Of course these are the words of the cleverest inventor alive. We can detect some minor, uxorious abbreviations in his tale. But we do have independent narrative or Olympian testimony at least for the most crucial adventures, the blinding of Polyphemos and the slaughter of the sacred cows. So all his accounts may well be true, which is not to say that he might not have touched up some exploits, for better effect upon the Phaiakian hosts.

What is claimed here is not an "influence," that Joyce should have picked up some clues from the *Odyssey*, but, perhaps vaguely, some kinship. Steadying our post-Ulyssean lenses "to a new focus" (*U* 141), we may uncover, or invent, features in an older text that we might otherwise not have cared to notice.

in medios loquos (*FW* 398.8)

Self-reflectiveness is a trademark of much recent story-telling. Joyce's later works, in particular, seem to have a self-awareness of their being artifacts. *Finnegans Wake* continually comments on its own nature, and infelicitous exculpations are never far off. *Ulysses* also more and more denounces itself as narrative scheming. Asides like "as said before" and even "as said before just now" (*U* 269, 276) are conspicuous avowals of the creator's handiwork. As against such narcissism, the *Odyssey* will appear simple and nobly primitive. On the other hand, its temporal arrangement is intricately contrived, in fact much more so than sequential *Ulysses*. The beginning, an address to the Muse, follows an epical convention. The goddess is to tell the story of that versatile man. After a brief plot summary the Muse, daughter of Zeus, is entreated to "tell us too" about the events just indicated. There is one little word, unstressed, in the closing line of the evocation, *hamothen*, and it stands for something like "from anywhere"—it is a little hint that narratologists should jump at. Perhaps they have.

It occurs here only and, unfortunately, it does not travel too well and is easily neglected in translation, or it is treated merely quantitatively (in "some part left," says Chapman; "snatch some portion of these acts," enjoins Pope). It may be taken to denote the origin of the information ("from whatsoever source you may know them," Samuel Butler), or else it is turned into a ponderous subordinate clause or a sonority like "beginning where thou will" (Palmer). Homer is much more casual, as though one professional were nudging another. The bard knows the Muse knows that the epic disposition of ten years and several strands of action is a formidable order, and that the handling of time alone entails many choices. In the *Iliad* the matter was easier to settle. For reporting the Anger of Achilleus it suffices to propose a starting point: "from where" (*ex hou*, Il. 1:6) the two heroes began to fall out. For the more intricate *Odyssey* the Muse is relieved of compositional deliberation, and we can almost hear a reassuring: "Don't bother—start any old place!"[3]

So there is a touch of artlessless which we realize is studied, a pretense; and the little adverb *hamothen* disguises and thereby signals both craftmanship and narrative consciousness. Odysseus himself is conscious of the same problem, where to begin, when about to tell his own adventures. "What shall I tell you first and what last?" (9:16), he asks and decides to begin with the end of the Trojan war, and to follow a straightforward chronological order. His sequential account is embedded in a complex time scheme, and this admirable Homeric manipulation is an instance of, as the *Wake* has put it, "modeln [in that German sense of shaping to specification] times." This can furthermore be echoed in the microstructure because of the multiple tenses and moods of the Greek language.

Epic bards were sometimes told where to begin. Odysseus had already directed the local singer, Demodekos, to "sing of the building of the wooden horse." This is worth a little digression. In a text scrupulously structured by a modernist we might be justified in treating *hippou*   *kosmon*   *aeison* (8:492)

[the horse's   building   sing]

as a recall of the opening of the *Iliad*: "*Meñin* (the anger) *aeide*
(sing. . . of Achilleus" (1:1). Odysseus is asking, after all, for a continuation of those earlier events. But Homer might not be like Joyce,
who can use Howth as a site to end *Ulysses* and to start off *Finnegans
Wake*, or who might, in his cyclical joining of the ending to the beginning of his last work, "along the. . . riverrun," not only echo a
Coleridgean sacred, subterranean river, but also the origins of his
own published works, "There's music *along the river*" (*Chamber Music*, I). That may not be plainspoken Homer's incidental linking. Still
it is odd to find a minor invocation of a tale within a tale imitating,
perhaps by chance, the beginning of its twin epic. And by one more
chance, since the demand is for *hippou kosmon*, the stratagem about
the horse, we might remember the *last* word of the *Iliad* as well:
hippodamoio ("Thus they held the funeral of Hector tamer of horses,"
I1. 28:804). Maybe coincidence, and maybe simply post-Joycean zeal-
ous projection? Still, from the safe ignorance of three millennia later,
we can always posit, for the sake of an argument, that Homer (or
his latest editor) knew what he was doing. Homer used *kosmos* here,
just three lines after Odysseus praised Demodokos for his compe-
tence, having sung the fate of the Achaeans *kata kosmon* (accurately,
in due order: 8:489).

The submission here is that Homer might in fact have contrived
what the text synecdochally suggests in the best Joycean fashion —
kosmos (that is to say adornment, arrangement, stratagem, order,
fashioning). If the Greeks had a word for structuring, it could have
been the verb *kosmeō*.

Very orderly himself, Odysseus ends *his* tale with the arrival at
Kalypso's island and his stay there; and he breaks off quickly, for he
has told that story already to a portion of his audience. "It is
irksome to tell a plain-told story a second time," he says, all but
doing it (12:453). By this negation, the *Odyssey* acknowledges its
own narrative principle, the parallactic doubling already referred to.
We have in fact heard the Kalypso affair not only twice by Odysseus, but before that by the poem's narrative voice, and twice by
Athene. The story of the adventures is brought back to its starting
point, where it was set in motion by that almost offhand *hamothen*.
We are now at the end of book twelve, exactly halfway through the
epic, at its structural middle.

And the identical same (*U* 649)

I now go on to report for the second time on the Proteus incident, the one of which we have two accounts as well. Proteus is *nēmertēs* (unerring, "who tells the truth," "whose speech is sooth"), he "knows" the depths of all the seas. A seer himself, he becomes visible in changing forms. We hear this, first, through his daughter (or rather, she indicates wisely, "he is said to be her father"). Her name is Eidothea, the goddess of *eidos* (shape, appearance, what can be seen). Dealing with illusions and reality, sense perception and knowledge, identity, likeness, trickery and disguises, the whole theme to be mythologised appears like an etymological deployment of the Indo-European root *weid* (to see), which lost its initial to become the Greek verb *eid* or *id*. Some forms of its elaborate system retain the old meaning of sight (as it is preserved in Latin *videre*, vision, etc.), while its perfect *oida* (I have seen) came to mean *know* (compare also its Germanic relatives "wit," "witness," "wise," German *wissen*, or even a semantic reunion like the *Wake's* "wiseable," 16.24). The passive *eidomai* means to appear, to seem. Other relatives are *eidos, eidolon*, idyll, or idea. What we see is what we think we know, it belongs to the ineluctable modality of the visible, "thought through my eyes" (*U* 37). The Proteus adventure is full of forms for seeing and knowing (and so is Joyce's second Sandymount strand scene, the Nausicaa chapter).

Eidothea proposes concealment and a fake appearance to trap the old wizard. She predicts that he will first (*prōton*) count (*arithmēsal*) all his seals (4:411; the adjective *prōtos* seems to be used here recurrently for homonymous reverberation). When Menelaos tells what actually happened, the wording varies slightly. Proteus, coming up to the seals, counted their number: "*lekto d'arithmon*" (4:451; *lekto* is an aorist form of the verb *legō*, to pick, number, count, recount, tell—*logos* was to become the most renowned member of the family). And as the first ones (*prōtous*) he counted (*lege*) the Greeks in ambush hidden under the sealskins: here *lege* is the imperfect tense of the same verb. And then, right after, we read, Proteus ". . . *lekto* . . . " So he is counting some more, and what might it be? The sentence continues: ". . . *kai autos*" (he himself). A jolt, and we need readjustment. He is not counting, but he himself *lies down* among the seals. The verb is from another root: *lech* (cognate with "lie" or *liegen*). The semblance was deceptive. We might have been mistaken.

It is not that this clash of two *lekto*-forms has never been noticed, but somehow commentators did not know what to make of it.[4] Of all the translators only Rouse at least tries to capture some link: ". . . counted the number; counted us first. . . he lay down himself *in the count;*" but even the addition does not tempt us with a wrong lead. For a Joycean what happens is simply that the listener has been drawn into the game of deceit. The reader has to sort out substance or accidents, truth or deceit, seals or human intruders, concealment and detection. The theme is acted out in the language, and the Greek inflection effortlessly offers a variety of forms, so that an identical activity can be expressed in different ways (*lekto/lege*); and the same phonetic appearance (or shape, *eidos*) does duty for two distinct doings. An identical *lekto* is not the same as another *lekto*; you cannot trust words ("lie" may not be "lie"). That, moreover, the shape *lekto/lech* is related to *lochos* and *lochaō* (a lying down in ambush and to ambush), links up with the ruse through which the tricky seer himself has been tricked, adds to the etymological functionality.

The device that Joyce used, and used widely in his Proteus chapter (think of "lap," "strand," "see," "close"; perhaps also "I, eye," "see, see," and all the rest), may be three thousand years old and has been largely overlooked in the meantime, to judge from the commentaries we have. I am fairly sure that Joyce, cunning or "knowing (*eidōs*) crafty tricks" like Proteus (4:460), never set eyes on the doubling of *lekto*. He did not have to, and neither did Shakespeare.

What do they think . . .? (*U* 284)

One reason why ambiguity, often mistermed "pun," tended to be disregarded or simply not registered for long periods, may have been its supposed ignobility. It is my guess that teachers of Greek may also have been responsible for its neglect. Teachers have to drive home distinctions, very often crucial trifles, like accents or the length of a vowel. Occupied as they would be with the nicities of Greek inflection, they would not have a class pause over the question why Homer, reputedly no mean manipulator of words, used the aorist *lekto* once only in the whole poem in the sense of counting, and almost juxtaposed it with an unaffiliated likeness, just in this passage. A pedantic, staid (let's think of our Victorian stereotype) teacher of old languages might not have encouraged observations like the following:

Agamemnon, a shade in Hades, speaks to Odysseus and mono-

maniacally dwells on the wrongs done to him by his treacherous
wife. Sweepingly, but understandably, he curses the whole sex, ex-
cepting only Penelope. His motive may be genuine, if envious, admiration, or it may be mere courtesy towards an old companion
who now stands before him to soon depart on his protracted way
home. Penelope, Agamemnon concedes, is "discreet and prudent in
all her ways" (Butcher & Lang), "a very admirable woman and has
an excellent nature" (S. Butler), "too wise, too clear-headed, sees
alternatives too well" (Fitzgerald). What a student has to spell out is
something like: she is wise and knows (*oide*) well (*eu*) in her mind
(*phrēsi*)—*mēdea* (11:445). That has to do with *mēdomai* (plan, plot,
consider); "knowing *mēdea* (counsels, prudence)" is a tag quite frequent. And it applies to Penelope, who *is* shrewd and loyal. But a
lewd student might spot an alternative word, identical, also *mēdea*,
in the dictionary, and apply that. It has occurred in the poem before. When Odysseus is about to brave Nausikaa and her maidens
on the beach, he covers his *mēdea* with a twig, the first gentleman of
Europe (6:129). To cut off a man's *mēdea* will later be a threat to a
beggar and a real punishment for disloyal Melanthios (18:87, 22:476).
So what is it that Agamemnon indicates that Penelope knows so
well? Surely our old schoolmaster would not incite a sniggering
class into probing this off-possibility too thoroughly. But what did
Homer, who knew and used both homonyms, have in his subtle
mind? Are we perhaps anachronistically psychologizing a formulaic
phrase with post-Freudian nastiness? Is it fair to imagine that
Agamemnon, in his morbid preoccupation with his wife's sexual in-
fatuation, could spitefully or unwittingly try to disquiet a former
war companion (whom he did not always trust or like, see *Iliad*
4:339, and who is still alive)? Who is to decide? Verbal suspicion,
justified or not, at any rate invigorates an otherwise routine phrase
and makes it disturbing. Joyce's Penelope is one who does have a
fair knowledge of male *mēdea* (*U* 742, 753, *et passim*), and this in the
sense that modernist writers seemed to devote so much attention to.
Molly's familiarity with *mēdea* helped to have *Ulysses* banned.

If *you*, having become duly suspicious, should now turn the various alternatives and aspersions over in your mind (as you should),
you would be living up to the activity of *mēdomai*—to take counsel,
meditate, measure, consider.[5]

produce your credentials (*U* 650)

All signals have to be treated with caution, and we also cannot tell what is or is not a signal, sign or *sēma*. Odysseus, on his return, has to disguise himself and to fake names and origins in order to find out whom he can trust. It takes skill to hide one's identity, but it is also difficult to prove it. Names are particularly unreliable, for anyone can make up a story. One's looks change with age, naturally or by divine interference.[6] Some bodily marks, however, remain as tokens of recognition, like the scar the nurse Euykleia discovers in one of the most memorable scenes. The scar does what a name cannot do. Names can be arbitrary or significant (*Odysseus—odyssamenos* is both, 19:407-9), but scars or, for that matter, tattoos, are silent and truthful testimony.[7] The feet of Odysseus are about to be washed, the nurse prepares cauldron and water (Leopold Bloom, home in his kitchen, puts the kettle with the water on and then washes his hands, and the secrets of the Dublin waterworks are revealed (*U* 670-72—an entirely different story). All of a sudden Odysseus remembers his scar: if the nurse touches it, she will recognize the wound and everything might come out. In one of the most evocative lines:

oulēn amphrassaito   kai   amphada erga   genoito
                                                                     (19:391)

[scar   would recognize   and   manifest   truth   would become]
                                                              (literally,
                                                              works)

the alliterative force is evident even to the Greekless reader, and the two *amph* -words become more significant when we learn that both of them are *hapax lagomena*, that is they occur here only. Joyceans might even become excited over a scene as trivial as a foot-washing, where an old wound is recognized (as it immediately will be) and something startling, a whatness, is revealed. Stephen Dedalus can get eloquent over such cases (*Stephen Hero*, p. 213). Being revealed is to be made *amphada*, a dialectal or even colloquial derivation of the verb *anaphainō* (to make appear, reveal, display, show forth). Homer, a moment before the hazardous disclosure, happens to use a near-synonym term of the one that young Joyce, and many later critics, was so fond of. The scene that follows literally and polytropically *is* an epiphany, and by some lucky chance, Homer almost called it so.

The (non)recognition fluctuations in book nineteen of the Odyssey are so subtle, both linguistically and psychologically, that they would need separate and extensive attention. Here I can only focus on that scar, *oulē*. Since it leads almost instantly to the naming of Odysseus, it would be tempting to link *oulē* to one of the non-Homeric variants of the name (which basically splits into an *Od* - and an *Ol/Ul* -lineage)—*Oulixes*, but there seems to be no philological evidence for this. Sounds and shapes, we know, are impostures. The scar will be mentioned seven more times, with one exception always in the accusative (since the scar is noticed, known, covered, inflicted, or suffered)—*oulēn*.

Before the famous foot-washing there has been a bristling first encounter between Odysseus, still a beggar, and Penelope who, most likely, does not yet recognize him. She is wary about anything reported about her lost husband. Calling himself Aithon and inventing some Cretan descent, he says that long ago Odysseus, on the way to Troy, had been his guest. Penelope wants some evidence: How did he look, what clothes did he wear, who was with him? Now Odysseus, making up fictional memories of meeting himself, is at his dexterous best. It is not easy, he says, you see, to remember things of twenty years ago, but he will try. And proceeds to recall the cloak Odysseus wore—it had a most marvelous brooch—and his doublet, and the one companion whom he can still name. But of course how is he to know that those actually were the clothes that his wife gave him for the journey; he might have gotten them from someone else along the way (19:218-48). It is all very common sense and most crafty. We also detect a Bloomian touch in the impression of the doublet being "like the skin of a dried onion." Penelope is convinced.

What clinched it is clearly that brooch of unique design and workmanship, with a "curious device" (*daidalon*). There is little doubt that the detailed description of the artwork—the earliest piece of pictorial life-like realism (19:226-34)—is the best proof of his veracity. Odysseus had begun, however, almost offhandedly and hesitantly, with a cloak, an unexceptional one. Unfortunately now, my presentation reverses the emphasis, directing attention precisely where it would not have been. I read the passage almost as a show Odysseus puts on of gradually remembering something from the past, not important at the time, in paraphrase like: Let me think. Ah! "A cloak (*chlainan*)—purple (*porphyreēn*)—made of wool (*oulēn*) he was wearing, of double fold (*diplēn*, 19:225-6).[8] And no one, surely, hearing the story for the first time, would give much thought to the common garment which only serves to introduce a marvel of epic acknowledgement, the depiction of the splendid brooch. It is not until a few minutes later, when we have come upon the revelatory scar, *oulḗn*, that we can turn the commonplace adjective woolly, *oúlēn*, into a potential identifying device, perhaps an auctorial overtone. Mind you, *oúlēn* (from *oúlos*, related to our "wool," occurring in its feminine accusative singular form only here), is slightly different from the noun *oulḗn*—a matter of accent, well discernible to a Greek ear, something that students of the language have to distinguish the hard way.

If Odysseus had wanted to signal, subliminally, a secret to his wife, or if Homer had wanted to communicate with his audience, that muted *oúlen* would have done the trick, a word that claims or proves nothing, yet spells a tiny message. All of this within a context of disguise and identification. Is this a cunningly wrought (*daidalon*) strategy? Penelope, we are told, "recognized the tokens" of circumstantial evidence, and the word for token is *sēmata* (19:250).

Semantic deviation of a phrase from its denotation is a technique that Joyce taught us. The signatures of the *Odyssey* are not usually read like that. We do not know whether we can take a slightly unnecessary remark, "and another thing will I tell you, and take it to your heart," occurring halfway through the listing of the clothes of Odysseus, at its below-surface level: *allo de toi ereō . . .* (19:236). If we take to heart what he said in his very first spoken words in the poem, in partly identical phrasing: *allo ti . . . mēdeai* (5:173), we get into deep waters. For there *allo ti* meant also note something other than what has ostensibly been said. If we now take *him* at *his* own previous word, an ordinary woolen cloak may be refunctioned into an incidental epiphany.[9]

previous intimations of the result (*U* 676)

Even *primarily* understanding Joycean phrases may depend on a second exposure later on, which is to say that reading, re-reading too, changes what we have read. It can clarify or add complexities. We cannot possibly account for the strange behavior of Bantam Lyons, who cryptically says "I'll risk it" and speeds off (*U* 86). That "it" will make belated sense when Bloom's "throw it away" has been drawn into a racing environment and accreted more fortuitous meaning from a religious pamphlet, so much so that even a wholly juxtapositional "hardly a stone*throw away*" (*U* 613) may set in motion an already intricate net of correspondences. Retroactive semantification is vital in *Finnegans Wake*. We do not expect it in Homer, though the Greeks were later to attribute ambiguity to their oracles, where decoding often trailed behind.

I can think of at least one tragically miniature example of delayed enlightenment. In the second book of the *Odyssey* an Ithakan assembly has been convened. The first person to rise is old, sage Aigyptios. Before he speaks, we are told that one of his sons, Antiphos, had gone away with Odysseus, that the savage Kyklos had killed him in the hollow caves, and—

pymaton   d'hoplissato   dorpon (2:20)

[last   (he) prepared   supper]

The Kyklops had "prepared (a, the) last meal." According to unstated laws of narrative pertinence, there must be some connection, but we are unable to deduce what it was. Translations, here representing reader response, go several ways. But one has to roam far afield to find versions that limit themselves to the simple statement of the original: A 19th century German rendering is: "das Mahl sich, das letzte, bereitend" (Hubatsch); and the same is expressed in a more recent French form: ". . . mais ce fut son dernier repas" (Jaccottet). Buckley needs a pronoun: "the cyclops . . . prepared for his last supper." The majority translate a different story, augmented by a decisive link: ". . . *on him* made a supper last of all" (Palmer); ". . . and made *of him* his latest meal" (Butcher & Lang).

In this view Antiphos is "last" in a meal as a passive victim. These readings are of course correct, but they are not what a novice listener to the tale could pick up. Translators anticipate and gloss, sometimes in creative amplification: ". . . who had cooked him too, and eaten him for his latest, and his last, feast" (T.E. Shaw); "The ravenous Kyklops in the cave destroyed him/Last in his feast of men" (Fitzgerald). Pope gave freest rein to his imagination:

But (hapless youth) the hideous Cyclops tore
His quivering limbs, and quaff'd his spouting gore.

All of this is in full, but predictive, awareness that the Kyklops used to feed on guests that dropped in. Of the companions of Odysseus, he took two at a time, on three recorded occasions. One might reopen the old question of *verbatim* against "free" translations, but what the responses bring out here are shifts in interpretation, all the way from a fairly innocuous domestic meal to a gruesome spectacle, and not, for example, a metaphoric licence, as in "The Russians, they'd only be an eight o'clock breakfast for the Japanese" (*U* 58).

It is the dangling adjective *pymaton* that seems to cause so much divergence in translation and to provoke officious paraphrases. What does the phrase really say? It has both an uninformed (present) and an enlightened (future) meaning, and this latter one is let out of the translators' bag too soon. Reviewed from the later perspective of the Kyklops adventure, *pymaton d'hoplissato dorpon* appears as a short-hand version of the much more detailed later report. After attending to several chores in the case, the Kyklops "seized two men" (*dyō marpsas*), and made ready (*hoplissato*) his supper (*dorpon*); this is the final one of three such outrages, the one, as we now can conclude, that involved hapless Antiphos (9:344). The first and most shocking demonstration of cannibalism, however, is the one most drastically evoked: it shows the victims' brains flowing forth, their limbs being cut, with mention of entrails, flesh and bones, all this around another *hoplissato dorpon* (9:29-3):[10] here clearly is the source for Pope's transferred quivering limbs and spouting gore. The visualisation has been anticipated.[11] The meal we first heard of was not the last one for the dining host, but the last feasting on the Ithakans—or else it was the last one Polyphemos could still enjoy seeing. The translations already quoted by Fitzgerald and Shaw, as well as Rieu's "when he made the last of his meal off Odysseus' men," are explicitly adequate synopses, but not what Homer said in less than half that many words.[12]

We may note in passing that a phrase for taking a meal, which could easily be dismissed as a bardic routine, has become full of suspense. There is at least one more retroactive overtone to *pymaton*. The Kyklops had guilefully promised a "guest-gift" in return for the stranger's name and then, when "Outis" introduced himself, craftily answered him: "*Outin* I will eat *pymaton* (last), . . . this will be your gift" (9:369-70). The threat will not be fulfilled, but the adjective has acquired more reciprocal punch. The more we read and remember (or, like good modernists, cross-reference), the more ominous each single term becomes. The suitors too will suffer their fateful last supper, as Odysseus announces to them before he takes up his bow: "now it is time to prepare *dorpon* for them. . ." (21:428). These meanings are not just "there" from the start, but gradually accrue, just as Joyce's words ("home," "key," "jingled," "four," or even "up") grow in resonance as we go along.

So the question has turned into what does our phrase mean *when*, and to *whom*? Time, reading time, is modeling our understanding in progress. We are given two accounts, only minimally overlapping. Odysseus, maybe in heroic caste-consciousness, has not mentioned the names of any of his subordinates in a conflict which is between an anonymous Kyklops—whose name will be revealed accidentally by his compatriots ("Polyphemos," 9:403, 407)—and a pseudonymous "Outis"—who finally gives away his identity in an uncautious lapse. The much more concise epic digression in Book Two supplements the self-centered story of the titular figure and shows, more humanely, the reverse of heroic survival—an individual with a name, a qualification (he was a spearman), and a bereaved father.

There is also parallactic ignorance. The novice reader is told that Antiphos has been killed (which he could never learn from the extensive Kyklops episode alone), but is unable to understand the exact nature of the meal. Aigyptios, the father, does not even know that his son is dead. In poignant irony the father is called "sage," literally "who . . . knew *myria*" (2:16), but for all the "numberless" things he knows, he cannot know what he would care most about, what happened to his son, and he still hopes the assembly might hear news of the expedition force coming back. Homer has deftly sketched a subsidiary tragedy of a father and a son. And once more a formula that has all the visible signs of a cliché, "knowing *myria*," has become almost harrowing.

A commentator, far less deft than Homer, has to muster an inordinate amount of verbiage and quotations (and, excuse me, transliteration), to show how "understanding" may come about slowly, sequentially, chancily, parallactically.

The above readings are all modeled on techniques that we may call Joycean. Joyce, at any rate, helped to teach them to us. As might be shown in much more ample detail, some of these techniques were already Homeric, and may have been overlooked. But, inevitably, I have offered not only interpretations, but also metachronic figments, or feints—for that is what fiction means: Latin *fingere*, "feign", or figure (all cognates of English "dough") go back to a root meaning to kneed, mold, form, or what in German could be expressed by *modeln*.

Which brings me commodiously back to the modernist fiction of the arch-modeler Joyce. In his last work, after *Ulysses*, he wrote that "Temp untamed will hist for no man" (*FW* 196.22). In the history book of Everybody no man may be Outis, and the author might condone the dislocution of a phrase close by (the context is a trial) into a comment on my own illicit tampering with an ancient model—" illysus distilling."

Notes

1. I may be making too much of a lexical suspicion nowhere recorded. The epithet *naulochus* turns up only once more, at the end of Book Two, where the task force of the suitors found a convenient harbour "for ships to lie in" (*naulochoi*, 4:846). The next lines say that the suitors are waiting for Telemachos, to kill him, "ambushing (*lochoōntes*) him."

Before Odysseus leaves for Kirke's house, he falls out with the lieutenant, who cautiously had not entered her place but came back to report. He now refuses to join the rescue party, for fear of being trapped again. Odysseus seems to overreact to the one companion who shares so much of his own prudence. His name is Eury*lochos*.

2. Joyce may have inverted this misconception in his Book of Deceptive Signs. Instead of a final reconciliation, we read of the origin of Earwicker's agnomen, an episode, with "a high perch atop of which a flowerpot was fixed"—a strange landlubber's device to trap earwigs which is mistaken for an aquatic implement, part of a fishing rod—"paternosters and silver doctors" (*FW* 31.1-8). In *Finnegans Wake* this is how the troubles *begin*.

3. Robert Fitzgerald shifts the choice of a starting point from the Muse addressed to the invoker, who specifies: "Begin when all the rest. . . had long ago returned. . . "

4. The most recent gloss on this that I could find says: "Il glocco di parole e chiaramente intenzionale." Omero, *Udissea*, Vol. I, Testo e commento a cura di Stephanie West, Milano: Arnoldo Mondadori, 1961, p. 356.

5. That words like *mēdomai* and *mēdea* are related to "measure," "metre," "meditate" and, moreover, cognate to "mode," "modern," "modality" and "*modeln*," merely shows that this is a small world of Indo-European roots. But it is intriguing to notice that the first instance of dubiousness by Odysseus is connected with *mēdomai*. When Kalypso, out of the blue, announces his sudden return, he says distrustfully: "Something else, goddess, you have in mind (*mēdeai*) than my return" (5:173). He knows, no one better, about the disparity of what people say and what they intend. I think it significant that the first words Odysseus ever speaks are "*Allo ti*"— "something else." Something-elseness is characteristic of his mind

and his cunning, it is a feature of the *Odyssey* and of Joyce's works, it is the life-force of *Finnegans Wake*. When I speculated on the *pers pro toto* validity of this opening hint ("Paratektonik oder Nichts gegen Homer," in *Nichts gegen Joyce: Joyce Versus Nothing*, Zurich: Haffmans Verlag [1983], p. 155-6), I had not even noticed that the first, exemplary speech is actually sandwiched between this common word denoting otherness: *"Allo ti. . .allo"* (5:173, 179).

6. Leopold Bloom's incongruous measurements have been explained in various ways. Mythologically, some obvious discrepancies in the size of Bloom's "chest . . . biceps . . . forearm . . . thigh. . . calf" (*U* 721) need not worry us, for Pallas Athena can diminish Odysseus for his role as a beggar (13:430f) and, at need, enhance his appearance: "Odysseus. . . showed his thighs, comely and great, and his broad shoulders. . . his chest and mighty arms. And Athene. . . made greater the limbs. . . " (Murray, 18:67-70).

7. Maud Ellmann has written about the linking of the scar with the naming of Odysseus in "Polytropic Man: Paternity, Identity and Naming," in *James Joyce: New Perspectives* (ed. Colin McCabe), Brighton: Harvester Press (1982), pp. 81ff. Her excellent essay relies on translations, in which identifying features easily get blurred.

8. The cloak is *diplēn*, "worn double"; another cloak that Odysseus (disguised) claims he was given by Odysseus (real) in a Trojan fictitious exploit, creating a lie of fascinating duality in order to wheedle a *real* cloak from Eumaias is also "of double fold" (*diplaka*, akin to Lat. *duplex*). Twofoldedness is typical of the Nostos-books of the *Odyssey*, but duplicity also suffuses the Eumaeus chapter of *Ulysses*, with its doubling of roles, events, identities, etc.

9. As though to reinforce such suspicions, the last description of the companion that the beggar remembers, Eurybates—who is "so much like-minded with Odysseus"—is *oulokarēnos*, literally "woolly-headed" (19:246).

10. Line 311 is identical, only the meal this time is *deipnon*, (taken in midday or, here, in the morning). A similar formula is used for the meal that the Laistrygonians make of one of the Greeks (10:116), so that this further disaster may become part of an expanding aura of secondary associations.

11. Homer is modeling times. Odysseus's report of the Kyklopian adventure narratively *succeeds* the brief mention in Book Two, but *precedes* it in actual time. Translators remodel the tidings for the reader's comfort and for facile instant consumption.

12. It is congruent that Joyce translators too are occasionally inclined towards glossing amplification. If my somewhat excessive list-

ing of metaphrastic evidence should undermine the readers' trust in translation generally, then we have to be grateful to Homer and Joyce for showing us *that*, too.

Translations of the *Odyssey* quoted:

Most of these translations are available in several editions. Since the citation of the original (5:173 = line 173 of book five) can always guide a reader to the corresponding passage, the page numbers have not been given.

Buckley: *The Odyssey of Homer*, literally translated by Theodore Alois Buckley. London: Bell & Daldy, 1867

Butcher & Lang: *The Odyssey of Homer*, done into English prose by S.H. Butcher and A. Lang. London: Macmillan and Co., 1887.

S. Butler: *The Odyssey of Homer*, translated by Samuel Butler Roslyn, N.Y.: Walter J. Black, Inc., 1944 (dated July, 1900).

Chapman: *Chapman's Homer*, Vol. II, *The Odyssey*. Edited by Allardyce Nicoll, Princeton University Press, 1958 (first published 1614-15?).

Fitzgerald: *Homer: The Odyssey*, translated by Robert Fitzgerald. Garden City, N.Y.: Doubleday, 1981.

Hubatsch: *Homers Odyssee*, In neuer Uebersetzung von Oskar Hubatsch, Bielefeld & Leibzig: Velhagen & Klasing, 1892.

Jaccottet: *Homère: L'Odyssée*. Traduction de Philippe Jaccottet. Paris: Francois Maspero, 1982.

Murray: *Homer: The Odyssey*. With an English translation by A. T. Murray. Loeb Classical Library. Cambridge, Mass.: Harvard University Press, 1910.

Palmer: *The Odyssey of Homer*. Translated by George Herbert Palmer. Boston and New York: Houghton, Mifflin and Co., 1899.

Pope: *The Odyssey of Homer*. Translated by Alexander Pope. London: Frederick Warne & Co., n.d. Published 1725-6 (the translators were Pope, Elijah Fenton, and William Broome).

Rieu: *Homer: The Odyssey*. Translated by E.V. Rieu. Harmondsworth: Penguin Books, 1946.

Rouse: *The Story of Odysseus*. A New Translation by W.H.D. Rouse, New York: Modern Age Books, Inc., 1937.

Shaw: *The Odyssey of Homer*. Newly Translated into English Prose by T.E. Shaw (Lawrence of Arabia). New York: Oxford University Press, 1932.

(   ):
Finnegans Wake and the Postmodern Imagination

Ihab Hassan

PREAMBLE

I have no title, only a phrase held together by an ambitious conjunction. The phrase is an invitation to place this most outrageous of
books, this parodic myth of all myths, this endless sound of language and its echolalias—I mean *Finnegans Wake*—help place it in
the field of our consciousness.

The invitation is collective, which gives me leave to wander and
license to digress within the limits of my time and everyone's patience. There are several questions that I hope to raise, and several,
no doubt, that will arise, unbidden, troublesome, spontaneous. But
all my own questions finally come to one:

> How does *Finnegans Wake* accord with, how does it make itself available
> to, the postmodern imagination?

Obviously, to argue the question is not to prove influences but
rather to speculate on concordances.

I confess it from the start: I am no deep reader of that book. I lack
the cryptogrammatic sensibility which rejoices in "The keys to.
Given" (628.15). I have little to say that will illumine its puns and
patterns, its susurrus and sources. Yet I am convinced that the work

stands as a monstrous prophecy that we have begun to discover (thanks to many deep readers) but have not yet decided how to heed.

Admittedly, Joyce was a man of many superstitions; repeatedly, he told Stuart Gilbert that the *Wake* included "premonitions of incidents that subsequently took place." But Joyce was not only superstitious; he was also increasingly vatic. He was Stephen and he was Dedalus; he became both Bloom and Ulysses; and his Penelope remained Nora as well as Flaubert. Yet in the end, in *Finnegans Wake*, Joyce glimpsed the great mystery beyond the Pillars of Hercules. Once again, the question returns: what is there for us to see in that Joycean vision beyond the seas?

Let me now end this preamble with a brief note on method. I want to present seven perspectives of the central question. Against these thematic perspectives, I will permit myself a counterpoint made of postmodern rumors and random reflections, through which the mind may pause or run. Fittingly, I close with a personal postamble.

COUNTERPOINT

In my notes, I have found these admonitions to myself: "Avoid puns and portmanteaus; leave Joyce to his imitative forms. Resist the temptation to quote from your 1969 Dublin Scenario; the 'Missisliffi' flows backwards only by moonlight. Quote, however, all the Joyceans present in the 1973 symposium—if possible." But these are only intentions. True gaiety in form surprises itself.

PERSPECTIVE I: A DEATH BOOK AND BOOK OF LIFE

The book is more determinedly cyclical than Vico and the very seasons of the unforgetting earth: "The seim anew" (215.22). This sometimes obscures for us the depth of its deathly hue. The *Wake* is not only Joyce's "funferall," designed "for that ideal reader suffering from an ideal insomnia"; it is itself a presentiment of ends. "*Finnegans Wake* will be my last book," Joyce said. "There is nothing left for me to do but die." Coincidentally, this book of night appears in 1939, when night descends on the world.

For humanist readers, for children of reason and history and a bourgeois social order, that is, for most of us, the unspoken intimation of this novel must be death of the self, death of the old reader himself. I must return to this topic later; here I only wish to signal the secret threat of the *Wake*. Make no mistake: this book of universals avers our mortality. Oliver Gogarty, who was so often and so interestingly wrong about Joyce—because he was in some perverse way right—says about the *Wake*: "To me it is like a shattered cathedral through the ruins of which, buried deep and muted under the debris, the organ still sounds with all its stops pulled out at once. . . ." Only Père Ubu, I suppose, went further: one must also destroy the ruins, he cried.

For the reader who happens also to be a writer, *Finnegans Wake* offers the aspect of a labyrinth with all its ends seemingly dead. We know the resistance that the book encountered. It was not only Alfred Noyes, Arnold Bennett, H. G. Wells, G. B. Shaw, Desmond McCarthy, Sean O'Faolain, and Oliver Gogarty who expressed their grave discomforts with the work; it was also, and more viciously, such modernists as Gertrude Stein and Wyndham Lewis. Even supporters balked. Mary Colum thought that *Finnegans Wake* would remain "outside literature," and Harriet Weaver grumbled about the "Wholesale Safety Pun Factory," and like a good English governess, scolded Joyce: "It seems to me you are wasting your genius."

Is *Finnegans Wake* outside of literature? Or is it pointing the way for literature to go beyond itself? Or, again, is it a prophecy of the end of literature as we have come to know it? These three questions are really the same question I have asked from the start. And I would answer all three: YES. That is why I call *Finnegans Wake* not only a death book but also a book of life, not simply an end but a progress as well.

COUNTERPOINT

A progress toward what? A new vision of universal consciousness?

How express my distaste, my desperation, my strange allegiance—all provoked by this book? Once, scholars and savants—Ernst Robert Curtius and Carl Gustav Jung, for example—understood Joyce little and liked him less. And now, without understanding Finnegans Wake a great deal more, men turn to the book like sunflowers to a secret sun.

Take Norman O. Brown or Marshall McLuhan or Michel Butor—or take Theodore Roszak and William Irwin Thompson, more pert and trendy still—all have something to say about the Wake. *Here is Brown: "Darkness at noon. A progressive darkening of the everyday world of common sense.* Finnegans Wake. *Second sight is the dark night."* Here is McLuhan:*

---

*Brown's Closing Time (1973) appeared after the writing of this essay.

"Finnegans Wake . . . *is a verbal universe in which press, movie, radio,*
TV merge with the languages of the world to form a Feenichts Playhouse or
metamorphoses." And Butor? He calls the Wake *the greatest single effort to*
transcend language by means of itself.

Whether we think with modernist Northrop Frye that the work is the
"chief ironic epic of our time" or think with various post-modernists—
Butor, McLuhan, Brown—this or that, the work still stands, like a word
ziggurat, teasing our sense of human possibilities. Yes, more than À la
Recherche du temps perdu, The Sound and the Fury, Der Zauber-
berg, Women in Love, *and even* Das Schloss.

Yet, how many ever read Finnegans Wake? *Ah, Mr. Wilder, though*
you say some works permeate the culture unread, the question still nags,
and nags.

PERSPECTIVE II:
HIGH ART, POPULAR CULTURE,
AND BEYOND

The *Portrait* depicts the Artist alone; *Ulysses* presents the Artist
seeking Everyman to be atoned; and *Finnegans Wake* gives "Allmen."
That, at least, is a plausible view of the work of James Augustine
Joyce. And there is the paradox that gives credence to this view:
Joyce was among the most autobiographical of artists and the most
impersonal, the most self-obsessed and also the most dramatically
universal. There is really no paradox at all: he simply pushed his
subjective will so far that it became superfluous to distinguish between subject and object, self and world. Like a Berkeleyan god, he
hoped to create the universe in his mind-languages, all but abolish-
ing God's original book. Paul Léon put it another way: "Continuous
self-confession, for Joyce, meant continuous creation. . . ." There is
a willed unity in Joyce's art and life. And it is precisely this willed
unity of the outcast mind that compels us to review the categories
not only of self and world but also of high art and popular culture as
they apply to Joyce.

We all know that none possessed a brow higher than "Sunny
Twimjim" (211.07). "The demand that I make of my reader is that he
should devote his whole life to reading my works," he said, and
though he said it smiling, he repeated it to make a bad joke deadly
earnest. Thus the ascetics of high art. Twelve hundred hours spent
on the composition of "Anna Livia Plurabelle" justified some mor-
tification on the reader's part. Herbert Read easily concludes: "Mr.
Joyce is the high priest of modern literature precisely because liter-

ature is a priesthood and has a sanctuary more inaccessible than the monasteries of Thibet. . . ." But there is another side to this picture: the face of Joyce on the cover of *Time* magazine. With infinitely more cunning than silence in his exile, Joyce succeeded in making *Finnegans Wake* the most famous of unread books.

Preposterous as it may seem to us, Joyce also believed that the *Wake* could appeal to a wide and varied audience, believed that his "Big Language" could win the common as well as the uncommon reader. And why not? The book, after all, abounds in wit and sentimentality, in folklore, ribaldry, and song; the sounds of the music hall, the pub, and the street crackle in its pages. The bizarre, the lowly, the gushy, the factual, the obscene—all crowd into his later work, hodge-podge, mish-mash, hurly-burly, pell-mell, together with the purest poesy. In the end, the distance between the sublime and the ridiculous is contracted into a pun and expanded into endless parody. Pop, which Leslie Fiedler identifies with postmodern, is never far from the edge of *Finnegans Wake*.

But the affinity of this book with popular culture is still more complex. When Joyce said to Jolas: "This book is being written by the people I have met or known," he was not suddenly overcome by modesty. The book of "Allmen" needs, in theory at least, a collective author. It requires also a communal reader. What else can a "Joyce industry" produce but such a reader? J. Mitchell Morse puts it more pleasantly: ". . . reading *Finnegans Wake* is a collective enterprise of no ordinary kind: what takes place is no mere quantitative gathering and mechanical assembling of parts into larger units, but a blending of objective and subjective elements—a kind of communion—in which one person's information calls from another's subconscious an inference that validates the conjecture of a third. Joyce has revived the magical function of the old bards and shamans, in what by convention we consider a most unlikely place, the seminar room."

Perhaps the seminar room is as close as most of us come to popular culture; or perhaps the seminar without walls will become itself the culture of a "deschooled society." The point I want to make is simply this: *Finnegans Wake* carries the tendencies of high art and of popular culture to their outer limits, there where all tendencies of mind may meet, there where the epiphany and the dirty joke become one. If this still be elitism, it is elitism of a special kind.

COUNTERPOINT

I wonder if Fendant de Sion will be provided at the banquet for Joyceans. "The Archduchess" at dinner?

I wonder, too, about "dreck." In Snow White, *Donald Barthelme says: "We like books that have a lot of dreck in them, matter which presents itself as not wholly relevant (or indeed, at all relevant) but which, carefully attended to, can supply a kind of 'sense' of what is going on." Is* Finnegans Wake *full of magical dreck? Does the refuse of an old consciousness remake itself into bricks of the new?*

There are other matters. Assume for the moment that the Wake *challenges the modernist idea of high art and in some ways prefigures the postmodernist idea of pop culture. Not only because of its mixed tone (after all, "Lil's husband got demobbed" earlier), not only because of its slapstick and obscenity, but also because of its myth of a collective mind in which the author himself must disappear as privileged person.*

No, I am not speaking of "impersonality" as Hulme, Eliot, or Pound spoke of it; I am thinking of the "death of the author" as Roland Barthes thinks of it. Barthes, that cool and canny semiotician, may seem an odd ally of Pop; but let us hear him anyway: "Once the Author is gone, the claim to 'decipher' a text becomes quite useless. To give an Author to a text is to impose upon the text a stop clause, to furnish it with a final signification, to close the writing." For Barthes, then—and here Morse unwittingly joins him—the true locus of writing is reading. Thus, "a text consists of multiple writings, issuing from several cultures and entering into dialogue with each other, into parody, into contestation; but there is one place where this multiplicity is collected, united, and this place is not the author, as we have hitherto said it was, but the reader. . . ."

What text could celebrate the "death" of the author and the "birth" of a new reader better than Finnegans Wake? *Ultimately, in another kind of literature perhaps, may not author and reader become true coevals? But for the time being, have we not witnessed the advent of a youthful reader, not Pop but its parody, a lexical player, amorous in* Ada, *agile in* Giles Goat-Boy, *skipping weightlessly in* Gravity's Rainbow?

PERSPECTIVE III: DREAM & PLAY
(AND LATER STRUCTURE)

The disorder of dreams, the purposelessness of play, the cunning of structure seem contradictory; yet it is on that contradiction that *Finnegans Wake* balances itself.

Actually, the balance is less miraculous than managed, a supreme act of prestidigitation. For as a dream book, the *Wake* is an effort of huge wakefulness. The comedy and wit of the work, which remind Arland Ussher of "the delicious absurdities of a Marx Brothers film," are intensely conscious of themselves. Whether Joyce ever dreamt or not, we must recognize that his words constitute a metalanguage, not a dream. Certainly the work obsessed him: "Since 1922," he says, "my book has been a greater reality for me than reality. Everything gives way to it." Obsession makes for hyperconsciousness. "What about the mystery of consciousness?" Joyce asked Budgen. "What do they know of that?" The dream element in *Finnegans Wake*, then, seen from the point of view of its author, is simply his freedom: his freedom to alter language and reality. The dream is literary fantasy. We are "whenabouts in the name of space?" (558.33).

COUNTERPOINT

Michel Butor suggests that Finnegans Wake *is not the description of a dream but a "machine for provoking and helping the reader himself to dream." Or rather, helping the reader to play. Play is the vice and joy of postmodernism; play is fatuousness but also fantasy.*

Think of all our fantasists and geomancers: Beckett, Barth, Bernhard, Burgess, Becker, Barthelme, Butor, Blanchot, Burroughs, Brautigan, Borges, Bichsel, Nabokov. Ronald Sukenick, himself one, speaks of still later writers as dancers of the Bossa Nova: "Needless to say the Bossa Nova has no plot, no story, no character, no chronological sequence, no verisimilitude, no imitation, no allegory, no symbolism, no subject matter, no 'meaning.'"

But that's not Finnegans Wake, *we all want to cry. Yet it is an ablation of the* Wake; *it is the* Wake *deprived of its paranoiac intentionality; it is the* Wake *without work, the surface as grimace, comedy as absurd and precise play. Whether or not he meant it to be so, when God became the Dreamer, everything became possible.*

PERSPECTIVE III: CONTINUED

Dream, then, becomes game, an exercise in fantasy and number. Above all, dream and play provide the invisible latticework of comedy. Someday, someone may devise a theory of comedy based entirely on *Finnegans Wake*. She (or he) may refer to the work of Hugh Kenner and Vivian Mercier on this zany subject; consider the goliardic, macaronic, parodic, satiric, and all other comic traditions; consult philosophers of every kind; ponder the statement of Karl Marx about history repeating itself, the first time as tragedy, the second as farce; and perhaps finally pray: "Loud, heap miseries upon us yet entwine our arts with laughters low!" (259.07). For myself, I simply want to note that comedy links dream, game, and structure in the *Wake*, that it objectifies dream and democratizes structure while relieving game from the logic of banality. From the smallest pun to the largest parodic pattern, comedy asserts its power, not only to amuse or even to surprise us, but far more to multiply meanings, to compound complexities. In this book, comedy is the tuning fork of language, vibrating in a vacuum, forever.

BRIEF COUNTERPOINT

Vacuum. Exactly!

Some would call the infinite vibrations of comedy nihilism. The parody of a parody of a parody that was once comedy. Eternity as absurd recurrence. No evaluation, no value. Is that what "The Gracehoper . . . always jigging ajog, hoppy on akkant of his joyicity" (414.22) has done to the novel?

Still, what major postmodern fiction is conceived but in the comic mode? And who are its ancestors but Joyce and Kafka? Unless it be that obscure man, Raymond Roussel?

PERSPECTIVE IV: STRUCTURE

What can I possibly add to this subject, except perhaps to suggest that all good structuralists go to *Finnegans Wake* on their way to heaven, and that is perhaps why they are so long in reaching their destination?

We know that the novel is both structurally over-determined and semantically under-defined. Its structural principles include numbers, symbols, leitmotifs, collages, montages, mythic patterns, simulated dreams, mystic correspondences, musical ratios, multiple and receding perspectives, game theories, parodies, puns, alliterations, and much else in the lexicon of classical rhetoric. Yet *Finnegans Wake* is not only supremely aware of itself as structure; it is also aware of the more obscure need to de-structure itself. "Samuel Beckett has remarked that to Joyce reality was a paradigm, an illustration of a possibly unstatable rule. Yet perhaps the rule can be surmised," Ellmann says. "It is not a perception of order or of love; more humble than either of these, it is the perception of *coincidence* [italics mine]."

Now coincidence as a structural principle means both identity and accident, recurrence and divergence. Coincidence implies the frightening disorder that every fanatic order itself implies. Four legs of a horse, four seasons, four evangelists. Is this the coincidence of secret design or of dementia in reality? To the very end, Joyce seems to have qualified his emergent vision of correspondences by his ineluctable irony. The more mystical he became—or is it merely superstitious?—the more ruthless his self-parody. His great Dedalian labor includes a deep instinct of unmaking.

Thus, on the one hand, *Finnegans Wake* acknowledges the totality of Joyce's artifice and effort. The ending of Book IV, for instance, may be read to include the endings of all his other works; and various passages of the *Wake* recapitulate the design of the whole novel. But the structure of the novel also reflects upon itself, and in so doing heightens its fictitiousness. The shady character of Shem the Penman, the pervasive motif of the Letter, the reflexive references to Joyce, the wry comments on the manuscript of the novel itself, its progress and reception—"Your exagmination round his factification for incamination of a warping process" (496.36)—all these are instances of artifice recognizing its own artificiality. Thus, on the other hand, *Finnegans Wake* accepts the gratuitousness of every creative act. Indeed, as we shall see, Joyce identified creation with original sin, the most necessary and gratuitous of all acts.

COUNTERPOINT

Shem the Penman, "Sniffer of carrion, premature gravedigger, seeker of the nest of evil in the bosom of a good word" (189.28), Shem, Cain, Satan, Nick and Glugg, Ishmael, Set, Taff and Mutt, Iago, Romeo, Bottom and Puck, Stephen Dedalus, James Joyce, "still today insufficiently malestimated notesnatcher" (125.21), "nay, condemned fool, anarch, egoarch, hiresiarch, you have reared your disunited kingdom on the vacuum of your most intensely doubtful soul" (188.15).

Ah, we say, here is a Portrait of the Artist as Nasty Man. But this artist, Shem Joyce, creates peculiarly postmodern forms and here is why:

a. Parodic Reflexiveness. *The novel that parodies and reflects upon its own structure is not new.* Gide's Les Faux-Monnayeurs (1925) *and* Gombrowicz' Ferdydurke (1937), *for instance, antecede the* Wake *in this, as does* Tristram Shandy (1760–1767). *But the genre, with its multiple, fractured, and ambiguous perspectives, becomes current only after the war in such diverse works as* Nabokov's Pale Fire, *Cortazar's* Hopscotch, *Borges'* Ficciones, *Genet's* Journal d'un voleur, *Beckett's* How It Is, *and Barth's* Lost in the Fun House.

b. *The Re-creation of Reality*. *The conventional ideas of time, place, character, plot are shattered; reality is re-created. In modernist literature this is sometimes achieved by a quasi-cubist breakdown of surfaces, as in the works of Gertrude Stein or Alfred Döblin; at other times it is achieved by dissolving surfaces, absorbing them into an interior language, as in the works of Proust or Faulkner. The first method appears quasi-objective, the second quasi-subjective; yet both remake reality in words. Joyce masters both these methods. In that sense,* Finnegans Wake *clears the way for both "neo-realist" and "surrealist" fictions—for Robbe-Grillet's* La Jalousie *and Butor's* Mobile *on the one hand, and Hawkes's* The Cannibal *and Wurlitzer's* Nog *on the other. In either case, the re-creation of reality requires us to abandon the distinction between objective and subjective categories within the pervasive fantasy of the work. Fact and fiction acquire the same aspect. This, too, is postmodern: Capote's "non-fiction novel,"* In Cold Blood; *Styron's "meditation on history,"* The Confessions of Nat Turner; *Mailer's "history as a novel, the novel as history,"* Armies of the Night; *even the New Journalism in America—all these perceive, however partially, that from a certain vantage, fact and fiction must blur. The enormous volume of the World is matched by even greater expansions of the Self until reality becomes a declaration of the mind.*

c. Nonlinear Form. *Circular, simultaneous, coincident—a mesh or mosaic or montage or Moebius time strip of motifs—that, too, is* Finnegans Wake. *We think of myth, music, the cabala, and electrical systems as prototypes of the nonlinear structure of the book, creating a perception that exists outside of conventional time and space. It is not only that time is spatialized as Joseph Frank has argued about the modern novel; in this work both time and space are fantasticated. By rejecting linear or discursive logic, by simulating dream, the* Wake *maintains itself in the "pressant" time and unlimited space of mind. Speaking of Marc Saporta's so-called "shuffle novel,"* Composition No. 1, *Sharon Spencer makes this pertinent point: "Saporta's narrative procedure takes from the dream a rationale for dissolving the conventional distinctions between memory (the past), desire (implying the future), and fantasy (suggesting present being) and for substituting a timeless and preeminently visual mode of organization." Though it appears idiosyncratic, Saporta's work shares with most postmodern fiction the assumption of nonlinear form, which is always visual and inevitably auditory but, above all, seeks to engage the mind directly.*

d. The Problematics of the Book. *Technologies have altered the nature of the book. From Marshall McLuhan to Michel Butor, writers have reflected upon this question; and in* The Stoic Comedians, *Kenner has spe-*

cifically noted the uses that Joyce made of movable type. It is plain for everyone to see: Finnegans Wake *employs footnotes, marginalia, lists, sketches, and a variety of types, and it defies sequential reading from cover to cover. More than other works, it is a mixed medium, both discontinuous and whole, visual and auditory, poetic and narrative. Some features of its format may recall the figures of Döblin's* Alexanderplatz Berlin, *the captions of Dos Passos'* U.S.A., *the blanks of Mallarmé's* Un Coup de dés— *may even recall* Gargantua et Pantagruel *or* The Book of Kells. *The same typographic features preview the experiments of John Cage, Ronald Sukenick, Donald Barthelme, Raymond Federman, and Eugene Wildman, to mention only some American postmodernists. But typography is not the real issue; the old concept of the book is at stake. "Throughout* Finnegans Wake," *McLuhan says, "Joyce plays some of his major variation on this theme of 'abcedmindedness'. . . . His 'verbivocovisual' presentation of an 'all nights newsery reel' is the first dramatization of the very media of communication as both form and vehicle of the flux of human cultures." One cannot help but wonder: what will the next verbisensual process of communication in our culture be?*

PERSPECTIVE V: EROTICISM

The eroticism of *Finnegans Wake* is inclusive as its life, varied as its language; yet it remains peculiarly Joycean. Margaret Solomon perceives sex as "Joyce's cosmic joke": "Taking upon himself the role of a God engrossed in sex—and using all the religious myths and symbols of creation to perpetuate his joke—was one way of using his jesuitical training in an act of defiance. . . ." But the *Wake* also goes beyond defiance, and the permutations of sex in it are, unlike Beckett's, both sacred and satiric.

The novel offers a non-Euclidean geometry of sex, as Ms. Solomon shows. People stand for genitals, and diagrams stand for people. Creativity is associated with both waste and generation. There are many entries and exits in nature, and many sensuous sides to every question. As above, so below; as in the beginning, so in the end. But as Fritz Senn notes: "The ups and downs and ins and outs are as erotic as they are political" in Joyce's night-book. The book contains everything Eros and Ellis and Kraft-Ebbing ever dreamed: romantic love, narcissism, coprophilia, incest, sodomy, onanism, lesbianism, voyeurism, exhibitionism, sado-masochism, impotence, every so-called perversion—not to mention the *osculum ad anum diaboli* of the Black Mass—as well as the fruitful love of HCE and ALP: "The galleonman jovial on his bucky brown nightmare.

Bigrob dignagging his lylyputtana. One to one bore one!" (583.08).

That is the mystery of love in the novel: the one coming from the many, the many becoming one again. The final point is not perversion but at-one-ment. Thus the composite sexuality of various characters, their male and female "bisectualism," which permits even Mohammed, Shakespeare, and Napoleon to invert their sex. Thus, too, the composite unity of the Earwicker family, which identifies father with sons, mother with daughter, and all with their incestuous counterparts. The sexual fall of Humpty Dumpty signals the eternal metamorphosis of word and flesh, seeking wholeness. Yet Darcy O'Brien says that affection and sensuality are rarely united in Joyce's life or work. Can it be so because final unity is always and wholly impersonal?

COUNTERPOINT

Eroticism in the postmodern age—there are plenty of dirty books now, dirty movies and dirty pictures—imagine Judge Woolsey at a screening of "Deep Throat."

But let us do our age justice.

Consider Norman O. Brown and Norman Mailer—Esalen Institute and Kinsey Institute—Grove Press and Olympia Press—Women's Lib and Gay Liberation—the Pill, Playboy, Penthouse, Portnoy, Pornotopia, and Pornopolitics—all express the dim desire to connect—express the desire and its failure—orgasm as program and sex as solipsism or ideology—yet a new erotic will persists in seeking larger configurations of itself—the death of the family (David Cooper) and the search for androgyny (Carolyn Heilbrun)—a new tribalism, a new polymorphousness and perversity—isn't Finnegans Wake *relevant?*

Certainly, but with a difference—it, too, affirms larger configurations of love—a love, however, closer to myth and mutability than to will and ideology—a love closer still to language—sex as the language of fantasy— "Psing a Psalm of psexpeans, apocryphul of rhyme" (242.30)—the sex speech of postmodern fiction?

PERSPECTIVE VI: THE LANGUAGE OF BABEL

"Although it uses the syntax of other languages," Strother Purdy says of *Finnegans Wake*, "it cannot be considered to be written in . . . the speech of any group." One wonders: Did Joyce seek to recover the unity of human speech before God said, looking down on the Tower of Babel: "Go to, let us go down, and there confound their language, that they may not understand one another's speech"? Frank Budgen remembers that Joyce once claimed to have discovered the secret of Babel; but Budgen never asked and we shall never know.

We can guess. Joyce senses that if reality can be identified with language, language can be identified with itself. This is not to deny his decreative fury in the *Wake*, his will to silence natural speech, tear asunder the mother's tongue. But Joyce's fury seeks "words" that can become im-mediately pure meaning. Harrowing 29 (?) of the world's languages, he also creates a metalanguage from the chaos of the world's phonemes, fusing the Viconian modes of hiero-glyph, metaphor, and abstraction.

Joyce, we know, also employs puns, stutters, riddles, seemingly to arrest the mind in discontinuities. But his puns become metony-mies; the stutters stress recurrence; and even riddles conceal a unity at the incestuous heart of the universe. However much he owed to the Jabberwocky of Lewis Carroll, Joyce's own language is less often analytic than synthetic. His "sentence" is a word in which syntax gives way to phonemic cluster. From the clear sentences of the ear-liest drafts to the packed, layered interpolations of the last, the pro-cess of Joyce's composition reveals a vast effort of syncretism in which all the elements of *Finnegans Wake* take part. When Biddy the Hen pecked out the Letter from the midden heap of time, she may have discovered the original language of Babel on a soiled pal-impsest. "Lead, kindly fowl!" (112.09).

COUNTERPOINT

There is another way of putting it. Finnegans Wake *is "a kind of Logos of the Einsteinian vision of the universe," William Troy wrote in the review which Joyce liked best. But the novel is also "associated with scriptures and sacred books, and treats life in terms of the fall and awakening of the human soul and the creation and apocalypse of nature," Northrop Frye has said. Can we then conclude that in the language of this work the old gnostic and the new technological dream meet, the dream of unifying mind and nature, science and myth, into a single truth—beyond matter?*

I cannot answer. But I am aware that the postmodern endeavor in liter-ature acknowledges that words have severed themselves from things, that language now can only refer to language. And what book, or rather what language, calls attention to itself as language, as ineluctably verbal and quite finally so, more than Finnegans Wake? *John Fletcher understands the influence of Joyce even on the most secretive stylist: "What Beckett really*

learnt from Joyce was the importance of words and how to make them per-
form in exercises irrelevant to their superficial meaning but faithful to their
essence. . . . "

The word has become essence indeed, essence or energy, subject to continuous change, yet indestructible and compact like that single book in Borges'
"The Library of Babel" which contains all books, past, present, and future,
in its infinitesimally thin pages.

PERSPECTIVE VII: TOWARD A UNIVERSAL CONSCIOUSNESS

As I draw to a close, my theme beccomes more obvious: *Finnegans
Wake* aspires to the condition of a universal consciousness. Consider
its design.

Item: Vico says: "Individuality is the concretion of universality, and
every individual action is at the same time superindividual";
so it is for Joyce, for whom no character is bound by this time
or that place.

Item: Characters are subject to a constant process of recurrence,
metempsychosis, and superimposition; and opposites—Shem
and Shaun, HCE and ALP—become the other.

Item: The actual and the possible, the historical and the fabulous,
have equal validity in eternity; in this gnostic view, Joyce follows Bruno; fact and fiction fuse.

Item: In a world of simultaneity, cause and effect coincide; eternity
and the instant merge in the Perpetual Now, as in mystic doc-
trines; sequence becomes synchronicity.

Item: Joyce chose the night world; as death is the great equalizer so
is sister sleep; and in our dreams we exchange all the symbols
of the race, without miserliness or shame.

Item: Whoever the Dreamer or Narrator may be, he is All; yet Bernard Benstock is also right: "On the creative level it is Joyce
himself giving form to what he has experienced and learned
and understood (in the same way in which the Demiurge,
creating the universe, dreams away its cycles of evolution)."

Item: The creative process, like the Holy Ghost, invades and unifies all media; television and telepathy, the famous Letter and spirit writing, film and shadows in Plato's cave, copulation and language, become one.

Item: The book wants to include everything; it is not an encyclopedia but a true universe; and through its correspondences of microcosm with macrocosm, it wants to become *the* universe.

The strategies of unification in the novel are as numerous as they have grown familiar. Yet I think many of us have allowed Joyce's demon, called Parody, to obscure this possibility: that the language of *Finnegans Wake* strains toward a gnostic truth. There is a sense in which the totality of the book, its effort toward a universal consciousness, fails to parody or subvert itself, fails to ironicize itself.

James S. Atherton: "Joyce does not deny the existence of sensible material objects. . . . But Berkeley's view of Laws of Nature which he describes in *Siris* as being: 'applied and determined by an Infinite Mind in the macrocosm of universe, with unlimited power and according to stated rules— as it is in the microcosm with limited power and skill by the human mind,' seems to me to be a possible source for the entire structure of the *Wake*."

William Troy: "Humanity is impressive not in its actuality but in its immanence. And this becomes something comparable to the conception of the Divine Idea of the medieval theologians— that which is capable of taking on matter but is itself infinite in time and space."

COUNTERPOINT

"Be that as it may, but for that light phantastic of his gnose's glow as it slid lucifericiously within an inch of its page . . ." (182.04), the postmodern writer might have been like others who have preceded him.

There is a new gnosticism taking hold of our age, a new insistence of Mind to apprehend reality im-mediately and gather more and more mind in itself, a new suspicion of matter, of culture, and even of language insofar as it derives not from the pure logos *but from historical circumstance.*

Much of this new gnosticism comes from technology. Buckminster Fuller speaks of "ephemeralization," whereby energy can be transferred with less and less mediation; Norbert Wiener suggests that man may some day "travel" by telegraph; Marshall McLuhan predicts that electric technology may "by-pass languages in favor of a general cosmic consciousness"; Paolo Soleri calls his new book The Bridge between Matter and Spirit Is Matter Becoming Spirit; *and Dr. José Delgado of the Yale Medical School states: "We are now talking to the brain without the participation of the senses. This is pure and direct communication—I call it nonsensory communication."*

Technology tends toward the direct action of mind on mind, tends toward new kinds of telepathy, telekinesis, and teleportation. Its noetic process, in fact, is similar to Teilhard de Chardin's threefold process—the "vitalization of Matter," the "hominization of Life," and the "planetization of Mankind"—ingathered in the "Noosphere." Thus a physicist, Gerald Feinberg, proposes universal consciousness as a rational goal for mankind in his aptly titled work, The Prometheus Project.

But the germ of the new gnosticism also invades the word-flesh of literature. It is not only William Burroughs who sees the word as a "virus" attacking our damaged "central nervous system," preventing us from enjoying "non-body experience." Less extreme in their utterances, perhaps, other postmodern authors, both of science and unscientific fiction, want to dissolve the given world, absorb its intractable and conditioned elements, into a vision, dream, or afflatus that may render even language redundant. Whether they are minimalists like Beckett and Borges or maximalists like Nabokov and Pynchon, one feels that they strain toward a region of articulate silence, of intelligent noise, fantasy-filled. This region, which I have too often attempted to explore, rings, as Susan Sontag says, with "an energetic secular blasphemy, the wish to attain the unfettered, unselective, total consciousness of 'God.'"

Is that not the cry of Finnegans Wake?

POSTAMBLE

"Traduced into jinglish janglage" (275.n6), *Finnegans Wake*, I repeat, stands as a monstrous prophecy of our postmodernity. In so many particular ways this seems to me so. But is that prophecy not ultimately hollow? The query leads to others, and that may be the way to end.

All my questions about Joyce, all my qualms really, seem to revert to his peculiar sense of Creation—I mean the creation of life, of people and stars and flowers. God created the world, and that, Joyce believed, was the original sin; for the creative act is always crooked. This flaw is in all generation, in sex as well as artifice. Thus Joyce could never see sex without the hidden taint and excitement of error. And suddenly I find myself wondering: did the lapsarian irony of this sensualist sometimes turn into final despair and thus turn into a kind of malice? In fact, how much malice lies in the mocking multiplicity of *Finnegans Wake*, and how much delight in the fullness of being? Adaline Glasheen refers to the "good-tempered nihilism" of the novel. Does the epithet also apply to the Joyce who wrote: "And from time to time I lie back and listen to my hair growing white . . ."?

Above all, why could Joyce never leave Dublin behind? Never, never, never, never, never. Whence this obsessive Imagination of Repetition? "mememormee," "mememormee" is the wail on the last page of "Finn, again!" Did Joyce really ever conceive a difference between birth and rebirth, occurrence and recurrence? And is not creation flawed precisely insofar as memory hovers over our copulation and lies in wait for the child as its *given* name?

These questions are perhaps too personal, and may seem too harshly put. Criticism, I know, has its own brand of malice, which I am not eager to display. Nor do I wish to disparage Joyce, who scarcely needs to be praised as a great novelist, among the very greatest to this day. The pilgrimages we all make to these symposia— Joyceans, crypto-Joyceans, meta-Joyceans, and para-Joyceans like myself—are often made in search of learning, sodality, and romance. Still, are they not all begun and concluded in his name?

Yet having emphasized the prophetic sense of Joyce's master riddle, part of me cries (yes, it is the cry of some exorbitant hope akin to pride): Human destiny may be larger than this vast, retrograde, and reversible riddle implies.

Movingly, Hélène Cixous writes: "After Bloom, the deluge, but Joyce had already prepared *Finnegans Wake* as an ark to contain all human myths and types; the world, in its blind lust to seek its own destruction, could wipe itself out, for *Finnegans Wake* had saved its symbols, its notations, and its cultural patterns."

Is this enough for the largest effort of the imagination in our time? Unabashedly, I would ask not only to save the heavy ark, nor only to seek the rainbow sign in the sky, but even to become the very matter of which all rainbows are made. Or perhaps more: NEW LIGHT. . . .

THE NEW SEXUALITY

The Joyce of Sex: Sexual Relationships in Ulysses

Morris Beja

In this essay, my aims will be to describe the sexual relationships the three chief figures in *Ulysses* have (or sometimes perhaps only seem to have) and to discuss why those relationships are the way they are, and where things stand at the end of the book. Obviously of primary concern is the sexual relationship between Leopold and Molly Bloom, and immediately we come upon an area where an effort to be as precise as possible goes against many of the assumptions that are usually made about this married couple. Of course everyone knows that Bloom and Molly have not had sex together for over ten years—since 27 November 1893, to be exact: that is, just before the birth and early death of their only son, Rudy. But what everyone knows is not always true, and Joyce is both meticulously precise and maddeningly vague, as he indicates that their abstinence has not been total. What they have not had is what the Ithaca chapter calls "complete carnal intercourse, with ejaculation of semen within the natural female organ"; instead, "carnal intercourse had been incomplete, without ejaculation of semen within the natural female organ."

For some reason, the term "incomplete," if noticed by critics at all, is apparently taken to mean "nonexistent," rather than "partial." But Bloom and Molly do have *some* forms of sexual activity with each other. Within just the last few weeks, for example, Bloom has—as Molly puts it—come on her bottom, and in the past he has performed cunnilingus. Indeed, when she thinks about her upcoming concert tour to Belfast and expresses doubts about the idea that Bloom and Boylan might both come with her—or, I suppose I should say, accompany her—her concern is not so much that she is afraid that Bloom would get sexually jealous as that he would get sexually active; and Boylan might be in the next room and hear, and *he* might get annoyed: "its all very well a husband but you cant fool a lover after me telling him we never did anything."

I am not trying to minimize the problems in Bloom and Molly's sexual relationship by pointing to the fact that their inactivity with each other is not absolute; rather, I wish to make sure that we realize what is *not* involved. And another thing that is clearly not involved is physical "impotence": despite the Citizen's question about Bloom, "Do you call that a man?" and Joe Hynes's answering reflection, "I wonder did he ever put it out of sight," Bloom can clearly achieve erection and ejaculate, as he does by masturbating over Gerty MacDowell; and, as we have seen, he has performed coitus interruptus with Molly, who is in fact of the opinion that he has "more spunk in him"—that is, more semen—than Boylan, who, she says, "hasn't such a tremendous amount . . . considering how big it is." If that is true, then it is no doubt especially wise that Bloom carries, as he does, a condom (or French letter). It is possible, as has been argued, that Bloom is a victim not of primary or physical impotence, but of secondary impotence, which entails the inability to perform actual sexual *intercourse*—or "complete carnal intercourse, with ejaculation of semen within the natural female organ"—or to perform it with some particular woman, from psychological rather than physiological causes. But I know of no specific evidence that that is so in Bloom's case; though who knows?—it would be one way out of it[1].

Of course, for her part Molly does engage in complete carnal intercourse on June 16, although the degree to which that is so can be exaggerated. For the first few of Boylan's ejaculations—just how many times he came is unclear, since the number increases each time Molly thinks about it (from "3 or 4 times" early in her monologue to "4 or 5" around the middle of it, to "5 or 6 times handrunning" toward the end)—Molly recalls, "I made him pull it out and do it on me." In other words, carnal intercourse with Boylan too was incomplete—until the last time, when, she says, "I let him finish it in me." It seems quite possible, even probable, that this is the first nonmarital act of complete carnal intercourse in which Molly has ever engaged. In any case it does seem to be the first day on which the affair with Boylan has been consummated. And I hope it is too late in the day to have to prove that the list of twenty-five lovers in the Ithaca chapter does not represent reality, but at the most Bloom's vague suspicions. Very vague, I would guess, for surely even he cannot really believe that she has slept with all twenty-five of those men; actually, even the likeliest candidate— Lieutenant Gardner, who incidentally is not on that list—almost certainly never went to bed with her. No doubt debating how much of an adulteress Molly Bloom is sounds rather like asking how much of a virgin someone else is, but facing the facts may help to put in perspective some long-held assumptions about Molly's sex life—and her character, which, for example, has been described by no less acute an observer than Robert M. Adams as that of "a slut, a sloven, and a voracious sexual animal." To Adams, Molly is "a frightening venture into the unconsciousness of evil"[2]—a declaration that strikes me as a frightening venture into the unconsciousness of moral criticism.

Still, however limited, Molly's infidelity is there for us to face, and it reflects important problems in her relationship with her husband and in their attitudes toward each other. It may be argued, indeed, that a home without complete carnal intercourse, with ejaculation of semen within the natural female organ, is like a home without Plumtree's Potted Meat: incomplete (even if one is less certain that, with it, the Bloom home would be an abode of bliss).

Critics have long been concerned over whose doing Bloom and Molly's lack of full sex with each other is (whose "fault" it is): is it Molly's? Bloom's? Something for which they are *mutually* responsible? (As the *Wake* has it, "so long as there is a joint deposit account in the two names a mutual obligation is posited.") In the Nighttown chapter of *Ulysses*, copulation and the question of "fault" are brought together when, instead of thinking of "felix culpa"—the "happy fault" or happy sin that caused the Fall—Bloom thinks of "copula felix"; but his "copula" isn't very "felix," so that leads to a feeling of "culpa." The question of responsibility no doubt matters to us as well, but ultimately laying blame is less enlightening than finding causes. I have suggested, however briefly, the role of some of the key men in Molly's life, and I shall get back to that. But first let us consider Bloom's attitude toward her—and, indeed, toward just about all the women we see enter his life and thoughts on June 16.

Without at all asserting that the best way to examine Bloom is from a Jungian perspective, I would like to suggest that it is helpful to consider his attitudes toward women in terms of Jung's concept of the Anima, and three of the most common manifestations of that archetype: the Mother, the Virgin, and the Temptress, or what Jung calls the Seductress. Molly is seen by Bloom in all three of those roles.

Certainly we need not dwell on the degree to which she fills a maternal role in his life, even in his erotic thoughts—as when, in the first chapter, in which we meet both of them, he looks down "on her bulk and between her large soft bubs." Other significant mother figures for Bloom include Mrs. Purefoy, of course, and Bella Cohen—who becomes Jung's loving and terrible mother, the devouring mother. Folklore is filled with figures corresponding to the devouring or terrible mother—as in *Snow White, Cinderella,* and *Hansel and Gretel.* In such a figure as the Indian goddess Kali, the terrible mother is loving as well, and the child's reaction may be similarly ambivalent. For the child may *wish* to be devoured, at least in the sense of longing for a return to the womb, a desire that itself may have sexual overtones—as in Joyce's letters of 1909 to his wife Nora, while he was in Dublin and she was back in Trieste. He wrote of his desire to return and make love to her: "My body soon will penetrate into yours, O that my soul could too! O that I could nestle in your womb like a child born of your flesh and blood, be fed by your blood, sleep in the warm secret gloom of your body!" In other letters that same month, he stressed the terrible aspect of the devouring mother, itself no less sexually exciting for him, by, for example, telling Nora, "I feel I would like to be flogged by you. I would like to see your eyes blazing with anger."

As far as I can tell, the figure of the Virgin is to Bloom a good deal less important than the other two, the Mother and the Temptress, and certainly much less central than the Virgin figure is to Stephen Dedalus, as we shall see. And especially in Bloom's world, "virgin" seems a relative term. Almost certainly, Molly entered his life a virgin, after a fashion. But she remembers her actions one day in Gibraltar with Lieutenant Mulvey: "I pulled him off into my handkerchief pretending not to be excited but I opened my legs I wouldn't let him touch me inside my petticoat." Because Mulvey was not permitted inside her petticoat, Molly remained, technically, a virgin—just as Gerty MacDowell's virginity may strike one as more technical than spiritual. Yet even while Gerty is obviously aware of what the dark stranger is doing with his hands while she

displays her hidden charms, she cannot quite admit it fully to herself, and so retains a certain naïve—indeed virginal—quality. But
she is also, as Bloom perceives, a "hot little devil." In other words,
she is (like Molly) both the Virgin *and* the Temptress, or Seductress,
or indeed Whore.

As Fritz Senn has observed, the Nausicaa chapter is the first of
three in a row in which we get "three archetypal manifestations of
the Feminine": the Virgin here, the Mother in Mrs. Purefoy during
the Oxen of the Sun chapter, and the Whore in Bella Cohen and the
prostitutes during the Circe chapter.[3] Of course, other women also
play the role of Temptress for Bloom—Molly, obviously, and Martha
Clifford, as well as women whom he fleetingly glimpses or thinks
of. But it is when Bella's role as Whore becomes blended with that
of the loving, terrible, devouring Mother that we get a sense of
Bloom's childish yet erotic submission, and our fullest sense of the
masochistic elements in his personality and sexual being.

Nevertheless, they have earlier been brought out in, for example,
his thoughts in the butcher shop about "the nextdoor girl," and her
"strong pair of arms. Whacking a carpet on the clothesline. She does
whack it, by George. The way her crooked skirt swings at each
whack." And when she walks away from him, "the sting of disregard" glows "to weak pleasure within his breast." To some readers, these traits suggest an element of femininity in Bloom:
Theodore Holmes speaks for a larger number of critics when he
writes that the overtones of Bloom's "effeminacy are unmistak-
able"—and that they are seen in the way he is "dominated," "vain,"
and "pathetic," and even in his "affinity for scents."[4] To other readers, and sometimes the same ones too, those and similar traits indicate that Bloom is actually "perverse." Even Vladimir Nabokov has
lamented that "in the sexual department Bloom is, if not on the
verge of insanity, at least a good clinical example of extreme sexual
preoccupation and perversity," indulging "in acts and dreams that
are definitely subnormal in the zoological, evolutional sense."[5] I
shall return to such attitudes toward Bloom (and toward what it is to
be feminine); but first, we ought to consider the third major figure
in the novel, Stephen Dedalus, whose attitudes toward women also
group them into similar patterns of Mother, Virgin, and Temptress.

Obviously, the chief archetypal Mother in Stephen's life is his actual mother, who is both loving and terrible—as well as devouring:
in the first chapter, he calls her a "ghoul," and a "chewer of
corpses." She is, then, symbolically like the Ireland he regards as—
in a phrase that appears in both the *Portrait* and *Ulysses*—"the old

sow that eats her farrow." But if Mrs. Dedalus represents in part Stephen's nation, she is even more emphatically connected with its church, and through and beyond that with the Holy Virgin, a figure much more important to Stephen than to Bloom. A number of the girls and women in the *Portrait* take on that role: Eileen, who in his childhood seems to him to reveal the meaning of "Tower of Ivory," and Emma (or "E.C."), and, of course, the girl wading in the water at the Bull Wall. But that girl on the beach—like Boylan's seaside girls and like Bloom's seaside Gerty MacDowell—also serves another role: that of the Seductress or Temptress. For while she is an "angel," she is a *"wild* angel," of *"mortal* youth and beauty," opening the "gates of all the ways of error and glory." Other such figures include, in the *Portrait,* Stephen's first prostitute, and Emma again (the "temptress," indeed, of his "villanelle")—and, in *Ulysses,* perhaps Florry and Zoe.

Perhaps. But so little is the Stephen of *Ulysses* tempted by those temptresses that we realize that sex in general now seems much less central to his existence than it had in the last half of the *Portrait.* He is twenty-two years old, but he thinks a good deal less frequently about sex than does the thirty-eight-year-old Bloom. Given the nature of Stephen's obsessions with sex in the *Portrait,* actually, we may be just as glad that he does not think all that much about it in *Ulysses,* for his desire in the earlier novel seems less to have sex with girls than to commit sin with them: "He moaned to himself like some baffled prowling beast. He wanted to sin with another of his kind, to force another being to sin with him and to exult with her in sin." Later, after the retreat sermons, Stephen thinks of his phallus as "a horrible thing," and he wonders: "Who made it be like that, a bestial part of the body able to understand bestially and desire bestially? . . . His soul sickened at the thought of a torpid snaky life feeding itself out of the tender marrow of his life and fattening upon the slime of lust."

One may be tempted to explain this horror of sex as disgusting and sinful by noticing that the same woman who has served as the chief exemplar for Stephen of both the Virgin and the Mother is in some respects the archetypal Temptress as well—Mrs. Dedalus. I do not wish to exaggerate the importance in Stephen's life of what the *Wake* will call the "eatupus complex," but it would be wrong to ignore its role altogether.

The first Temptress with whom Stephen has sexual intercourse is, of course, the actual whore—the prostitute in the *Portrait*—and when she says, "Give me a kiss," we are told: "His lips would not bend to kiss her. He wanted to be held firmly in her arms, to be caressed slowly, slowly, slowly. . . .But his lips would not bend to kiss her." That reluctance recalls the teasing he had endured while a little boy early in the novel:

> Wells turned to the other fellows and said:
> —O, I say, here's a fellow says he kisses his mother every night before he goes to bed.
> The other fellows stopped their game and turned round, laughing. Stephen blushed under their eyes and said:
> —I do not.
> Wells said:
> —O, I say, here's a fellow says he doesn't kiss his mother before he goes to bed.
> They all laughed again. (AP 14)

The question continues to bother Stephen: "He still tried to think what was the right answer. Was it right to kiss his mother or wrong to kiss his mother? What did that mean, to kiss?"

What it means to kiss—especially, to kiss one's mother—remains important to him. Years later, during his conversation with Cranly about his first major act of rebellion against his mother (his refusal to perform his Easter duty), Cranly claims that "whatever else is unsure in this stinking dunghill of a world a mother's love is not." Stephen's reply to that is interestingly oblique: "Pascal, if I remember rightly, would not suffer his mother to kiss him as he feared the contact of her sex." Cranly's response—"Pascal was a pig"—concentrates on Pascal; ours may concentrate on Stephen. We may think as well of his intense reaction to Davin's story about the peasant woman who had invited him to stay the night in her cottage—a woman who, Davin believes, was pregnant ("carrying a child"): another maternal Temptress.

In *Ulysses*, these themes remain subdued, although they may help explain why this young man's thoughts are so seldom about sex, despite his tendencies toward freedom of thought in so many other realms. The first time the theme of the mother appears at all in *Ulysses*, it is in the context of a relevant allusion, to Swinburne, when Mulligan asks, "Isn't the sea what Algy calls it: a grey sweet mother?" Swinburne's actual phrase is "great sweet mother," in his poem "The Triumph of Time":

> I will go back to the great sweet mother,
> Mother and lover of men, the sea.
> I will go down to her, I and none other,

Close with her, kiss her and mix her with me;
Cling to her, strive with her, hold her fast. . . .

In *Ulysses*, immediately after that allusion we get the first reference to the dream in which Stephen's mother has come to him in "her wasted body," "mute" and "reproachful." Clearly, Stephen's relationship with his mother is not without his resentment over what it is doing to him. In the Oxen of the Sun chapter, when everyone is talking about whether the doctor during a difficult birth ought to try to save the mother or the baby, Stephen is the only one to opt for the baby.

In *Ulysses*, then, we have two men and a woman who seem to have varied but pronounced problems in the sexual realms of their being. Probably the most important problem that they all share is that their sexual lives are cut off from their emotional lives: from love. None of them has completely satisfactory sex with a person whom he or she truly loves. In one of the "Notesheets" for *Ulysses*, Joyce writes: "Love? excuses all: Coition without love in & out of wedlock not desired." Yet without romanticizing, sentimentalizing, or minimizing all these problems, I hope to show that it is conceivable that they are either resolved by the end of the novel or, more certainly, shown as less catastrophic and problematic than they at first seem to be.

In regard to Molly's infidelity again, and Bloom's reaction to it, we have seen that one critic sees in Bloom's marriage evidence that he is "dominated," and that consequently his behavior reveals "effeminacy." Less extremely, Stanley Sultan laments that by serving Molly "ignominiously," Bloom fails to be the "master in the household." And according to Darcy O'Brien, Bloom's "unmanly weakness epitomizes the slavishness Joyce so lamented in his countrymen."[6] But I wonder: what ought Bloom to do in order to prove himself "manly" or "masculine"? Should he slap Molly around a bit? Or, avoiding such violence, should he leave in a huff? Do we really fault Leopold Bloom because he does not display the sort of machismo that would gain the admiration of someone like the narrator of the Cyclops chapter?

These are, of course, rhetorical questions, and I hope that the answers to them seem as obvious as answers to rhetorical questions usually are. For my point is that Bloom's attitude toward Molly's infidelity may in part—not entirely, to be sure: I am trying not to exaggerate but to set up what I perceive as a proper perspective—be correct, arguably heroic, even wise. He is not the possessive, dominant male that husbands are "supposed" to be, and for that he is the subject of ridicule within the novel and sometimes of ridicule, or sad sympathy or condescension, in criticism about the novel; but his mode of behavior seems to me not quite so clearly wrong-headed as those responses to him would suggest. In the Ithaca chapter, Bloom's "equanimity" in the face of Molly's affair is explained by his realization that her infidelity is "not as calamitous as a cataclysmic annihilation of the planet in consequence of collison with a dark sun," and is "less reprehensible than theft, highway robbery, cruelty to children and animals," and other transgressions that are meticulously listed—and finally is "not more abnormal than all other altered processes of adaptation to altered conditions of existence, resulting in a reciprocal equilibrium between the bodily organism and its attendant circumstances."

Few men in Bloom's "attendant circumstances" would or could display such "equanimity," to be sure. Certainly not James Joyce: when he was misled into believing in 1909 that Nora had once been unfaithful to him, his reaction seems to have been crazed. Personally, I doubt if that indicates that he was thereby stronger than Bloom. Rather, instead of showing that Bloom is weaker, it seems to me to indicate that Bloom is a *better* man—a better *man*—than his creator. But I do not mean to be condescending toward James Joyce either: the fact that he could not share his creation's attitude does not lessen his insight and discovery. Or if it does, then we may say of him what Stephen says of Shakespeare: that his "loss is his gain," as "he passes on towards eternity in undiminished personality, untaught by the wisdom he has written or by the laws he has revealed."

Even Bloom's resorting to masturbation may not be so contemptible as many critics—all of them, no doubt, themselves people with admirably active sexual lives—have assumed it to be, but instead may be a recourse to an outlet less destructive than others that (for various reasons we have not yet pursued) he avoids. It is probably an exaggeration to say, as Richard Ellmann does, that "Joyce has found an aspect of masturbation which every writer on the subject, from Rousseau to Philip Roth, has missed. For the first time in literature masturbation becomes heroic."[7] But it is an exaggeration that serves as a healthy corrective to the snickering or clucking of the tongue that usually goes along with discussions of Bloom's sex life.

Nor do I have much patience with those who regard Bloom's general sexual bents as "perverse." Bloom may have—he does have—masochistic traits, for example; but that in itself does not make him "a masochist." And the equation between Bloom's so-called weakness and submissiveness and his so-called effeminacy and un-manliness strikes me as abominable. Bloom is "the new womanly man": there are worse things to be. I recognize that Bloom's an-drogyny, like every other serious theme in the novel, is undercut and treated ironically: consequently, Bloom also has latent ambidex-terity; and he so wants to be a mother; and he sometimes seems less an adrogynous being than a hermaphrodite or transvestite. Yet his androgyny is no less real for all that, and no less to his credit. As Oliver St. John Gogarty long ago observed about Joyce, he "was gifted with a seriousness that was unremitting and could resist even his own jokes."[8]

In recent Joyce criticism, there has been an increasing willingness to become aware that Bloom transcends the usual male stereotypes; unfortunately, there has not been a corresponding willingness to recognize that Molly transcends the usual female ones. Yet to dis-miss Molly Bloom as Joyce's male projection of a woman is, while accurate, beside the point—as it would be to speak that way of Emma Bovary and Flaubert, or Anna Karenina and Tolstoy, or as it would be both accurate and beside the point to dismiss Bloom as a gentile's Jew, or Joe Christmas as a white man's Black, or Heathcliff, Lydgate, and Septimus Warren Smith as women's men.

After all, to whom does Molly seem to be an archetypal Mother or earth goddess—this woman who has had one surviving child in an Irish Catholic world where families as large as the Dedaluses' (Mrs. Dedalus had fifteen children) are quite common? Not to us, I sub-mit, and not to herself, surely, and not so much to Joyce the artist either. It is primarily for and to Bloom that she takes on that role. Thus Bloom's sexual problems may not be entirely different from some of Stephen's. But in any case a key question is what in Bloom's psyche more than in hers makes Molly seem to him an ar-chetypal Mother. A facile Jungian critic might explain everything away, once again, in terms of "projection," but the forces behind Bloom's attitude are neither easily dismissed nor easily understood. One such force seems to be his *need* to deify her, for if she is a goddess, then she is unattainable: who could fault him for avoiding sex with, and being submissive to, a goddess? Yet even that, al-though I think it is an operative element in his attitude, is perhaps more a mode of rationalization than it is a source.

Surely a key fact in his attitude toward Molly as an archetypal Mother is Bloom's sense of guilt and loss over the death of their son, Rudy. But while the relationship between sex and Bloom's agoniz-ing over Rudy's early death is often recognized, it is also often seen in overly simplistic terms. Bloom and Molly's lack of sex does, to be sure, date from, and arise out of, that event, but it is nevertheless a gross oversimplification of their lives, problems, and attitudes, and of the issues involved, to explain their abstinence entirely or merely as a primitive form of birth control. Otherwise, why do we explicitly learn from Molly's monologue that, in their last sexual act that afternoon, she let Boylan finish it in her?

Much more importantly, Bloom seems to have taken upon himself the role of the child Rudy, who was lost to him and Molly, and of the child they shall now never have, because of his or her or their fears as a result of Rudy's early death in infancy.[9]

One is tempted to get a bit exasperated at this point and observe that actually the Blooms are not childless: there is, after all, Milly. And of course one's exasperation would be justified. Still, if we wish to understand and not simply to judge with self-righteous superiority, we must acknowledge the significance of the fact that Bloom's only *son* has died in infancy; and for a Jew, maybe even more than for most men with other heritages, even Irishmen, a son can be immensely important.

(There is a nice little story that illustrates my point, so I hope it is not too much of a digression. A man went to see his rabbi quite distraught, seeking advice, because his son was going to marry a Roman Catholic woman—and not only that, he planned to convert: "My own son!" the man said, "My own son with a new religion!" The rabbi sorrowfully replied, "*You* have a son? *I* have a son! My son is going to shave his head and become a Buddhist monk. My own son with a new religion!" The man was shocked that such a fate should befall a rabbi, and he asked him what he had done, and the rabbi replied, "What should I do? I went to God with my problem." "And what did God say?" "He said, '*You* have a son? *I* have a son!'")

With such a context, for good or bad, it comes to Bloom to seem as if *he* is all they have left, so it is as if he becomes Molly's son, with Molly—from his perspective—"in the attitude of Gea-Tellus," and himself in that of "the childman weary, the manchild in the womb." My point is not that he has always been fixated in infantile sexuality, for which I see little or no evidence; his motivation is psychologically much more complicated than that, though the results may not be all that different.

Nowadays, of course, we are less reluctant to acknowledge the erotic elements in maternal relations than we used to be, and to that extent, if you will, we have learned to be Joyce's contemporaries.

But we also inevitably recognize the forces working against that aspect of human sexuality. However symbolic and unconscious the relevance of the incest taboo will seem here, it may nevertheless be in large part what makes it seem impossible to Bloom to have complete carnal intercourse with Molly, given the fact that he is, however vicariously, her child. Consequently, Bloom recognizes the need for other men to take on the role in the mother's life that the child cannot fulfill. But if someone else can take on the role of husband-lover, then presumably it is also possible for someone else to fulfill the role of the child—of Rudy, or of the unborn child—as well. Enter Stephen Dedalus.

Now if Stephen becomes, as it were, Rudy—as, for example, in the climactic vision at the end of the Nighttown chapter, but in many more subtle passages and ways as well—we have already seen that Bloom too is associated with Rudy, or "is" Rudy. And if all A are B, and all B are C, then all A are C as well; and, indeed, Stephen and Bloom *are* identified with one another: they have been baptized into the church by the same priest; they share an uncanny number of thoughts or allusions or images all day; and at one point in Nighttown they even look into a mirror and see reflected back a single image (that of Shakespeare). They well may be called Blephen and Stoom. Moreover, this identification entails (more or less unconsciously in Bloom's mind, a bit less so in Molly's) the possibility that Stephen may take on the symbolic role of Molly's lover, or dream lover.

But if, from the perspective of Bloom's needs, the Stephen/Bloom identification stresses Stephen as a son, from the perspective of Stephen's needs it stresses his going beyond dependence on the father. In *Ulysses*, despite critical tradition, Stephen does not so much "find" a father as identify with him. He must leave behind childish things; the trouble is, that is just as difficult to do in sexual realms as in others, or more so. But one way for this to happen—a mode that is psychologically beneficial for Stephen and artistically feasible for Joyce—is to have Stephen cast aside his childish stance by identifying with the father.

One may wonder, assuming that all this is not simply wrong, if a corollary might be that Bloom will assume or resume his full roles as husband and adult, enabling us to agree, at least in this instance, with the Joyce who once told Frank Budgen that Jews "are better husbands . . . better fathers, and better sons." But we cannot really know, since we do not follow the lives of our protagonists beyond the early morning hours of June 17, and Joyce never produced a

Ulysses II, or a *Ulysses Sails Again*. In any case, I do not mean to suggest that Bloom will—or that wouldn't it be nice if only Bloom would—take over and become head of his household. Joyce, after all, shows that we can be heartened rather than disappointed that Bloom is not built that way.

On the other hand, no doubt it would be pleasant or agreeable to think that he and Molly could resume complete carnal intercourse. But things have probably gone on too long now for that to be at all likely. As the Ithaca chapter puts it, "the parties concerned, uniting, had increased and multiplied, which being done, offspring produced and educed to maturity, the parties, if now disunited were obliged to reunite for increase and multiplication, which was absurd, to form by reunion the original couple of uniting parties, which was impossible." Anyway, Joyce has shown that maybe things are not so awful the way they are, or at least that they could be worse.

Oddly, Bloom for all his deficiencies in respect to sexuality, becomes the ironic yet serious exemplar in this novel of love—I mean the opposite of hatred. And we may sense that for Stephen, the identification with Bloom entails an identification not only with fatherhood—important as that is—but also with all that Bloom represents or exemplifies in other ways, including his values. If so, then at the end of his day Bloom has a right to his satisfaction and to his feeling that he has "sustained no positive loss" and "brought a positive gain to others. Light to the gentiles."

Notes

1. For cogent presentations of contrasting views, see Marilyn French, *The Book as World: James Joyce's "Ulysses"* (Cambridge: Harvard University Press, 1976), pp. 147-48, and Suzette A. Henke, *Joyce's Moraculous Sindbook: A Study of Ulysses* (Columbus: Ohio State University Press, 1978), p. 93n. In his lectures on *Ulysses*, Vladimir Nabokov also refers at least twice to Bloom as "impotent": *Lectures on Literature*, ed. Fredson Bowers (New York: Harcourt Brace Jovanovich, 1980), pp. 350, 352.

2. *James Joyce: Common Sense and Beyond* (New York: Random House, 1966), p. 166.

3. "Nausicaa," in *James Joyce's "Ulysses": Critical Essays*, ed. Clive Hart and David Hayman (Berkeley: University of California Press, 1974), p. 282.

4. "Bloom, the Father," *Sewanee Review* 79 (Spring 1971): 249.

5. *Lectures on Literature*, p. 287.

6. Stanley Sultan, *The Argument of Ulysses* (Columbus: Ohio State University Press, 1964), p. 132; Darcy O'Brien, *The Conscience of James Joyce* (Princeton: Princeton University Press, 1968), p. 183.

7. *Ulysses on the Liffey* (London: Faber and Faber, 1972), p. 133.

8. *As I Was Going down Sackville Street* (London: Reynal and Hitchcock, 1937), p. 299.

9. I wish to express my gratitude to Ellen Carol Jones for the discussions and arguments that first led me to examine this possibility closely and with full seriousness.

Joyce's Consubstantiality: Woman as Creator

Robert Boyle, S.J.

"The God of the Creation," model in the fifth chapter of *Portrait* for Stephen's notion of the artist, seems to be exclusively male— "paring his fingernails." So it was with Flaubert, originator of the analogy, and I suppose with the young Joyce too. But as I attempt to chart out the windings of Joyce's developing imagination, I seem to see an effort to involve woman in that Creator image. Joyce, I believe, used Trinitarian background to effect a union between male and female acting as one in his final Creator, with the female not only consubstantial but finally predominant. In Joyce's mature treatment of his Trinitarian divine artificer, I venture to assert, the Third Person, aptly designated by Catholics as Creator in the life of grace in the New Dispensation, is female.

The Pigeon House, as a power plant and as a symbolic home for the Holy Spirit, plays a role in my own construct of Joyce's development. Early on, in "An Encounter," as Bernard Benstock wittily established (in "Joyce's Rheumatics: The Holy Ghost in *Dubliners*," *The Southern Review*, xiv,i,January,1978), Father Butler's *not* being at the Pigeon House helps to stress a general absence of the Holy Spirit. Mahony had "asked, very sensibly, what would Father Butler be doing out at the Pigeon House." The emphasized adverb suggests that practical Mahony, like Tom Kernan, is more sensible than spiritual. At any rate, in joining the adventurous quest, he expects to see something more sensibly exciting than the Jesuit priest. His quest fails, but the story, for me, remotely prepares the stage for a much larger drama in which the Holy Ghost at least flies over the Pigeon House, and the dull priest is replaced by a priestess, perhaps a goddess, for whom the Pigeon House may be a power source.

That power plant lies between Howth and the Sandycove Martello Tower. A mock mass takes place, on the first page of *Ulysses*, atop the Tower. On almost the last page, a goddess broods atop Howth—"I wouldn't answer first only looked out over the sea and the sky I was thinking of so many things" (*U* 782). As I imagine her, she is looking at the Martello Tower, and her look necessarily passes over (perhaps also through) the Pigeon House. The priestly robed figure on the top of the Tower, whistling for the completion of the transsubstantiation, exists some sixteen years after Molly's pensive look, but time does not limit the vision of a divine being. And that whistle is addressed to the Power from on high, Who descended upon Mary to effect the Incarnation and Who, in Catholic attribution, effects the Sacrament of the Eucharist (and all other Sacraments). Buck's own reference to the Pigeon House I find in his "switch off the current," which unites the Scriptural Power with the electric energy from the power plant. And indeed Hopkins found electricity a good symbol for the power of the Holy Spirit—"O at lightning and lashed rod" in Stanza Two of the *Deutschland* and the electric charge, subtle and invisible but powerful, in the brooding Holy Ghost of "God's Grandeur." The rushing Pentecostal wind may be found also on the Tower, at least in a small way, in the three Trinitarian whistles. I have no trouble, in the large context Joyce provides for me, in hearing Buck's whistle (answered, I take it, by two responding whistles from Buck's waiting friends in the Forty Foot below) reach back through time to sound, on some deep symbolic level, in the ears of that goddess thinking of so many things on Howth.

One of the things she has thought in the conventional present time of Bloomsday is that poets "all write about some woman in their poetry well I suppose he wont find many like me" [*U* 775]. In her final words she conflates her first kiss on Gibraltar with Bloom's kiss on Howth, so time is subject to her. If one observes with care Joyce's many subtle suggestions of an identification of Molly with the Holy Spirit, I believe that it can be further realized that Molly, Joyce's "clou" to immortality, gives life to the world of *Ulysses*.

To see his creating Imagination as woman, the goddess Stephen wanted to adore as her priest, I observe Joyce utilizing especially two aspects of Catholic Trinitarian belief: a) the Third Person of the

Trinity, whose proper name is Love, binds together (as it were) the Father and the Son; b) the Third Person—celebrated in the ancient "Veni, Creator Spiritus," "Come, Holy Ghost, Creator blest"—carries the creating Word of St. John's Gospel into the renewed universe. Noting somewhere along the line that the Hebrew word *ruah* (breath, wind) in the opening lines of *Genesis*, "the spirit of God moved on the waters," is feminine, Joyce could have found, and I think did find, a basis for Catholic dealing with the Third Person as feminine rather than as masculine.

"Wisdom" (Hebrew feminine "hokmah"), the attribute of God as Creator [*Proverbs* iii:19], is personified as a woman in *Proverbs* iv:5-9, vii:4, ix:16 (see the splendid commentary in *The Anchor Bible*). She speaks and acts with authority, like a goddess, and the Church applies Wisdom liturgically both as a proper name to the Holy Spirit, "God's gift" [*Proverbs* ii:6], and by way of allegory to the Blessed Virgin. In "Oxen of the Sun," young Stephen builds an oration around the *Song of Songs* (linking his mother with the Bride, ". . . with a kiss of ashes hast thou kissed my mouth" *U* 393), through the Fates ("The aged sisters draw us into life" *U* 394), to a climactic celebration of the creator of this universe (". . . lo, wisdom hath built herself a house, this vast majestic longstablished vault, the crystal palace of the Creator. . . " *U* 394). [That "crystal palace" prepares for "the crystalline world" of *FW* 186.] And note that the Creator of this palace is the woman of *Proverbs* ix:1. *The Anchor Bible*, represented in this volume by R.B.Y. Scott, explains: "The house of Wisdom is the 'habitable world' (viii 31) of which she is the 'uniting force' (viii 30), the constructive power of reason in Yahweh's creation" (*The Anchor Bible*, vol. 18, p.76—and note how neatly that "uniting force" coincides with my treatment in my *James Joyce's Pauline Vision*, p. 52: ". . . the suggestion that Molly as Holy Spirit effects the binding of Bleephan.") All this seems to me lovely background for the Homeric earth-goddess who rules over *Ulysses*, if one is willing to extend "reason" beyond neo-Classical bounds.

Further, Bloom's final vision of Molly, "big with seed" [*U* 737], involves, as I see it, a montage of the interesting Euclidean circles of her buttocks superimposed on Dante's final vision of the circles of the Trinity. I find one of the preparations for this on *U* 702, where "the mystery of an invisible person" is denoted by a Pentecostal "visible splendid sign" which, I believe, undoes the destructive darkness effected by "Time's livid final flame" on p. 583. Dante's frustrated effort to distinguish clearly the outline of a human figure in the center circle, in the final lines of *Paradiso*, is expressed in terms of a geometer's frustrated effort to square the circle. Bloom, as he focuses upon Molly's anus (the black dot of ink into which Bloom disappears), perceives himself as "the manchild in the womb" and squares the magic egg of the roc (and perhaps of the Rock of Gibraltar) and the natural egg of the auk which might nest on Howth. A basis is thus supplied, in this montage, for my imagination to perceive an analogy between a divine Person and the life-giving Molly.

Joyce, at any rate, could find other precedents for regarding the Holy Spirit as feminine. Note, for example, the difference between the masculine "mighty wings" of Milton's impregnating epic dove and the gentle mothering breast of Hopkin's dove, in "God's Grandeur," brooding "over the bent world" (an attitude Joyce may have shared even if he did not see Hopkins's poems at College—I consider it likely that he did see them, since Hopkins's Jesuit friends, in Joyce's college years, anxious to publish them but blocked by Bridges, would tend to share them with students interested in literature; silence does not wipe out the possibility). The Fanders catechism (cf. "Joyce's Catechisms," Harry Staley, *JJQ* Winter, '69) which Joyce certainly did study and in part memorized, speaks of the Holy Spirit's procession from the mutual love of the Father and the Son, a solid background for the studious Pesciolines' squiggling about "the poissission of the hoghly course" [*FW* 245]. The catechism calls the Third Person "Spirit of Love, Capital Dispenser of all supernatural gifts and graces," "giver of life," expressed in Pentecostal "fiery tongues" which lead to the speaking in diverse languages. Molly, of the "plump bare generous arm" which "flung a coin over the area railings" [*U* 226], and ALP, dispensing gifts from her bottomless bag, express human aspects of divine Love. Molly, especially if she is seen as a development of the strangely powerful woman of Joyce's (not Stanislaus's) arrangement of *Chamber Music*, of the temptress of the villanelle, and of the sacrificing Jew's daughter of Stephen's ballad (*U* 691), fits well in the Dantean slot Joyce prepares for her as the human symbol of the invisible Third Person of the Trinity. For the artist, at least, that person is more properly called Creator than is the Father (see my analysis of the part Joyce assigns to each Person of the Trinity in human artistic production, *Pauline Vision*, pp. 21-22). And consider Stephen's claim that "all flesh" comes to the human artist in his more perfect post-creation ("in the spirit of the maker all flesh that passes becomes the word that shall not pass away" *U* 391). Joyce's maker, as I see him in his ultimate development, is androgynous.

More even than Molly, ALP seems to me to give flesh to a feminine claim to superiority in creativity over the Father and the Eternal
Son. ALP reveals to me her own easy exercise of divine power when
she takes over the Petrine power of binding and loosing in the Sacrament of Penance ("The keys to. Given" FW 628). Shaun has set
himself up as a priest [FW 187-8], Shem is being crushed beneath
the omega of doom and not yet waked by the alpha of dominical
domination, ". . . and lo, you're doomed, joyday dawns and, la,
you dominate" [FW 194], and ALP slootheringly slides in, easily dis-
missing all the nonsense in the cleansing flow of her wash-water.

At the next and final great climax of the book, she adverts with
her own dying and waking words to first things, "First. We pass
through grass behush the bush to. Whish!" [FW 628]. With these
powerful words I conclude my own study of Joyce's imagination
[Pauline Vision, p.103]. I see in them first of all the birth of a human
being through the mother's pubic bush (a contrast indeed to the
perverse "Crab (a bushranger)" of Mulligan's portrait of the masturbating artist, U 217). Then I see in that "bush" (or I think I do) an
echo of and contrast to Theseus's claim that imagination is untrust-
worthy and non-rational since it transmogrifies bushes into bears
[Midsummer Night's Dream, V,i,22]. But most of all in "Whish!" I hear
the rushing wind of Pentecost, the Holy Spirit creating a brave new
world. Note with the perceptive Adaline Glasheen, in A Wake Di-
gest, p.74, how that word includes the creative power of the Father
in the Tetragrammaton (IHWH) and the redeeming power of the
Son (IHS). And note with me how in its very sound and meaning it
denotes the Postcreation Power of the Holy Spirit, enkindling in us
the fire of divine love (words of the prayer, "Come Holy Ghost,"
that the young Joyce, like every Catholic in his time, recited daily in
chapels and classrooms).

And I see ALP in her following words looking toward Finn renewed by her ("Finn, again!") and toward the thousands, like Abra-
ham's descendants, to come ("Till thousendsthee"). And, finally
compressing into one magnificent word the solemn words which
another ghost had said to his son—"Remember me" [Hamlet,I,v,91]—
she adds an infinite dimension (so to speak) and reveals in her word
her own divine Trinitarian depths.

Joyce's procedure here strikes me, as I attempted to express in
James Joyce's Pauline Vision, pp. 95-6, as a Trinitarian one similar to
that of Hopkins in "As kingfishers catch fire . . ." In my discussion
in my book I speak in a general way of Hopkins's punning on "I"
and "eye" to suggest the activity in the redeemed world of the Per-

sons of the Trinity. I shall be more specific here. The octet of Hopkin's sonnet states that the proper being, the "haecceitas," of creatures is revealed in their proper act. The sestet of the sonnet is:

> I say more: the just man justices;
> Keeps grace: that keeps all his goings graces;
> Acts in God's eye what in God's eye he is—
> Christ. For Christ plays in ten thousand places,
> Lovely in limbs, and lovely in eyes not his
> To the Father through the features of men's faces.

In these punning lines that first "I" is the speaker's own human personality, expressing, like the acts of all the other creatures in the octet, its own being in its act. This human being, however, exceeds all those less-than-human material creatures by being able to produce an act of love.

But, the sonnet says, though the act of the human "I" naturally says "myself" (as do the proper acts of the other creatures), by an incomprehensible miraculous joining it says *more* than "myself." It also says "Christ." And that means, in Trinitarian belief, that it also says "Infinite Love." Thus the three "I's" that incomprehensibly operate in the one God are also now present in this one loving human "I."

In the puns in the following lines, the single "I am" which names God for Moses in *Exodus* 3:14 here becomes three Johannine "eyes," two singular and one plural. The first "God's eye"—bringing to my mind the symbol painted in the sanctuary of the church in which I learned about God, a triangle with a huge open eye in it ("the Trinity sees you")—suggests the "I" of the all-knowing Father, the First Person. The second "God's eye" suggests the "I" of the Word which expresses that infinite knowledge—"In the beginning was the Word, and The Word was with God, and the Word was God. He was in the beginning with God; all things were made through him . . ." *John* I:1-3—the Second Person. At Pentecost the Word sends forth into our world the Third Person, the Holy Spirit. Thus "lovely in eyes not his" expresses the Spirit in us, our sharing in the inner life of the Trinity in union with the mutual Love between the Father and the Son. That plural "eyes"—at once the eyes of the redeemed and the Beauty that infuses them—expresses the Third Person active in the human world we know.

I see Joyce working along similar lines in his own effort to see ALP as the Holy Spirit. ALP had written of the "three men in him" [FW 113]. She now moves, in one sense, to replace the Father as Creator—so I interpret her queenly act in assuming to herself King

Hamlet's sacred command, the behest of the typical literary father in "Scylla and Charybdis." She modifies that command, fitting it to herself by finding now three persons in herself, with the third one dominant. In her own version of the "Memorare" addressed to the Blessed Virgin by Catholics, she combines the "me" of the senior Hamlet with the "I" of the God of Moses, now revealed as the Trinity, and produces three "me's." Since, like the Holy Spirit revealed to Christianity, she brings into the divine Triangle all those humans who consent to come, she can in this context claim to be more of a "me" than are the other Persons, in line with the kind of analogy which Hopkins uses. "More," as in Hopkins's "I say *more*," operates to express here too that infinite expansion, so to speak, which can encompass all creatures in a loving union. "Thousendsthee," which on a contrary level can suggest the "thous" of the children ending the "thee" of the Father, can on a Trinitarian level express the new life—"Array! Surrection" [*FW* 593]—to which "whish" lifts my imagination. ALP, as I see her, is allied to that incarnating Power which moved Stephen to produce his own poetic word, the villanelle; to the Power who on the Martello Tower was called to assist in Buck's mocking Eucharist and in the Bloom kitchen to supply substance for the mass-product; to the Power that covers the phony Shaun of *FW* 409-10—"there does be a power coming over me that is put upon me from on high out of the book of breedings"; and to the lovely Power which now on the final page comes upon the book and all of us as she speaks her magic Trinitarian word with the Miltonic emphasis in the double vowel of its final syllable and, bringing the other Persons into her triumphant feminine orbit, spreads her own "whitespread" brooding wings over this postcreated verbal universe: "mememormee" [*FW* 628].

CONTEMPORARY PHILOSOPHY

The Modernist Age:
The Age of James Joyce

Morton P. Levitt

James Joyce left Dublin in 1903 at the age of twenty-one. He would return only three times thereafter—once to attend his mother's funeral; once to serve as manager of the first movie theatre in Ireland, as passing an enterprise; and once to immerse himself in the physical and moral landscape that would become *Ulysses*. After January 1910, he remained on the Continent, conspicuously removed from his homeland, in Trieste, Zurich and Paris—the most cosmopolitan of writers. At the same time, he was the most insular of writers, writing of nothing but Ireland, nothing but Dublin, in fact, writing home constantly for details of Dublin life, Dublin history, Dublin geography. With *Thom's Post Office Directory* at his elbow, he created his own map of the city, one that he boasted would outlive the physical city, that was more real and vital and convincing than historical Dublin. Of course he was right—as anyone who has seen what passes for urban renewal in Dublin will attest. Not even Demolition Ireland, that most ubiquitous of Dublin symbols, can destroy the city of Joyce. Those Joyceans who religiously take Bloomsday tours through what remains of his city, those less dedicated tourists who turn a corner and discover with a shock a Joycean landmark— on my last visit, it was the City Arms Hotel, where the Blooms once had lived along with Dante Riordan, and then later, in Ennis, the Queens Hotel, once owned by old Rudolph Bloom—such travelers affirm the conviction that the city of Joyce and the city of history are inextricably linked and that, of the two, the fictional Dublin may well be preferable.

Yet Joyce's city is not all of Dublin. As we follow lower-middle-class salesman Leopold Bloom and fallen, almost classless, would-be-writer Stephen Dedalus on their wanderings through the city, we perceive that theirs is only a part of Georgian Dublin: the city which Joyce has preserved is essentially a lower-middle-class city, inbred, decaying, unaware that this will be the last generation in Ireland for the Empire which built this beautiful city and which kept hostage its people. There is no hint of any of this in *Ulysses*. It is not as social historian that we read Joyce.

There are other critical clichés fostered by *Ulysses* that are also not quite right. Joyce chose Dublin as his setting, he tells us, because it was large enough to serve as model of the modern metropolis and yet not too large to prevent the kinds of crossings and re-crossings, personal connections and missed connections, which make up so much of his view of urban life. This is perhaps true, in a symbolic sense, because we accept Joyce at his word. But his Dublin, in which hardly anyone works at a job demanding more than a few hours a day and many work only at sociability, is hardly representative of modern urban life in the West. We are not likely to find Henry Adams' Dynamo here (and Molly Bloom makes a most curious Virgin to erect our edifices to). We see the fringes of imperial trade on the Liffey, see the fringes of education and scholarship, of communications, medicine and religion, see the crumpled edges of Irish political life reflected in drunken arrogance and wishful daydreaming. But it is not as political historian either that we read Joyce.

Nor do we come to Joyce as a representative Irish literary figure. It is true that he followed the Irish pattern of exile and distance and irony and just a touch of sentimentality about what he had left behind him. But Joyce makes clear throughout his work what he thinks of the Irish literary world: he would not want to be thought its representative figure. Not that there might be such a danger: to an American visiting Dublin on Joycean business, the local attitude toward Joyce, and toward his overseas admirers, is dramatically clear: they wish that we would go away (or at least come only as tourists) and allow him to go away, too. Joyce has had little enduring influence in his homeland. (Even the bench dedicated to him on St. Stephen's Green faces the wrong way and must be shared with his convivial, failed father, a more acceptable Dubliner.) We do not read Joyce, it seems, for any reasons that have very much to do with

Ireland. We read him because he left Dublin behind him, because he became at last a universal author, the greatest of modern novelists, eponymous hero of the age: The Modernist Age might more tellingly be labeled The Age of James Joyce.

II.

Only now, when the death of Modernism has been almost universally proclaimed, have we begun to be concerned much with the origins of the movement. The problems of affixing a birthdate are obvious: do we follow Henry Adams, see the year 1900 itself as cataclysmic and assume that the new literary movement must inevitably follow the new century? Or do we look to some specific event, such as the death of Edward VII or the outbreak of the Great War or the first Dadaist stirrings during the war? One widely admired date is 1922, which saw the publication of *The Waste Land* and *Ulysses*, the principal texts of the period. There was also in that year *Jacob's Room*, which serves as the starting point, in technique and theme, for Woolf's mature fiction, and in the following year *Kangaroo*, so significant a step on the philosophical pathway leading to Lawrence's *Plumed Serpent*, as well as the first stories of Hemingway. In 1924, Breton issued the First Surrealist Manifesto, and *The Magic Mountain* appeared. We might go on, balancing our dates and our documents to fit our critical needs for another decade at least: the posthumous publication of Kafka's novels and of the final volumes of *A La Recherche Du Temps Perdu* and the appearance of *Parade's End* in the mid-1920s; Faulkner's creative explosion in the final years of this decade and the opening years of the next; Beckett's first significant efforts in the mid-1930's; the completion, after many years and many revisions of Kazantzakis' *Odysseia* in 1938 and of *Finnegans Wake* in 1939. And then there is Conrad, whose major works were completed before any of these were begun, or perhaps even contemplated.

It is an intriguing exercise, this effort to date so nebulous an event, and obviously futile. But it appeals to our need for scholarly symmetry, and besides, confident that the period has surely expired, we have the leisure as literary historians to define its boundaries and contemplate its resources. For few of us would deny that Modernism is among the richest of literary epochs and, in particular, the great age of the novel. Yet we are likely to reflect, in sadness no doubt, upon its discontinuity from earlier tradition: what was formerly seen as one of the strengths of the period—its sense that a new age demanded a new art, free of the encumbrances of the past that had sapped both age and art—is now viewed as its major defect. In denying the past, we are told, in elevating the individual artistic performance of the moment over the accumulated heritage of the past, the Modernist artist (and Joyce is said to be the prime villain in this) has cut us off from our history, has sacrificed the communal wisdom for mere technical brilliance, has deprived us of the hard-earned lessons of our humanity. Modernist art, in this widely held view (especially in England), is distinctively and consciously anti-humanist; for humanism to be resurrected in our time, Modernism as a creative force must be denied. It is a neat formulation, this conviction that we can recover the surety of tradition—that we can regain our humanity—by denying a mere few decades of art (a half century at most) and just as obviously wrongheaded. Perhaps our concerns should lie elsewhere than with dating; we may well need to reconsider our basic understanding of Modernist forces and effects, and Joyce may be our prime means to do so.

It is partly the growth of a new post-Modernist sensibility in all the arts which leads us to herald Modernism's demise; in part, as well, it is a kind of historical necessity. For if the Modernist Age was a time of literary giants and of gigantic, often unbearable historical events; and if we live today in a more human-sized world—giantism's inevitable aftermath—yearning desperately for events, historical and literary alike, which we can more comfortably control—then it would seem apparent that Modernist fiction, as exemplified by *Ulysses* and *Finnegans Wake*, with its limitless expectations and urges, can speak to us and for us no more. The new sensibility is indisputably in process; the historical necessity seems equally clear—although we may find it deplorable. But the conclusion seems to me not at all so inevitable. My own sense is that Modernism, in its fiction in particular, is still very much alive, still continuing to change and to grow, and that claims for its demise are a sign of our cultural insularity.

I am convinced as well that we are wrong to insist that Modernism represents a break from our humanist heritage. It may be apparent only in retrospect, and we may need to ignore the claims of some of their critics and of some of the Modernists themselves: but from the perspective of the most self-destructive half-century in human history—after Dachau, Hiroshima and My Lai—the Modernist novel seems humanist indeed: accepting human limitations, to be sure, but affirming human potential and dignity; appearing to deny man's most hallowed clichés of self-image, even at times to deny his presence (and the presence of God) but evidencing in fact great faith in our ability to endure, to prevail, to adapt to the most dehumanizing of man-made circumstance and to retain in the process some at least of our deepest values, the most significant of them. And in all of this Joyce is the representative figure. We act as if it were the Modernist novelist who invented the insane world that he so well and movingly describes.

III.

Artists are not alone in admiring the symmetry and conviction of symbolic dates and events: how else explain the fixing of Romantic beginnings by critics to the publication of the *Lyrical Ballads* in 1798 when the unheralded *Songs Of Innocence* had appeared almost a decade earlier? If we need a symbolic moment to posit as the first Modernist act, I would offer that day in 1909 when James Joyce, shortly after the birth of his daughter, Lucia, decided to rewrite *Stephen Hero* and to make of it *A Portrait Of The Artist As A Young Man*. Richard Ellmann points out that the theme of *A Portrait*, "the gestation of a soul," is consistent with the new facts of the artist's own life; that its opening images develop directly out of that life; and that Joyce was "encouraged" in his new state of mind and affairs "to work and rework the original elements in the process of gestation."[1] I would hazard, however, another understanding of that act, a rather different symbolic significance for Joyce and for us, a meaning drawn less from the artist's own life than from his observation of the life around him: a rather different offspring.

The narrative of *Stephen Hero*—such of it as survives—is in a form perfectly appropriate to the Edwardian state of affairs which it describes: an elaboration of late Victorian social views, of Victorian attitudes toward art and the role of the artist, even of Victorian omniscience. When the earlier Stephen Dedalus accuses Emma Clery of betraying him with Cranly, we know that he is wrong. We know this because the essentially omniscient Edwardian who describes the scene has informed us that she is innocent: he has shown us already the attempted public seduction and her inevitable, perhaps wished-for rejection of her would-be lover. There is none of the potential ambiguity here of the later Stephen's accusation. Even in *A Portrait*, we believe that Stephen is acting unjustly, that he is fabricating this betrayal—as he will fabricate others—because of his need to be isolate, to be betrayed, to fit the Romantic conception of the artist which Joyce always maintained. But in *A Portrait* we are not quite certain; we cannot indisputably contest Stephen's claim because we have been shown no evidence; we must not dispute the artist's essential veracity however much we suspect that he forges his deeds and his words. We understand that he is one of those who will sacrifice his life for his art, that he will demean not merely his friends but himself if it will satisfy the demands of his art, that he will gladly subjugate accepted norms of truth to what he conceives of as a higher truthtelling. Thus we suspect him. But because we are limited to what Stephen himself will admit of his life, we cannot be quite certain. Even on this supposedly higher level of truth, the ambiguity remains.

When the Victorian and Edwardian novelists made use of narrative omniscience, they were reflecting a worldview which harbored few uncertainties. The opening scene of *A Portrait Of The Artist As A Young Man*, with its sharply limited perspective, is a consciously symbolic act warning us that that old dispensation has irretrievably altered. The change in point of view is both sign and measure of this change in worldview.

The opening scene of *A Portrait* thus puts us on notice that the comfortable Victorian world is no more. Thrust without warning into a consciousness which cannot order the events it observes, which is incapable of distinguishing among levels of truth or even of sorting out its own sensory perceptions, the reader understands at once that he is in a new world, with changing forces and shifting boundaries, with none of the certainty that the Victorians desire and that he himself has long been accustomed to. Joyce's use of point of view in *A Portrait* is not perfect or perfectly consistent; glimpses of omniscience break through even here. But the symbolic import of this narrative act is inescapable: for a new world a new vision is needed, a new lens to penetrate and elucidate the new reality. Yet the change from *Stephen Hero* to *A Portrait* and beyond—from the young Joyce's point of view to the young Stephen's and eventually to Bloom's and HCE's—is both actual and symbolic, reflecting in this duality the dual perspectives of the mature art of Joyce and of Modernism as a whole: these are real people in Joyce's fiction and not merely symbols. We admire Stephen and perhaps despise him; we recognize that the irony is Joyce's irony and not ours alone; we acknowledge the ambiguous stance which we must adopt toward his world. Such ambiguity is the central focus of the Modernist vision and of all Modernist art.

But it was not Joyce or any of the Modernists who invented this state of mind and affairs; the conditions of the world were ambigu-

ous long before the novelists appeared to make them so: Vietnam
was hardly the first war to crystallize a civilization in ambiguity. For
all of Europe, the Great War—and the chain of events leading inex-
orably to it and out of it—was a kind of greater Vietnam, destroying
expectations along with lives, long-accepted versions of truth along
with national boundaries and seemingly eternal political facts, ideals
and visions of men along, it seemed, with humanity itself.

Yet because the shape of man is distorted—as it is in the contem-
poraneous Cubist painting—because human experience is unlooked
for and unhappy and because man and experience alike are viewed
through an unlikely series of prisms and lenses, this does not necessarily mean that the role of man in Modernist fiction has been de-
humanized. We react ambiguously to Stephen and to his greater
successors, Leopold Bloom and HCE. But we react to them as men,
not as mere symbols or forms. No character in literature is more
palpable than Bloom. There is none whom we know so deeply and
so well; few about whom we care so intensely; few whose humanity
so makes us aware of our own. There are times when we scorn
Bloom and wish to distance ourselves from him; his is a way of life
that most of us would like to deny, with lesser expectations, a lesser
sense of achievement. But Bloom retains his dignity and his human
concern, even a heroism of sorts, a mythic stature that affixes him in
lower-middle-class Dublin at the start of Henry Adams' century and
raises him somehow above it. This is not the mythic view of Modernist art as propounded by Eliot—based on irony and scorn for
man's present condition, a superstructure of form and control for
the artist that is rooted in the past rather than a guide to the nature
of man in the present. The Joycean view is more basic, more truly
mythic and less brutally ironic, closer to the spirit and intention of
the ancient fertility figures whom Bloom at times echoes.[2] That we
can see Bloom's endurance, his will to live his life with dignity and
even with a certain clumsy grace, his commitment to human needs
and involvement: that we can see him as potentially heroic despite
the irony and beneath the burden of naturalistic detail, is a sign of
Joyce's own commitment to humanism. The times are difficult, to be
sure, and man's potential has indisputably lessened: but he remains
at the center of Joycean and Modernist concern, and his values—the
old humanist values, altered but still recognizable—are in the end
affirmed once again.

IV.

I have been speaking of Joyce as if his art could stand for all Modernist art. This is not to deny the very real differences—artistic, philosophic and human differences—which exist between Joyce and Mann, or Joyce and Proust, or Joyce and Kafka. Nor is it necessarily to imply that Joyce ranks unreachably above tham as a novelist, that his is the sole meaningful point of view of the age or that he is more deeply committed than they are to humanist affairs. The glory of the fiction of the Modernist Age is that it possesses four such masters— and many others, Faulkner, Woolf, Gide, Nabokov, Svevo, Broch, Kazantzakis and Hemingway among them, who are lesser only by comparison, who in another age would be giants. This diversity may make the period difficult to delimit or to define, but it leaves other, more fruitful tasks to the critic. For it seems indisputable to me that this is the great age of the novel. And Joyce, despite his individuality, is its eponymous hero, symbol (in part because of his individuality) of its artistic and human commitment: the Modernist Age is truly the Age of James Joyce.

In Joyce we find that marriage of sensibility and technique which is characteristic of the period as a whole; he provides in his life the model of the Modernist artistic endeavor; his work makes manifest both the apparent extremes and the actual means which distinguish this age from all others. The developing body of his fiction establishes its critical poles—from the Edwardian *Stephen Hero*; to *Ulysses*, the most representative and, I believe, the major work of the century; to *Finnegans Wake*, which might almost be called the first post-Modernist text. In Joyce we find in detail the most significant Modernist innovations and concerns; the concern for devising a narrative point of view which will most suitably convey a changing world-view (not simply stream of consciousness, as some have claimed, but many other variations of both interior and exterior views); the awareness of time as a phenomenon of the individual mind and not of the clock, as a force which operates in each of our lives and not simply as an objective measure of their passing; the ironic tone which alone can reflect these changing perspectives, another function of point of view; the erection of tight and elaborate metaphoric structures which demand that novels be read as closely now as sonnets alone were once read—and necessitating the rise of a new critical approach to fiction, the New Criticism so-called; the recognition that in myth we may test out not only our ties with societies of the past but the present status of our own society; the diminished yet central vision of man surviving, of man persisting, a revised yet still powerful humanist vision. In all of this, Joyce serves as exemplar for his generation.

But rather than create a list of the characteristics of the Joycean (read Modernist) novel, we need urgently to investigate some of our most hallowed critical clichés arising from Modernism: the assumption, for example—seemingly approved by the novelists themselves—that Modernist fiction was an elitist activity, designed solely for those few readers who were willing to fulfill Henry James' implied contractual obligation and devote to the novelist all the energy and time and intelligence at their disposal. Yet my own teaching experience convinces me that *Ulysses*—and with it virtually every other Modernist text—is accessible to most readers with patience, a moderate experience as readers and a moderate intelligence, a minimum of help from outside and a goodly degree of good will. Parts of the novel—the Stephen parts primarily—are difficult and dense, perhaps, at times, needlessly so. But there is little about Bloom—his language, his experience, his emotions—that we cannot touch at first hand, that does not touch us. I reject the implicit paradox that this book about the great common man, if you will, is reserved for uncommon men.

Another of the assumed critical truths about the Modernist novel is the significance of the cool and objective, aloof and distant attitude which we attribute to its makers. "The artist," says the young Stephen Dedalus, following Flaubert, "like the God of the creation, remains within or behind or beyond or above his handiwork, invisible, refined out of existence, indifferent, paring his fingernails."[3] Such aloofness we interpret as a deficiency of ethics, a retreat from humanity. Modernist art, comments Ortega y Gasset in *The Dehumanization Of Art*, "is an explicit act of dehumanization."[4]

Following Flaubert and eliminating the novelist as a middleman who intercedes between character and reader, the Joycean point of view reweaves the fabric of Victorian fiction and depicts a new world from which certainty has fled, in which even objective reality can no longer be unquestioned. The apparent result of Stephen's youthful obiter dicta, some half century later, is the feverish perspective of an Alain Robbe-Grillet narrative, his rejection of metaphor because it is centered in man, his explicit denial of humanism. But it is wrong to link Robbe-Grillet too closely with Joyce and the Modernists: his dictates are, in fact, a reversal of their practice; it is unwise as well to identify the young Stephen with the mature Joyce:

much of what Stephen says about art in *A Portrait* is repudiated in the novel itself and in the subsequent novels.

Similarly, when T.S. Eliot ordained in the essay called "Ulysses, Order, and Myth" in 1923 that Joyce had used myth as "a way of controlling, of ordering, of giving a shape and a significance to the immense panorama of futility and anarchy which is contemporary history,"[5] we assumed that he was speaking for all the Modernists both about necessary artistic technique and about the nature of the world confronting the artist. It seems quite clear today, however, that Eliot was speaking not of *Ulysses* but of *The Waste Land*, that Joyce's use of myth is very different from his and from what he describes in his essay, that the poet's worldview is more conservative, closer to despair and much less humane than that of Joyce and most of the other Modernist novelists. For no character in literature is more fully realized than Bloom, no day more profoundly chronicled than Bloomsday; and the Modernist narrator—distant, aloof, uninvolved as he seems—is by no means unaware of or unconcerned with the condition of man.

The author-as-God has indeed been eliminated from the Modernist narrative as it is developed by Joyce; the burden is now on the reader-as-man. He must supply the narrative answers (if there are answers to be found) or even the questions once willfully raised by the all-knowing, all-powerful Victorian author; he must collaborate with his author in constructing the framework of character and event; he must provide with his involvement a human focus. His is a much less comfortable position than that of the Victorian reader, his world less predictable and easily harmonious. But it is an accurate reflection of the world beyond fiction (fiction's goal, after all), and it is not lacking totally in values. For if we interpret humanism as the willingness to accept responsibility for our deeds and even for our vision of reality, and the dignity that may accompany such acceptance, then surely the position of the Modernist reader—and of Modernist author and character as well—is at least as humanistic as those of their predecessors.

V.

From those contemporary novelists for whom Joyce serves as a metaphor of the potential of the novelist—in humanistic theme as well as Modernist technique: I think, for example, of the early Michel Butor and Claude Simon, of John Barth and E.L. Doctorow and, in a negative sense, Thomas Pynchon, of Carlos Fuentes, Gabriel García Márquez, Guillermo Cabrera Infante and many others—from his followers we learn that Joyce, once deemed a mere parochial Dubliner, is actually the most universal of artists; that Joyce, seen in his own day as a rebel and rejected by some even today for his presumed denial of tradition, is in fact our bridge to the past, as well as expositor of our present.

Writing of that fearful year 1900 and of what is for him the symbol of the new age, Henry Adams declares in his *Education*, in the chapter entitled "The Dynamo and the Virgin," that "the dynamo itself was but an ingenious channel for conveying somewhere the heat latent in a few tons of poor coal hidden in a dirty engine-house carefully out of sight; but to Adams the dynamo became a symbol of infinity. As he grew accustomed to the great gallery of machines, he began to feel the forty-foot dynamo as a moral force, much as the early Christians felt the Cross. . . . For Adams's objects its value lay chiefly in its occult mechanism."[6] The very real James Joyce, self-exiled from Dublin, and his very palpable fictions, at once parochial and universal in import, have become for the novelists and critics of our age a similar symbol: a great and powerful metaphor that both threatens us and promises salvation. The Argentine writer Jorge Luis Borges perhaps puts it best in the poem called "Invocation to Joyce":

> What does our cowardice matter if on this earth
> there is one brave man,
> what does sadness matter if in time past
> somebody thought himself happy,
> what does my lost generation matter,
> that dim mirror,
> if your books justify us?
> I am the others. I am all those
> who have been rescued by your pains and care.
> I am those unknown to you and saved by you.[7]

Joyce has gone further beyond Dublin than perhaps even he had realized.

Notes

1. Richard Ellmann, *James Joyce* (New York, 1959), p. 307.

2. See my essay "A Hero for Our Time: Leopold Bloom and the Myth of *Ulysses*," in Thomas F. Staley, ed., *Ulysses: Fifty Years* (Bloomington and London, 1974), pp. 132-46.

3. James Joyce, *A Portrait Of The Artist As A Young Man*, Viking Press edition (New York, 1956), p. 215.

4. José Ortega y Gasset, *The Dehumanization Of Art And Other Writings On Art And Culture* (Garden City, 1956), p. 21.

5. T.S. Eliot, "Ulysses, Order, and Myth," in Seon Givens, ed., *James Joyce: Two Decades Of Criticism* (New York, 1963), p. 201.

6. Henry Adams, *The Education Of Henry Adams* (New York, 1946), pp. 380-81.

7. Jorge Luis Borges, *In Praise Of Darkness*, trans. Norman Thomas diGiovanni (New York, 1974), p. 93.

Introduction to
The Decentered Universe
of *Finnegans Wake*

Margot Norris

STRUCTURE AND LANGUAGE

Thanks to the patient toil of its dedicated explicators, the major contours of Joyce's *Finnegans Wake* have gradually come into focus in the thirty-five years since its publication. Yet while more allusions, motifs, and linguistic details are continually coming to light, the intellectual orientation of the work remains largely obscure.

The attempt to assess the teleology of *Finnegans Wake* has always presented critics with a dilemma: the choice between a radical and a conservative interpretation of the book. A radical interpretation would maintain that *Finnegans Wake* subverts not only the literary status quo but the most cherished intellectual preconceptions of Western culture as well—a position most clearly maintained in the pioneer studies of the work. Yet in these early studies, such as *Our Exagmination*,[1] the weakness of the radical interpretation also becomes apparent. While proclaiming the revolutionary nature of *Work in Progress*, the writers lack scholarly pegs on which to hang their theories and finally resort to ad hoc analogies to support their theses. In contrast, the conservative critics, who have dominated *Wake* criticism for the last thirty years, possess a small but scholarly arsenal: the stylistic and thematic conservatism of the early manuscript drafts, the inclusion of traditional, even arcane, literary material in the work, Joyce's admission that the work's structural and philosophical models are derived from a sixteenth-century metaphysician and an eighteenth-century philosopher, and finally, Joyce's own decidedly reactionary tastes. Even the recently published *A Conceptual Guide to "Finnegans Wake,"*[2] which aims at a comprehensive study of the work, embraces this conservative tradition by approaching the work as a novel: "along with the problem for the reader of deciphering Joyce's language goes the stumbling block of figuring out the narrative or the plot."

Joyce is himself partly responsible for this unsettled state of affairs. Throughout the progress of his writing, he sent friends and disciples scurrying to reference books that would unlock the secret of a phrase or passage, while his comments on the overall purpose and construction of the book remained enigmatic and vague—often phrased in negative terms that suggest what *Finnegans Wake* is not, rather than what it is. "I might easily have written this story in the traditional manner. . . . Every novelist knows the recipe. . . . It is not very difficult to follow a simple, chronological scheme which the critics will understand. . . . But I, after all, am trying to tell the story of this Chapelizod family in a new way. . . ."[3] We are left to wonder about the nature of this new way of telling the story. Joyce's sanction and supervision of *Our Exagmination* was clearly an effort to answer this question. Yet while approving his disciples' defense of his work on radical grounds, he failed to supply them with a theoretical base other than his references to Bruno and Vico.

Since the time of these pioneer *Wake* critics, an enormous amount of detailed explication of the text has become available, and new tools for critical investigation have emerged that make it possible to examine more thoroughly those aspects of the work that resist novelistic analysis. With these advantages, I hope to resume the radical viewpoints of the early critics and demonstrate the extent of the challenge that Joyce offered not only to conventional literary modes but also to many of the epistemological presuppositions of our culture. My argument will be based on the assumption that Joyce did not mount this challenge in a vacuum, but that knowingly or unknowingly he participated in those intellectual currents of early-twentieth-century Europe, whose destructive impact depended on a profound revision of the understanding of language. Eugene Jolas, a close personal friend and colleague of Joyce's, was extraordinarily sensitive to these currents. "The real metaphysical problem today is the word," he writes in *Our Exagmination*. "The new artist of the word has recognized the autonomy of language."[4] Jolas also connected Joyce with the literary experimentalists of the day.

> Léon-Paul Fargue, one of the great French poets of our age, has created astonishing neologisms in his prose poems. . . . The revolution of the surrealists, who destroyed completely the old relationships between words and thought, remains of immense significance. . . . André Breton, demoralizing the old psychic processes by the destruction of logic, has discovered a world of magic in the study of dream via the Freudian explorations. . . . Miss Gertrude Stein attempts to find a mysticism of the word by the process of thought thinking itself.[5]

At the time Jolas proclaimed "the revolution of the word," modern theoretical linguistics was in its infancy.[6] Ferdinand de Saussure's *Course in General Linguistics* was published in Paris in 1910 but appears to have gone unnoticed by contemporary writers. And yet we find in *Finnegans Wake* that intellectual shift which locates meaning in relationships and structure rather than in content—a shift formalized by Saussure's recognition of the arbitrary nature of the linguistic sign and his focus on the synchronic laws of language.

Among the many shocks administered to the Victorian mentality during the early twentieth century, the power and scope of the unconscious in human life was perhaps the least sensational but the most enduring. Freud's discovery of the extent to which man's psychic and emotional life is controlled by his unconscious adumbrated the complex role that language plays in that process. Psychoanalyst Jacques Lacan has recently restored this aspect of Freud's theory to prominence.[7] But those marvelously complicated workings of the unconscious that give us language were not truly recognized until Noam Chomsky's devastating refutation of behaviorist linguistic theory in the 1950s. Further evidence of man's lack of self-knowledge and impaired understanding of his condition ultimately served to raise criticism to the status of a highly self-conscious, creative act. In recent times this brand of self-reflexive criticism has expanded to many disciplines in a movement known broadly as structuralism. The theoretical roots of the structuralist method lie in linguistics, but its application ranges across the diverse human sciences, with particularly interesting developments in anthropology, psychoanalysis, and philosophy.

Structuralism presupposes that the organization of psychic and social life is based on similar unconscious laws and that the structures that underlie various human activities—language, family relationships, religious worship, social communications, for example—

are therefore isomorphic. Consequently, relationships rather than substances, structures rather than contents, provide significant sources of meaning in human institutions and systems of communication.

Structuralist theory is stubbornly at variance with those prevailing political and social philosophies that exhibit a distinct behaviorist bias, an underlying faith that man is shaped by the external forces of his environment and that human betterment depends on the improvement of that environment. Yet it is precisely this conflict that helps to illustrate the suitability of the structuralist approach to Joyce's work. In their grim depiction of the spiritual "paralysis" that Dublin visits on its citizens, *Dubliners* and *A Portrait of the Artist as a Young Man* (hereafter cited as *Portrait*) affirm the oppression of the individual by society and its institutions. But while Joyce is unconcerned with melioration in these works, his theme of exile does promise hope of escape. The local use of mythic patterns in *Portrait* expands in *Ulysses* to a massive mythic structure that ascribes the condition of the individual not merely to accidents of environment but to certain constant predispositions in his own nature and in the order of things as well. For example, the "brutal" fathers in *Dubliners*, Farrington and Little Chandler, are so crushed by their environments that they take their anger and frustration out on their small sons. But father-son relationships in *Ulysses* have become symbolic and complex. Stephen's *Hamlet* theory and numerous mythic analogues isolate recurrent difficulties that plague the hierarchical systems in which men relate to each other and to their gods. In *Finnegans Wake* the notion of an "environment"—which depends on an empirical belief in the separation of inner and outer, subjective and objective, mental and physical—completely disintegrates. Characters are fluid and interchangeable, melting easily into their landscapes to become river and land, tree and stone, Howth Castle and Environs, or HCE. We find in the *Wake* not characters as such but ciphers, in formal relationship to each other.

For all his reticence on the subject, Joyce did provide a single helpful clue to orient our approach to his new universe. Preceded by a theory of correspondences that he derived from Hermes Trismegistus and Swedenborg (cf. *P*, p. 244), his last work employed the thought of Giordano Bruno, which he summarized as follows: "His philosophy is a kind of dualism—every power in nature must evolve an opposite in order to realise itself and opposition brings reunion etc etc."[8] Besides its resemblance to Hegelian dialectic, Bruno's philosophical dualism adumbrates the binary opposition of phonemes, which provided a central insight into the nature of linguistic meaning: meaning inheres not in sounds themselves—"d" and "t," for example—but in the contrast or difference between them, so that we can distinguish "dime" and "time." The concept of binary opposition is a cornerstone of the structuralist method. "But when, as in structuralism, substance is replaced by relationship, then the noun, the object, even the individual ego itself, becomes nothing but a locus of cross-references: not things, but differential perceptions, that is to say, a sense of the *identity* of a given element which derives solely from our awareness of its *difference* from other elements, and ultimately from an implicit comparison of it with its own opposite."[9] I will try to use this method in a central, integrated approach to the entire work, its narrative structure, its themes, the nature of the discourse (point of view), and the technical and aesthetic aspects of the language.

DREAM THEORY

For all its stylistic innovations, *Ulysses* ceased to bedazzle critics and readers and started to "make sense" once the plot and story line were discovered and understood. Similar attempts to transcend the pyrotechnics of *Finnegans Wake* have more or less failed. Story lines and plots have had to be plugged with hallucinations and dreams within dreams. Yet annoying questions concerning the nature of the figures, events, and language have persisted all the same. I have tried to approach *Finnegans Wake* with an abiding trust in Joyce's artistry and professional experience and a modicum of trust in my own good sense as a reader and critic. I have resisted the promptings of armchair psychology to chalk up the puzzling and confusing nature of the work to Joyce's mischief, malice, or megalomania. And after much study, thought, and irritation, I have come to the conclusion that the key to the puzzle is the puzzle. In other words, expecting the work to "make sense" in the way *Portrait, Ulysses*, or traditional novels "make sense" implies a conceptual framework and epistemology that Joyce strongly intimated he wanted to undermine. *Finnegans Wake* is a puzzle because dreams are puzzles—elaborate, brilliant, purposeful puzzles, which constitute a universe quite unlike any we know or experience in waking life.

Although Freud's influence on Joyce is argued convincingly by Frederick J. Hoffman in his early essay[10] and endorsed by Atherton,[11] Clive Hart's preference for the *Upanishads* as the source of Joyce's dream theory[12] makes some restatement necessary. Joyce's reference to Freud's *The Interpretation of Dreams* in *Finnegans Wake* (338.29) is supported by ample evidence that he read the book with care and applied the techniques of dream-work to the *Wake*. Virtually every one of the "typical dreams" described by Freud[13] constitutes a major theme in *Finnegans Wake*. "Embarrassing Dreams of Being Naked," which often find the subject naked before strangers, are reflected in the voyeurism of the three anonymous soldiers in the Phoenix Park incident. Freud points out that frequently the strangers in such dreams represent familiar persons: the *Wake's* soldiers represent HCE's sons, who view their father much as the sons of Noah viewed their father. Explaining dreams about the death of beloved persons, Freud discusses both sibling rivalry and the simultaneous incestuous and murderous feelings between parents and children. All of these taboos are at issue in the mysterious sin in *Finnegans Wake*. In fact, Freud reports a dream that contains a cluster of the elements found in the Phoenix Park incident. It shows "two boys struggling," like the *Wake's* enemy twins, with one of them fleeing for protection to a maternal woman, like ALP hiding the "lipoleums" under her skirt hoop to "sheltershock" (8.30) them. Freud interprets the woman as representing both an incestuous and a voyeuristic object for the boy. "The dream combined two opportunities he had had as a little boy of seeing little girls' genitals: When they were *thrown down* and when they were *micturating*. And from the other part of the context it emerged that he had a recollection of being *chastised* or threatened by his father for the sexual curiosity he had evinced on these occasions."[14] Freud's dream resembles the homework chapter, II.2, where the boys examine their mother's genitals and one boy strikes the other in punishment. The merging of the boy with the threatening father in Freud's dream also recurs frequently in a merger of father and son in the *Wake*. Furthermore, the notion of voyeuristically watching girls urinate is a repeated Phoenix Park/Waterloo image. Freud discusses both children's games and examinations or academic tests as bearing sexual significance in typical dreams, a concept manifested in Chapters II.1 and II.2 of *Finnegans Wake*.

The dream universe is structured differently from the mental universe of conscious life because meanings are located in different places. One explanation for the encyclopedic nature of *Finnegans Wake* is that the dreaming psyche attaches items of knowledge or information from the waking consciousness and invests them with totally different meanings. The key to the new meanings is hidden in the connection between the two thoughts. For example, "Waterloo" means a famous Napoleonic battle to the waking mind. In the Wakean dream world it also means a place for urinating. If "Waterloo" reminds the dreamer of a juvenile chastisement for watching girls urinate, then the sexual and historical references to the place become linked by the common theme of humiliating defeat. Because meanings are dislocated—hidden in unexpected places, multiplied and split, given over to ambiguity, plurality, and uncertainty—the dreams represents a decentered universe. Since this dream universe is so unlike waking life, the critical techniques designed to explore the traditional novel are unsuitable to the study of a dream-work. To examine various aspects of this decentered world, I have borrowed the ideas and tools of theoreticians in a variety of fields who share an interest in the structures of the systems they study.

The narrative structure of *Finnegans Wake*. . . appears more intelligible in the light of the modern myth theories of anthropologist Claude Lévi-Strauss than it did through attempts at finding correspondences to the Gilbert scheme for *Ulysses*. Lévi-Strauss's myth theory suggests a plausible reason for Joyce's "new way" of telling a story by collocating versions of the same event rather than developing a chronological plot. Furthermore, Lévi-Strauss's concept of the homology of myth and dream suggests a way of relating individual and social experience in *Finnegans Wake* without recourse to the Jungian concept of a "collective unconscious." While Lévi-Strauss argues that myths and dreams are governed by the same unconscious structures and that the meaning of myths and dreams resides in the relationships between their elements, Jungian theory posits the significance and persistence of the nature of types and images in the personal and racial memory.

The relationships between Wakean figures have such complex functions that a series of interlocking approaches was required. . . to describe them adequately. Insofar as these relationships are power relationships, they constitute a destructive and repetitive system that is reflected in the theories of Vico, Freud, and Hegel. Vico's socioreligious history is based on endless cycles produced by mankind's progress from one age to another as power relationships change. The sexual dynamic of the Freudian family is based on unconscious power relationships that were operative in establishing primitive society. The power relationships implicit in Hegel's Master-Slave dialectic relate the concept of the fight to the emergence of human consciousness—a notion elaborated on at the psychoanalytic level by Jacques Lacan. The paradoxical nature of society as simultaneously lawful and repressive is reversed by the anarchic Oedipal drives in the *Wake*, which create a decentered dream world that is without law, but free.

The dream permits the dreamer's relationship to himself to assume dramatic form as he uses the disguises and defenses provided by the dream mechanism to communicate to himself about himself. Philosopher Martin Heidegger's theory of inauthentic being helps to explore the ontological condition of the dreamer through his comportment toward guilt, truth, and death.

Another chapter explores dream language as poetic language, using Lacan's theories of language, repression, and poetry. It is the function of a dream to simultaneously conceal and reveal the nature of the "true" or unconscious self, a task accomplished through the structural operations described by Freud. Such techniques of dreamwork as displacement, condensation, and distortion, correspond to the tropes that create the dense, ambiguous, polyvalent language of the work. The tension in the language, which bars semantic certainty or simplicity, signifies the decentered universe it expresses.

My final chapter treats the philosophical implications of expressing a decentered universe—a problem formulated by philosopher Jacques Derrida as a critical dilemma. In Joyce's case, the problem is technical—the need to find a language to depict a world in which identities are unstable, speakers are deceptive and lack self-knowledge, the point of view is not unified, and the society depicted is anarchic.

Throughout this discussion I have spoken of a dreamer and of the dream of *Finnegans Wake* as though there is indeed a single dreamer and I know exactly who he is. Well, I don't know who he is. To say that Joyce is the dreamer tells us nothing useful. To say that the dreamer is Finn or Earwicker ignores the significance of ambiguous identities in the dream. Wakean figures are interchangeable because characters in dreams are fictions created by the dreamer—including fictions of himself. In other words, the dreamer is invested in all of his characters in certain ways, and the characters that represent himself are no less fictional than any of the others. I suspect that we are to assume a single dreamer, since the same obsessions inform all the themes narrated by the different voices. The different speaking voices may therefore represent different personae of the dreamer relating different versions of the same event. For example, since a single dreamer can be a father, a son, and a brother all at once, he can play out an Oedipal drama in his dream, in which he takes the parts of Laius, Oedipus, and Creon all at once. In this way he can express many conflicting feelings simultaneously. I speculate that it makes no difference whether one supposes a single long dream, with constant repetition of the same theme, or a group of serial dreams, each dealing with the same theme. It seems plausible to suppose that the dreamer is male, since the major conflicts appear to afflict male figures. But sex, like everything else, is mutable in dreams. The question "Who is the dreamer?" is a question properly addressed not to the reader but to the dreamer himself, who discovers in the dream that he is by no means who he thinks he is.

Notes

1. Samuel Beckett et al., *Our Exagmination Round His Factification for Incamination of Work in Progress* (New York: New Directions Books, 1962).

2. Michael H. Begnal and Fritz Senn, eds., *A Conceptual Guide to "Finnegans Wake"* (University Park: Pennsylvania State University Press, 1974), p. x.

3. Eugène Jolas, "My Friend James Joyce," in Seon Givens, ed., *James Joyce: Two Decades of Criticism* (New York: Vanguard Press, 1963), p. 11.

4. Eugene Jolas, "The Revolution of Language and James Joyce," in Beckett et al., p. 79.

5. Ibid., pp. 84-85.

6. The available evidence indicates that Joyce attended a lecture on experimental linguistics by Père Marcel Jousse in 1931, although its effects on *Finnegan's Wake* are uncertain. See Richard Ellmann, *James Joyce* (New York: Oxford University Press, 1965), p. 647. Joyce's personal library contained virtually no works on linguistic theory per se. Thomas Connolly in *The Personal Library of James Joyce*, does list H. L. Mencken's *The American Language* and texts on auxiliary languages, Charles Kay Ogden's *Basic English and Debabelization*, "with a Survey of Contemporary Opinion on the Problem of Universal Language." Other language books in the personal library incude foreign language dictionaries and dictionaries of slang, as well as texts on usage and etiquette: Basil Hargrave's *Origins and Meanings of Popular Phrases and Names Including Those Which Came into Use during the Great War*, also *English as She is Spoke: Or a Jest in Sober Earnest*, and Ogden's *Brighter Basic: Examples of Basic English for Young Persons of Taste and Feeling*. See Thomas E. Connolly, *The Personal Library of James Joyce: A Descriptive Bibliography* (Buffalo: The University of Buffalo Bookstore, 1957); Ronald Buckalew, "Night Lessons on Lan-

guage," in Begnal and Senn, pp. 93-115, also contains a helpful discussion of Joyce's linguistic background.

7. Jacques Lacan, "The Function of Language in Psychoanalysis," in Anthony Wilden, *The Language of the Self* (Baltimore: The Johns Hopkins University Press, 1968).

8. James Joyce, *Letters of James Joyce*, ed. Stuart Gilbert (New York: Viking Press, 1966), 1:226. From a letter to Harriet Shaw Weaver dated 27 January 1925.

9. Frederic Jameson, "Metacommentary," *PMLA* 86, no. 1 (January 1971):14.

10. Frederick J. Hoffman, "Infroyce," in Givens, pp. 390-435.

11. James S. Atherton, *The Books at the Wake* (New York: Viking Press, 1960), pp. 37-39.

12. Clive Hart, *Structure and Motif in "Finnegans Wake"* (London: Faber and Faber, 1962), Chapter 3.

13. Sigmund Freud, "The Interpretation of Dreams," in *The Standard Edition of the Complete Psychological Works of Sigmund Freud*, trans. James Strachey (London: The Hogarth Press, 1953-74), 4:241-76.

14. Ibid, p. 201.

NEOTERIC PSYCHOLOGY

Closing Time:
An Interlude of Farce
Norman O. Brown

In the meantime, waiting
waiting
Abide Zeit's sumonserving, rise afterfall.   FW, 78
Waiting for the return of the theocratic age
to greet the return of the gods
                         (Heidegger
                         (H.D. *Tribute to Freud*
   The while we, we are waiting, we are waiting
for. Hymn.   FW, 609

Plato:
   There is an era in which the god himself assists
the universe on its way and helps it in its rotation.
There is also an era in which he releases his control.
Thereupon it begins to revolve in a contrary direction under its own impulse. At last, as this cosmic
era draws to its close, disorder comes to a head. The
few good things the universe produces are polluted
with so great a taint of evil that it hovers on the very
brink of destruction, both it and the creatures in it.
Therefore at that very moment the god who first set
it in order looks down upon it again. Beholding it in
trouble, and anxious lest racked by storms and con-

fusion it suffer dissolution and sink into the bottomless abyss of differentiation, he takes control of the helm once more. *Politicus, 269C, 273D*

In the meantime, an interim
in the time of the Not yet. *FW, 3*

*In Nowhere has yet the Whole World taken part of
    himself for his Wife;*
*By Nowhere have Poorparents been sentenced to
    Worms, Blood and Thunder for Life*
*Not yet has the Emp from Corpsica forced the
    Arth out of Engleterre;*
*Not yet have the Sachsen and Hudder on the
    Mound of a Word made Warre;*
*Not yet Witchywitchy of Wench struck Fire of his
    Heath from on Hoath;*
*Not yet his Arcobaleine forespoken Peacepeace
    upon Oath;* *FW, 175*

In the interim, an interlude
    during this swishingsight teilweisioned *FW, 345*
an interlude of farce.
Finnegans Wake is his farced epistol to the hibruws. *FW, 228*

Etymology of farce: stuffing.
Make a farce with livers minced small. Pigge farced with sage. With what stuffe our old historiographers have farced up their huge volumes. *O.E.D.*
Farce, or satire:
Satire. Scaliger's derivation of this word from *satyr* is untenable. It is from *satura* (full of variety, *saturated*), *satura lanx*, a hotchpotch or olla podrida. *Brewer's Dictionary*
Finnegans Wake:
    My wud! The warped flooring of the lair and soundconducting walls thereof, to say nothing of the uprights and imposts, were persianly literatured with burst loveletters, telltale stories, stickyback snaps, doubtful eggshells, bouchers, flints, borers, puffers, amygdaloid almonds, rindless raisins, alphybettyformed verbage, vivlical viasses, ompitter dictas, visus umbique, ahems and ahahs, imeffible tries at speech unasyllabled, you owe mes, eyoldhyms, fluefoul smut, fallen lucifers, vestas which had served, showered ornaments, borrowed brogues, reversi-

bles jackets, blackeye lenses, family jars, falsehair shirts,
Godforsaken scapulars, neverworn breeches, cutthroat ties,
counterfeit franks, best intentions, curried notes, upset
latten tintacks, unused mill and stumpling stones, twisted
quills, painful digests, magnifying wineglasses, solid ob-
jects cast at goblins, once current puns, quashed quota-
toes, messes of mottage, unquestionable issue papers,
seedy ejaculations, limerick damns, crocodile tears, spilt
ink, blasphematory spits, stale shestnuts, schoolgirls',
young ladies', milkmaids', washerwomen's, shopkeepers'
wives, merry widows', ex nuns', vice abbess's, pro vir-
gins', super whores', silent sisters', Charleys' aunts',
grandmothers', mothers'-in-laws', fostermothers', god-
mothers' garters,   FW, 183

A farce, or compost heap:
   He dumptied the wholeborrow of rubbages on to soil
here.   FW, 17
   Puffedly offal tosh!   FW, 419
   What a mnice old mness it all mnakes! A middenhide
hoard of objects!   FW, 19

An interlude of farce
an interval
   between shift and shift   FW, 293
   between explosion and reexplosion (Donnaurwatteur!)
Hunderthunder!)   FW, 78
The Ginnungagap: the name given in the Icelandic
Eddas to the interval of timeless formlessness between world aeons.
   Somewhere, parently, in the ginnandgo gap between an-
tediluvious and annadominant.   FW, 14
An interval of timeless formlessness
an *interregnum:*
   Whenever the Roman constitution fell temporarily
in abeyance because the succession of supreme mag-
istrates was accidentally broken, the transitional
period was designated an *interregnum.*
An interval intercalated:
   An intercalary period stands outside the regular
order of things. Intercalary days tend to degenerate
into seasons of unbridled license; they form an inter-

regnum during which customary restraints of law and morality are suspended.
Interregnum, or Saturnalia
satire for the Saturnalia.
Interlude interpolated.
Definition of farce: The word was orginally applied to phrases interpolated in the litany between the words *kyrie* and *eleison;* to similar expansions of other liturgical formulae; to passages in the vernacular inserted between the Latin sentences in chanting the epistle.

His farced epistol.

Subsequently the name for the interludes of impromptu buffoonery which the actors in the religious dramas were accustomed to interpolate in their text.
Bob Dylan:
    There must be some way out of here
    Said the joker to the priest.
The Origin of Attic Comedy:
not the *eirōn* or the *alazōn* but the *bōmolochos*
                  altar-ambusher or altar-snatcher
    James Joyce, altar-boy turned altar-snatcher.
This is the way that Shem built:
  —*The hoax that joke bilked.*
  —*The jest of junk the jungular?*
  —*Jacked up in a jock the wrapper.*
Joyce celebrates the Feast of Fools
  Tis jest jibberweek's joke.

The festival of the subdeacons which is held on the Circumcision or on Epiphany or the Octave of the Epiphany is called the Feast of Fools. (*'Festum hypodiaconorum, quod vocamus stultorum.'*) This festival flourished chiefly in the cathedral towns of France, though there are traces of it in other countries. It varied, of course, at different places and times, but the general character of the rejoicing is perfectly clear, for it took the form of a complete reversal of ordinary custom. The transformation began with the singing of the Magnificat at Vespers, when

Frazer,
G.B. IX, 328

O.E.D.
FW, 228

F. M.
Cornford

FW, 511

FW, 565

the words 'He hath put down the might from their
seat and hath exalted the humble and meek' were
repeated again and again, while the *baculus* or staff
of office was delivered into the hands of one of the
despised sub-deacones who as 'bishop or Pope or
King of Fools' led his fellows into the stalls of the
higher clergy, to remain there and usurp their functions for the duration of the feast. This transference
of authority was the signal for the beginning of the
most astonishing revels. As soon as the higher
clergy shed their authority the ecclesiastical ritual
lost its sanctity. Even the Mass was burlesqued.
Censing was done with pudding and sausages.
Sometimes an ass was introduced into church, while
the Prose of the Ass was chanted:

> 'Orientis partibus
> Adventavit Asinus,
> Pulcher et fortissimus,
> Sarcinis aptissimus.'

On these occasions solemn Mass was punctuated
with brays and howls, and the rubrics of the 'office'
direct that the celebrant instead of saying *Ite missa est*
shall bray three times *(ter hinhannabit)* and that the
people shall respond in similar fashion.

E. Welsford,
The Fool,
202

Ritual clowns in primitive religion
the "Fools Lodge," or "Society of Contraries,"
violate taboos and thereby acquire magical power.
"You shall regard nothing as sacred."
Shocking stunts, just like Shem:

L. Makarius
in *Diogenes,*
69 (1970),
44–73

this mental and moral defective

FW, 177

seeker of the nest of evil in the bosom of a good word.

FW, 189

The Zuni clowns used to drink bowls full of urine
and feed on excrament and all sorts of filthy matter.
Shem wrote *crap in his hand, sorry!*

He shall produce nichthemerically from his unheavenly
body a no uncertain quantity of obscene matter not pro-
tected by copriright in the United Stars of Ourania.

FW, 185

This was a stinksome inkenstink

The worst, it is hoped, even in our western playboyish
world for pure mousefarm filth.

FW, 183

The Zuni clowns ridicule people

Shem scrabbled and scratched and scriobbled and skrevened nameless shamelessness about everybody ever he met. FW, 182

Other traits characteristic of ritual clowns are "reverse behavior" and "backward speech." From his birth, the mythical Koshari, father of the Sia clowns, "talked nonsense, talked backward." The Zuni clowns say the opposite of what they mean. Like a crazy fellow. Speaking a strange language. As in *Finnegans Wake*.

It is what Michelet called "the great satanical principle that everything must be done in the reverse order."

Kish is for anticheirst,
and the free of my hand to him! FW, 308

This interlude of farce
the time of *Finnegans Wake* is intermission time
   incipit intermissio FW, 278
not *incipit tragoedia*.
There's just that Shakespeare fellow left to beat, said Nora Joyce

He was avoopf (parn me!) aware of no other shaggspick, other Shakhisbeard, either prexactly unlike his polar andthisishis or procisely the seem as woops (parn!) as what he fancied or guessed the sames as he was himself. FW, 177
Joyce's answer to Shakespearian tragedy:
                incipit intermissio
  Lights, pageboy, lights! FW, 245
The moment of *Finnegans Wake* corresponds to the exit of the king from the play within the play in *Hamlet*:

  Enterruption. Check of slowback. Dvershen. FW, 332
  You're well held now, Missy Cheekspeer, and your panto's off! FW, 257

Farce makes a farce out of tragedy.
Have you evew thought, wepowtew,
that sheew gweatness was his twadgedy?   FW, 61
Empson, *Some Versions of Pastoral*, p. 5: "There was a
performance of *Hamlet* in the Turk-Sib region which
the audience decided spontaneously was farce."
Karl Marx, *The Eighteenth Brumaire of Louis Bonaparte*,
p. 1: "Hegel says somewhere that, upon the stage of
univrsal history, all great events and personalities
reappear in one fashion or another. He forgot to add
that on the first occasion, they appear as tragedy; on
the second, as farce."
Tragedy, comedy, farce
the forms of politics are the forms of theater
bourgeois comedy, the happy ending   H. Rosenberg
tragic confrontation of antagonists
                    the agony
Class-struggle as the continuation of tragedy
Waiting for Lefty—
Is the proletariat the new collective hero
            waiting to go on stage
            another actor on the stage of history
            a new actor in a neo-classical revival
            as in 1848—
            Karl Marx of *The Communist Manifesto*—
Or is the proletariat the sober reality of the human
condition
—the necessity of labor—
to be disclosed after the show is over
after the farce has ended
    and none so soon either shall the pharce for the nunce
come to a setdown secular phoenish.   FW, 4
Waiting for lefty, Waiting for Godot,
waiting to stop the show, the farce
waiting to bring the house down.
    History is a nightmare from which I am trying to
awake.   Ulysses, 34
    The play thou schouwburgst, Game, here endeth. The
curtain drops by deep request.   FW, 257
    Roll away the reel world, the reel world, the reel world!
CHERCHONS LA FLAMME!   FW, 64

Farce is the mode of consciousness in which a people take leave of their history
"The iron statue of Napoleon will crash from the top of the Vendôme column."   Marx
No more Greek revival
let the dead bury the dead
no more ghosts.
Waiting for a new dawn.
   Calling all downs. Calling all downs to dayne. Array! Surrection!   FW, 593
   You mean to see we have been hadding a sound night's sleep? You may so. It is just, it is just about to, it is just about to rolywholyover.   FW, 597
The necessity of farce:
it takes a farce to see a farce
Marx's paradoxes in *The Eighteenth Brumaire*
it is not sober political analysis: it's a riot.
Marx clowning
Abbie Hoffman clowning
John Cage clowning
What Karl Marx really meant is *Finnegans Wake.*
"Literary bolshevism," brother Stanislaus Joyce called it.
   Stannie was a santryman and drilled all decent people. Caddy went to Winehouse and wrote o peace a farce.   FW, 14
Farce, or operetta—
               the swan song of dying civilizations—
   For a burning would is come to dance inane.   FW, 250
   Are you not danzzling on the age of a culvano?
Siar, I am deed.   FW, 89
Operetta—
"It's divine idiocy, its heavenly sclerosis," to quote the Polish novelist Witold Gombrowicz, "provide a perfect artistic symbol for the absurdity of outworn conventions, for paralyzed social and political structures."   *New York Times,* March 9, 1970
Finnegans Wake is Joyce's *gaiety pantheomime*   FW, 180
               or *chrisman's pandemon*   FW, 455
   Every evening at lighting up o'clock sharp and until further notice in Feenichts Playhouse. (Bar and conveniences always open, Diddlem Club douncestears.)   FW, 219

*With futurist onehorse balletbattle pictures and the Pag-
eant of Past History worked up with animal variations
amid everglaning mangrovemazes and beorbtracktors by
Messrs Thud and Blunder. Shadows by the film folk,
masses by the good people.*   FW, 221
   *The gist of the pantomime, from cannibal king to the
property horse, being, slumply and slopely, to remind us
how, in this drury world of ours, Father Times and
Mother Spacies boil their kettle with their crutch. Which*   FW, 599–
every lad and lass in the lane knows. Hence.   600
Farce is the mode of demystification
the tragic mode remystifies
   "Love Remystified"
the tragic mode is solempne.
The necessity of farce of *Finnegans Wake*
in order to have our archetypes without Jungian solemnity or Yeatsian occultism.
   —*How culious an epiphany!*   FW, 508

Farce is vulgarization
   (Stoop)   FW, 18
      (please stoop)   W. C.
"It is imperative that we sink"   Williams
   *HYPOTHESES OF COMMONEST
   EXPERIENCES*   FW, 286
Here Comes Everybody.
No more heroics
instead of Aristotle's leading families, *our low hero*   FW, 184
   *O! the lowness of him was beneath all up to that sunk
to!*   FW, 171
   Lowest basemeant in hystry!   FW, 535
Farce is the theater of impotence.
In a situation of general social paralysis
stasis, sterility, stereotypification
the aim is not the seizure of power, but the dissolu-
tion of power.
Karo Marx in *The Eighteenth Brumaire*
demolishing the cult of the leader
bringing Napoleon's statue down.
Abbie Hoffman. "We are outlaws, not organizers."
Organizers are big pricks.

Beyond history, beyond tragedy, beyond genital organization of the body politc.
Farce is the theater of impotence
the clown is the castrated penis   Fenichel
the little fellow; Charlie Chaplin.

Farce is nihilism.
   Nixnixundnix.   FW, 415
Joyce wore his eyes out looking at Europe and
seeing nothing.
And of Irish history he said: Two bloody Irishmen in
a bloody fight over bloody nothing.
Finnegans Wake: Putting Allspace in a Notshall.   FW, 455
   All marryvoising moodmoulded cyclewheeling history. FW, 186
Avoiding Jungian solemnity or Yeatsian occultism
we take refuge in the Void, the Nothing:
   *It was allso agreenable in our senegear clutchless, tour-
ing the no placelike no timelike absolent, mixing up pet-
tyvaughan populose with the magnumoore genstries,
lloydhaired mersscenary blookers with boydskinned pigt-
tetails and goochlipped gwendolenes with duffyeyed dol-
ores; like so many unprobables in their poor suit of the
improssable.*   FW, 609

A tale
   Told by an idtio, full of sound and fury,
   Signifying nothing.   *Macbeth*, V, v
King Lear is also *Much Ado About Nothing*
         Tomfoolery
Enter Lear, with Cordelia dead in his arms
         My poor fool is hang'd!   *Lear*, V, iii
Beyond tragedy and farce
is the fusion of these opposites.
The final pages of *Finnegans Wake*
literature at the breaking point
breaking down
breaking into tears.
   The poignt of fun where I am crying to arrive you at. FW, 160
This intermingling of hilarity and fear is, eth-
nologically speaking, sufficient to betray the presence of the clown.

Just as in the romantic theory of the *mélange des gen-*
res in literature, the Zuni clowns represent both   Makarius
gravity and hilarity.
In *Finnegans Wake*, the twins Hilary and Tristopher
Giordano Bruno's motto: *In hilaritate tristis, in tristitia*
hilaris.
   I am not leering, I pink you pardons. I am highly sheshe
sherious.   FW, 570
Beyond tragedy and farce
to the fusion of these opposites
is
back
back to the original goat-song out of which both
tragedy and satyr-play, those *siamixed* twins,   FW, 66
by separation arose.
        We know nothing and can know nothing
                      but
        the dance, to dance to a measure
        contrapuntally,   W. C.
             Satyrically, the tragic foot.   Williams

Tragoedia = goat-song
   What then agentlike brought about that tragoady thun-
dersday this municipal sin business?   FW, 5
        This municipal sin business—is he talking
        about Kent State?
   That tragoady thundersday
Finnegans Wake is *that fishabed ghoatstory*   FW, 51
HCE is *Hircus Civis Eblanensis*, old goat-citizen   FW, 215
             of Dublin
Giles Goat-Boy is out of *Finnegans Wake*   John Barth
   Got by the one goat, suckled by the same nanna, one
twtich, one nature makes us oldworld kin.   FW, 463
Goat-song or satyr-play
satyr-play or satire
Scaliger's derivation of this word from satyr is rein-
stated when we go joycing
            letting punplays pass to ernest.   FW, 233
   That tragoady thundersday
or *Satyr's Caudledayed Nice.*   FW, 415
   For the triduum of Saturnalia his goatservant had pa-
raded hiz willingsons in the Forum.   FW, 97

Saturnights pomps, exhabiting that corricatore of a
harss, revealled by Oscur Camerad.   FW, 602

Finnegan Beginnagain
we are back again
before the Birth of Tragedy
before the Gods of Greece
something more elemental.

What does that synthesis of god and goat in the
satyr mean? (Nietzsche). I estimate the value of hu-   *Ecce Homo,*
man beings, or races, according to how necessarily   XV, 4; II, 4
they cannot understand the god apart from the
satyr.
Said the joker to the priest.
Mais regardez donc ce Joyce: il est tout à fait grecque.
C'est le satyre sur un vase grecque!   Ellman, 612
Something more elemental
the hour of the beast—"pawses"   FW, 221
   It darkles, (tinct, tint) all this our funnaminal world.   FW, 244
Not Pater noster but *Panther monster.*   FW, 244
Pan-ther: all beast.
When the leopards break into the temple and drink
the wine from the sacred chalice.

The hour of the beast, or the barbarian
   The wild main from Borneholm has jest come to crown.   FW, 331
   The whool of the whaal in the wheel of the whorl of the
Boubou from Bourneum has thus come to taon!   FW, 415
   One two three. Chours! So come on, ye wealthy gen-
trymen wibfrufrocksfull of fun! Thin thin! Thin thin! Thej
olly and thel ively, thou billy with thee coo, for to job a jig
of a crispness nice and sing a missal too. Hip champouree!
Hiphip champouree! O you longtailed blackman, polk it up
behind me! Hip champouree! Hiphip champouree! And,
jessies, push the pumkik round. Anneliuia!   FW, 236
   One stands, given a grain of goodwill, a fair chance of
actually seeing the whirling dervish, Tumult, son of
Thunder.   FW, 184
Waiting for the return of the gods
witnessing the return of barbarism
                       the new barbarians

Engels, on *The Origina of the Family, Private Property*
and the State:
the origin—the coming-into-being and the passing-
away—
"Indeed, only barbarians are capable of rejuvenating
a world laboring under the death throes of unnerved
civilization."
Vico is right
Engels is right—
    Here is that synthesis that Gramsci sought:
    Vico and Marxism reconciled—
Mao is right—
    The Great Cultural Revolution was to detach
communism from civilization. The civilized world
looked on and could not believe its eyes.
Waiting for the return of the gods
witnessing the return of barbarism
The new barbarians
   returning to primitive simplicity of the first world of
peoples   NS, 1106
to recognize the gods
to greet them
Dei dialectus soloecismus—the dialect of God is   *Love's Body,*
                       solecism.   239
God does not speak good English.
Not atticism but solecism.
Barbarism.

Barbarism, or speaking with tongues
          as in *Finnegans Wake*
          polyglot turning into glossolalia
Pentecost
   wordloosed over seven seas crowdblast in cellellene-
teutoslavzendlatinsoundscript.   FW, 219
   In the buginning is the woid, in the muddle is the
sounddance.   FW, 378
Instead of the sentence, the sounddance.

AVANT GARDE MUSIC

From
Writing for the Second Time through *Finnegans Wake*

John Cage

In 1939 I bought a copy of *Finnegans Wake* in a department store in Seattle, Washington. I had read the parts of *Work in Progress* as they appeared in transition. I used outloud to entertain friends with *The Ondt and the Gracehoper*. But even though I owned a copy, no matter where I lived, the *Wake* simply sat on a table or shelf unread. I was "too busy" writing music to read it.

In 1942 Janet Fairbanks asked me for a song. I browsed in the *Wake* looking for a lyrical passage. The one I chose begins page 556. I changed the paragraph so that it became two and read as follows:

> "Night by silentsailing night, Isobel, wildwood's eyes and primarose hair, quietly, all the woods so wild, in mauves of moss and daphnedews, how all so still she lay, neath of the whitethorn, child of tree, like some losthappy leaf, like blowing flower stilled, as fain would she anon, for soon again 'twill be, win me, woo me, wed me, ah weary me! deeply, now evencalm lay sleeping.
>
> "Night, Isobel, sister Isobel, Saintette Isobelle, Madame Isa Veuve La Belle."

The title I chose was one of Joyce's descriptions of her, *The Wonderful Widow of Eighteen Springs*.

I remember looking in later years several times for other lyrical passages in the *Wake*. But I never settled on one as the text for another song.

In the middle 'sixties Marshall McLuhan suggested that I make a musical work based on the *Wake's* Ten Thunderclaps. He said that the Thunderclaps were, in fact, a history of technology. This led me to think of Jasper Johns' *Painted Bronze* (the cans of ale) and to imagine a concert for string orchestra and voices, with the addition towards the end of wind instruments. The orchestra would play notes traced from star maps (*Atlas Borealis*) but due to contact microphones and suitable circuitry the tones would sound like rain falling, at first, say, on water, then on earth, then wood, clay, metal, cement, etc., finally not falling, just being in the air, our present circumstance. The chorus meanwhile would sing the Thunderclaps, which would then be electronically transformed to fill up the sound envelopes of an actual thunderstorm. I had planned to do this with Lejaren Hiller at the University of Illinois 1968-9, but *HPSCHD* took two years rather than one to make and produce.

Due to N. O. Brown's remark that syntax is the arrangement of the army, and Thoreau's that when he heard a sentence he heard feet marching, I became devoted to nonsyntactical "demilitarized" language. I spent well over a year writing *Empty Words*, a transition from a language without sentences (having only phrases, words, syllables, and letters) to a "language" having only letters and silence (music). This led me to want to learn something about the ancient Chinese language and to read *Finnegans Wake*. But when in this spirit I picked up the book, Joyce seemed to me to have kept the old structures ("sintalks") in which he put the new words he had made.

It was when I was in this frame of mind that Elliott Anderson, editor of *TriQuarterly*, wrote asking me to write something (anything, text or music) for an issue of the magazine to be devoted to the *Wake* (In the wake of the *Wake*). I said I was too busy. I was. I was writing *Renga* and had not yet started *Apartment House 1776* the performance date of which had already been set. Anderson replied that his deadline could be changed. I refused again and again. He persisted.

Anderson was not the first person to bother me by asking me to do something when I was busy doing something else. We continually bother one another with birthdays, deadlines, celebrations, blurbs, fund raising, requests for information, interviews, letters of introduction, letters of recommendation. To turn irritation into pleasure I've made the practice, for more than ten years now, of writing

mesostics (not acrostics: row down the middle, not down the edge).
What makes a mesostic as far as I'm concerned is that the first letter
of a word or name is on the first line and following it on the first line
the second letter of the word or name is *not* to be found. (The second letter is on the second line.) When, for instance, we were in a
bus in Northern Michigan on our way to hunt morels (Interlochen
music students were asking me what a mesostic was), I wrote

"Music . . .

(the M without an O after it)

"Music
cOnducted . . .

(the O without an R) (the word "performed" would not have worked)

"Music
cOnducted
in sp R ing . . .

(the R without an E)

". . . by tr E es: . . .

(the E without an L)

". . . dutch e L m disease."

To bring my correspondence with Elliott Anderson to a temporary
halt, I opened *Finnegans Wake* at random (page 356). I began looking
for a J without an A. And then for the next A without an M. Et-
cetera. I continued finding Joyce and James to the end of the chapter. I wrote twenty-three mesostics in all.

I then started near the end of the book (I couldn't wait) for I knew
how seductive the last pages of *Finnegan* are.

my lips went livid for from the J oy
of fe A r
like alMost now. how? how you said
how you'd giv E me
the key S of me heart.
J ust a whisk brisk sly spry spink
spank sprint Of a thing
i pit Y your oldself i was used to,
a C loud.
in p E ace

Having found these, I looked for those at the beginning and, finally, as Joyce had done, I began at the end and continued with the
beginning:

J ust
A
May i
b E wrong!

for S he'll be sweet for you as i was
sweet when i came down out of
me mother.
J hem
Or shen [brewed by arclight]
and ror Y end
through all C hristian
minstr E lsy.

The bracketed words are the ones I'd have omitted if it were just
now I had written them. There were choices to be made, decisions
as to which words were to be kept, which omitted. It was a disci-
pline similar to that of counterpoint in music with a cantus firmus.
My tendency was towards more omission rather than less.

J ust a whisk brisk sly spry
spink. . .

became

J ust a whisk
Of
pit Y
a C loud
in p E ace and silence.

And a further omission was suggested by Norman O. Brown, that
of punctuation, a suggestion I quickly acted on. Subsequently, the
omitted marks were kept, not in the mesostics but on the pages
where they originally appeared, the marks disposed in the space
and those other than periods given an orientation by means of *I
Ching* chance operations. Where, in all this work, Joyce used italics,
so have I. My marginal figures are source pages of the Viking Press
edition of *Finnegan*.

Stuck in the *Wake*. I couldn't get out. I was full of curiosity about
all of it. I read *A Skeleton Key*. . . . Ihab Hassan gave me his book,
Paracriticisms, and two others: Adaline Glasheen's *a second census of
finnegans wake* and Clive Hart's *Structure and Motif*. . . . I continued
to read and write my way through all of *Finnegans Wake*.

Finnegans Wake has six hundred twenty-five pages. Once finished,
my *Writing Through Finnegans Wake* had one hundred fifteen pages.
My editor at Wesleyan University Press, J. R. de la Torre Bueno,
finding it too long, suggested that I shorten it. Instead of doing that,
I wrote a new series of mesostics, *Writing for the Second Time Through
Finnegans Wake*, in which I did not permit the reappearance of a
syllable for a given letter of the name. I distinguished between the
two J's and the two E's. The syllable "just" could be used twice,

once for the J of James and once for the J of Joyce, since it has neither A nor O after the J. But it could not be used again. To keep from repeating syllables, I kept a card index of the ones I had already used. As I guessed, this restriction made a text considerably shorter, forty pages in all.

My work was only sometimes that of identifying, as Duchamp had, found objects. The text for *TriQuarterly* is *7 out of 23.* Seven mesostics were straight quotations, e.g., this one from page 383:

> he J ust slumped to throne
> so s A iled the stout ship *nansy hans.*
> froM liff away.
> for natt E nlaender.
> a S who has come returns.

In such a case my work was merely to show, by giving it a five-line structure, the relation of Joyce's text to his name, a relationship that was surely in these instances not in his mind, though at many points, as Adaline Glasheen cheerfully lists, his name was in his mind, alone or in combination with another name, for example, "poorjoist" (page 113), and "joysis crisis" (page 395).

When I was composing my *Sonatas and Interludes,* which I did at the piano, friends used to want to know what familiar tunes, *God Save the King* for instance, would sound like due to the preparations between the strings. I found their curiosity offensive, and similarly from time to time in the course of this work I've had my doubts about the validity of finding in *Finnegans Wake* these mesostics on his name which James Joyce didn't put there. However I just went straight on, A after J, E after M, J after S, Y after O, E after C. I read each passage at least three times and once or twice upside down. (Hazel Dreis, who taught us English binding, used to tell us how she proofread the *Leaves of Grass,* an edition of which she bound for San Francisco's Grabhorn Press: upside down and backwards. When you don't know what you're doing, you do your work very well.) J's can thus be spotted by their dots and by their dipping below the line which i's don't do. Difficult letters to catch are the commonest ones, the vowels. And the consonants escape our notice in empty words, words the mind skips over. I am native to detailed attention, though I often make mistakes: I was born early in September. But I found myself from time to time bursting into laughter (this, not when the *Wake* was upside down). The play of sex and church and food and drink in an all time all space world turned family was not only regaling: it Joyced me (in places, that is, where Thoreau hadn't, couldn't, where, left to myself, I wouldn't've). I don't know whom to connect with Joyce ("We connect Satie with Thoreau"). Duchamp stands, I'd say, somewhere between. He is, like Joyce, alone. They *are* connected. For that and many other reasons. But that's something else to do.

I am grateful to Elliott Anderson for his persistence, and to the Trustees of the James Joyce Estate for permitting the publication of this work.

New York City, May 1977

I

wroth with twone nathan J oe   3
A
Malt
jh E m
S hen

pft J schute
sOlid man
that the humpt Y hillhead of humself
is at the kno C k out
in th E park

J iccup   4
the f A ther
Most
h E aven
S kysign

J udges
Or
deuteronomY
wats C h
futur E

pentschan J euchy
ch A p
Mighty
c E ment
and edifice S

the J ebel and the   5
crO pherb
fl Y day
and she all C asually
ansars h E lpers

J ollybrool
A nd
strupithuMp   6
and all th E uproor
aufroof S

to f J ell
his baywinds' O boboes
all the livv Y long   7
tri C ky
troch E es

whase on the J oint
wh A se
faoMous
old E
a S you

J amey
O ur   8
countr Y
is a ffrin C h
sorac E r this is

the grand mons in J un this is
the A lps hooping to sheltershock
the three lipoleuMs this is
th E ir
legahorn S

                    J innies
                is a cOoin her
              phillipp Y   9
                dispat C h
          to irrigat E the willingdone

                    the J innies
                   font A nnoy
              bode belchuM
                  bonn E t
                to bu S by

this is the hinndoo waxing ran J ymad   10
                    fOr
        the hinndoo seebo Y
                    C ry
        to the willingdon E . . . .

FOR THE SINGER

THE WORDS OF THIS SONG ARE ADAPTED FROM PAGE 556 OF
JAMES JOYCE'S FINNEGANS WAKE.
SING WITHOUT VIBRATO, AS IN FOLK-SINGING.
MAKE ANY TRANSPOSITION NECESSARY IN ORDER TO
EMPLOY A LOW AND COMFORTABLE RANGE.

FOR THE PIANIST

CLOSE A GRAND PIANO COMPLETELY (STRINGS + KEYBOARD).

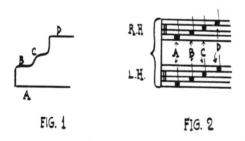

FIG. 1   FIG. 2

FIG. 1 SHOWS A CROSS-SECTION OF THE PIANO SO CLOSED. 'A'
INDICATES THE UNDER PART OF THE PIANO STRUCTURE,
AND IS NOTATED AS SHOWN IN FIG. 2 ON THE 1ST SPACE
OF THE PERCUSSION STAFF; 'B' INDICATES THE FRONT
PART OF THE KEYBOARD-LID, 'C', ITS BACK AND HIGHER
PART (THEY ARE NOTATED RESPECTIVELY ON THE 2nd +
THIRD SPACES); 'D' INDICATES THE TOP OF THE PIANO.
♩ = PLAY WITH FINGERS ; ✗ = PLAY WITH KNUCKLES
OF CLOSED HAND.

THE WONDERFUL WIDOW OF EIGHTEEN SPRINGS

John Cage

John Cage's instructions to the performer on how to rap a closed piano case and the first few bars of his The Wonderful Widow of Eighteen Springs, *his setting of a passage from* Finnegans Wake. *(Copyright © 1961 by Henmar Press, Inc. Reprinted by permission of C.F. Peters Corporation.)*

Texte

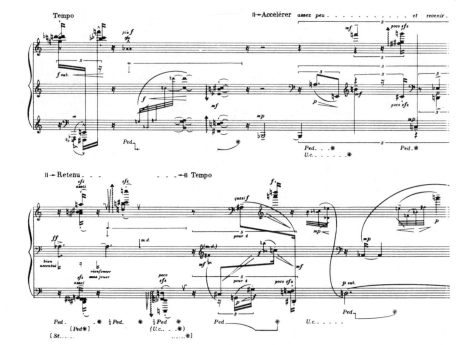

Under the influence of Joyce, Pierre Boulez used such literary section titles as "Chapter," "Text," "Gloss," "Parenthesis," and "Commentary." Here the "Texte" of Sonata III for piano. (From Pierre Boulez - TROISIEME SONATE POUR PIANO, FORMANT - TROPE "TEXTE." © Copyright 1961 by Universal Edition (London) Ltd., London. All rights reserved. Used by permission of European American Music Distributors Corporation, sole U.S. agent for Universal Edition.)

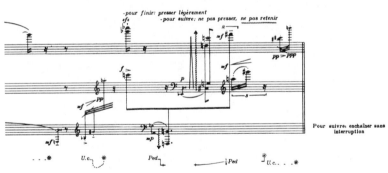

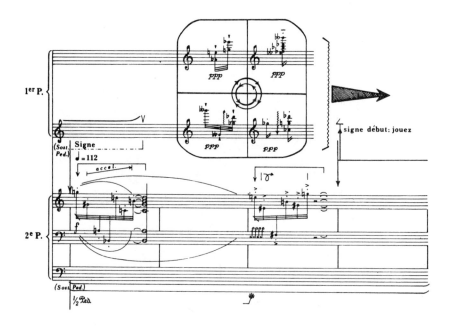

Pierre Boulez reflected Joyce's cyclic structures and aleatory techniques in the two pianos of Structures II. *(From Pierre Boulez - STRUCTURES - DEUXIEME LIVRE (1961). © Copyright 1967 by Universal Edition (London) Ltd., London. All rights reserved. Used by permission of European American Music Distributors Corporation, sole U.S. agent for Universal Edition.)*

ABSTRACT ART

The Double Image Of Modernism: Matisse's Etchings For Ulysses

Shari Benstock

What we know of the circumstances surrounding the Limited Editions Club 1935 publication of Joyce's *Ulysses*, illustrated with line drawings by Henri Matisse, is sketchy—legend having supplanted meager fact. Richard Ellmann's account of the proceedings in his biography of Joyce suggests that the artistic crux of the matter is to be found in Matisse's ignorance of the text. In contradiction to this suggestion, George Macy (then publisher of Limited Editions) recorded his surprise at Matisse's announcement to him in 1934 that after a quick page-through of Stuart Gilbert's translation of the novel, "he had observed how Joyce's *Ulysses* was divided into episodes corresponding to Homer's *Odyssey* and would Macy agree therefore to his making six etchings based on Homer's *Odyssey* which could then be published in the Joyce volume."[1] Joyce would have liked to believe (perhaps *did* believe) that Matisse knew "the French translation very well," as he wrote to T. W. Pugh in August, 1934. Wherever Matisse came upon the Homeric correspondences in

---

[1]Alfred J. Barr, *Matisse: His Work and His Public* (New York: The Museum of Modern Art, 1951), p. 249.

Ulysses (perhaps from Gilbert's study of the epic backgrounds to the novel), he did not know the novel well, and to the extent that he needed to know about it to begin work on the line drawings, he consulted Eugene Jolas during a week-end visit to Jolas' summer residence in Utelle. Ellmann relates that after a brief introduction to the work by Jolas, Matisse "went his own way, in the late summer and early fall of 1934; when asked why his drawings bore so little relation to the book, he said frankly, 'Je ne l'ai pas lu.' "[2]

The relationship that Matisse's drawings bear to Homer's *Odyssey* is presumably of less import, then, than their apparent disregard of Joyce's text. Thus, the usual exclamations of surprise from Joyceans ("But they have nothing to do with *Ulysses!*") may well be accurate enough, and might even have been Joyce's own remarks. And if one were suspicious as to the motives that impelled an American publisher to solicit a French painter to illustrate a book written by an Irishman and based, in some degree, on a Greek epic, art critic Thomas Craven's denouncement of the drawings might well serve as the last word on the efficacy of such a project: "as it turned out, Matisse delivered to Mr. Macy a bunch of studio sweepings having no discoverable connection with anything in Homer or Joyce."[3] An effort to render that "discoverable connection" has produced this study; although Matisse clearly chose to approach the Homeric materials directly, rather than through Joyce, a closer examination of the six illustrations and the sketches for them suggests that Matisse's method rather cleverly complemented that of the *Ulysses* text in ways that even Joyceans, much less art critics, might appreciate. . . .

The Matisse illustrations, if we can call them that, approach their subject gnomonically, assuming a narrative background that is barely hinted at, much less developed. In this respect their technique might be said to resemble Joyce's effort in *Dubliners*, where meaning is shadowed forth by a method of intimation: we measure what is "there" by what is not "there." But even a statement such as this does disservice to these drawings and to Matisse's artistic method, since it implies that his effort should be defined in terms of Joyce's. In fact, this unusual textual setting legislates against such an approach by providing an opportunity for two important figures of modernism to approach the same allusive materials—Homer's epic poem—from different viewpoints, through dissimilar mediums, ex-

---

[2]Richard Ellmann, *James Joyce* (New York: Viking Press, 1957), p. 687.
[3]George Macy et al., *Quarto-Millenary: The First 250 Publications . . . of The Limited Editions Club* (New York: Limited Editions Club, 1959), p. 36.

ploiting discrete aspects of the subject. Matisse's line drawings,
then, are as "Matissist" as Joyce's text is "Joycean." In examining
the counterpoint of text against illustration, it may prove valuable
first to comment on specific aspects of Matisse's method, subor-
dinating speculation about his knowledge of *Ulysses* to the more appropriate realm of guesswork, and to assess the drawings as works
of art in their own right rather than merely as illuminations of a
primary narrative subject. More valuable still might be a broader
assessment of the modernist principles that seem to have guided
these respective creations, the ways in which Matisse and Joyce may
have shared similar insights into Homer's classical world and its re-
fraction in art and literature of the early twentieth century.

It is a hallmark of modernism that art is unceasingly self-conscious, constantly probing the motivations behind its own production, inspecting the means through which the initial impetus is
turned into a completed work of art, preoccupied with the tenuous,
often obscure, relationship between artist and artifact. Joyce's pen-
chant for introspection and self-scrutiny is well known, but the impulse is no less evident upon examination of Matisse's work. These
two artists share an almost compulsive stylistic self-consciousness,
but the pattern of their questioning differs significantly. Whereas
Joyce's artistic development occurs in a nearly linear, predetermined
progression that treats the same subject matter (Dublin and Dubliners) in a increasingly complex rhetoric, beginning with the scru-
pulous meanness of *Dubliners* and arriving at the verbal embel-
lishments of *Finnegans Wake*, Matisse's progress appears to be
circular. . . .

In choosing scenes from *Ulysses* to illustrate, it is significant that
Matisse focused on the women in Homer's epic, choosing to draw
three females (Calypso, Nausicaa, and Circe), only one male (Polyphemus, although Odysseus is present in this illustration as well as
in Nausicaa), one landscape (Ithaca), and a final plate which shows
a barely representational bag of winds (Aeolus). In the six plates and
nineteen drafts which are included with the plates, it is the female
form which dominates. Interestingly, however, Matisse did not
choose to illustrate Penelope, who—in *Ulysses*, at least—remains the
quintessence of all that is female, two of whose cardinal points
(breasts and bottom) were favorite subjects for Matisse's delicate
lines, and whose symbolic 8 turns on its side to become the sign of
infinity, or the "countersign" for Bloom's eternity—a figure that offers the rounded curves common to Matisse's women. It is Molly
Bloom who contains all possibilities for a delineated human, female

shape—one which is curved, oblate, self-contained, and eminently opulent. But Molly as Penelope is foreshadowed by Calypso, Nausicaa, and Circe—all of whom are somehow contained within her earthy femininity—and Matisse's rendering of these women suggests in graphic terms the outlines of Molly's "adipose posterior female hemispheres, redolent of milk and honey and of excretory sanguine and seminal warmth, reminiscent of secular families of curves of amplitude, insusceptible of moods of impression or of contrarieties of expression, expressive of mute immutable mature animality" (*U*, p. 734).[4] The "curves of amplitude" described so excessively and compulsively in Joyce's prose are superscribed by Matisse in sparse, extended lines, devoid of detail. And any one of Matisse's women might have been—or become—the Penelope/Molly of the "mellonous rump."

That immutable mature female animality which so enthralled Joyce is best represented in Matisse by the Calypso sketches (see figures 1 and 2). What is troublesome to the reader of *Ulysses* (or *The Odyssey*) is the double female image, portrayed either in the grip of passion or conflict—or some hybrid including both. The upper figure in the first sketch is seen swooping down on a semi-reclining female whose rounded abdomen suggests pregnancy and whose posture is one of resistance, using the left foot and arm to ward off the encroaching figure. The rhetorical basis for this depiction of Calypso is speculative at best, since Homer's epic in no way suggests that she is a "double" or in any other way functions in a dual role. She is described, singularly, as "a nymph, immortal and most beautiful."[5] Neither does Homer hint at some kind of female warfare in this episode, although there is another female goddess hovering over Calypso's island cave. Pallas Athena's intervention in human concerns is by means more subtle, however, than direct confrontation or conquest: she employs Hermes (a male) as her intermediary in releasing the enthralled Odysseus from Calypso's charms (Book V, p. 82). Joyce is of little more help than Homer in illuminating Matisse's intent: his Calypso rules the chapter in which we first meet Leopold and Molly Bloom, and she is graphically represented in the *Bath of the Nymph* which hangs over the Bloom bed. But Calypso is physically present in this chapter as Molly herself (who remains *in* the bed), and who—for most of the hour—keeps Bloom

[4]James Joyce's *Ulysses*; parenthetical page references are to the 1961 Random House edition.
[5]*The Odyssey*, trans. Robert Fitzgerald (Garden City, N.Y.: Anchor Books. 1963), Book I, p.2. Hereafter cited parenthetically in the text.

within the confines of her own cave: the bedroom. While it is possible that Matisse imagined in this episode a kind of mental grappling, present in Odysseus' mind if not in Bloom's, between the wife to whom he longs to return and the cave-queen who has kept him enchanted for so long, the implied conflict present in the early versions of this plate has been replaced by a complex evolution of form, one female growing out of another.

It is highly likely that one of the thematic tools Jolas provided Matisse in their discussions was the link between Molly and the nymph Calypso that exists in the concept of "metempsychosis," the word in *Ruby, Pride of the Ring* which Molly does not understand and which is "illustrated" for her by Bloom in an example. The particular example is suggested by the picture of the nymph at her bath ("Naked nymphs: Greece"): "Metempsychosis, he said, is what the ancient Greeks called it. . . . What they called nymphs, for example" (*U*, p. 65). Possibly the intertwined figures are supposed to represent the notion of such a spiritual evolution. The shapes of the women are strikingly alike, suggesting a similarity of type—huge of thigh and breast, with ovoid faces and firm, rounded breasts—to which Bloom, as modern Odysseus, is fatally attracted.

Importantly, the alterations between the first sketch and the last (there are two more which intervene) indicate a change of artistic direction: the raised arms of the upper figure in the first plate suggest a flailing motion against which the lower figure resists, though the expression of swooning on the face of the reclining figure makes the tone of the sketch ambiguous. By the final plate (figure 2), however, the upper figure has developed a large left arm which extends onto the lower figure and ends with its mid-forearm sunk into the bosom of the reclining figure. As the plate has evolved, the thighs of both women have ballooned in typical Matisse fashion, the women have lost all distinguishing features—eyes, nose, mouth, hair, hands, and feet—and the breasts have become disproportionately small, appearing to be almost arbitrarily placed on the human frame. Matisse has moved from the representational to the symbolic as he does in each of the illustrative plates, distilling in the final drawings figures that are hairless, faceless, almost inhuman models. The "action" of this illustration hints at a rhetorical construct which is not present in the picture, not present in *The Odyssey*, and only subjectively evident in *Ulysses*: the possible evolution of Molly out of Calypso through a figural "transmigration of souls." The hint of gestation present in the voluptuous lower figure of the first plate may have given birth in the final drawing to a graphic metempsychosis.

That the figures seem to have lost their individuality, perhaps even their femininity by the final frame is significant, too, since if Molly Bloom is also Calypso, she is so only on an abstract, symbolic, and nonhuman level.

If the double image of Calypso is problematic for Joyce's *Ulysses*, the triple image of Nausicaa is not. Although Matisse's decision to illustrate three women posed in a line (see figure 3) may have been arbitrary, it seems more than coincidental that in *Ulysses* Gerty Mac-Dowell (the resident Nausicaa) is accompanied by Cissy Caffrey and Edy Boardman on Sandymount strand. And while Homer is unclear as to the precise number of maids accompanying his Nausicaa ("Princess and maids delighted in that feast; / then, putting off their veils, / they ran and passed a ball to a rhythmic beat, / Nausikaa flashing first with her white arms"—Book VI, p. 102), Joyce is not: "The three girl friends were seated on the rocks, enjoying the evening scene" (*U*, p. 346). Apart from the triumvirate of women present in this sketch, it adheres in all other respects to Homer's account, even to the extent of clothing the females in quasi-Greek garb gazing at a naked Odysseus; this first sketch is "realistic" even to the degree of giving facial features and individualized expressions of the figures. By the final plate (figure 5), the women have been denuded and divested of all distinguishing features; they have become "modern" rather than "classic," and the rhetorical import of the encounter with Odysseus has been dismissed.

There are five sketches for the Nausicaa plate, more than for any other illustration except The Blinding of Polyphemus, and two of these are of Odysseus alone. As in *Male Model*, the figure is muscular, with an obviously powerful physique, rippled with sinuous fiber (see figure 4). But in the various sketches of Odysseus Matisse appears to be experimenting with the mood he wishes to create in his epic hero. The first composite sketch clearly shows a surprised Odysseus, caught unaware in the embarrassment of his own nakedness (figure 3), while the sketch of Odysseus alone (figure 4) shows less obvious surprise, and the facial expression hints at supplication rather than alarm, as the arm gesture beckons rather than dismisses. By the final lithograph (figure 5), however, the extended arm and flattened hand clearly indicate Odysseus' desire to have the women depart, and the head—now devoid of facial features—illustrates in its rigid backward thrust and the sweep of hair, tossed back as if by a wind, the need to push away the intruding females. The stance is aggressive and powerful, and the movement of the form is toward the women, evident in the outstretched hand and bended knee, whereas the mood is clearly one of fending off, keeping the intruders at bay.

The tone of this sketch is in keeping neither with Homer's description of the scene nor with Joyce's in which Bloom is the observer, clearly within view of the girls, but shadowed by the falling dusk of the summer evening. In Homer's version, Odysseus is not discovered by the women, as he seems to be in Matisse's sketch, but is described as advancing upon them:

> He pushed aside the bushes, breaking off
> with his great hand a single branch of olive,
> whose leaves might shield him in his nakedness; . . .
> Odysseus had this look, in his rough skin
> advancing on the girls with pretty braids;
> and he was driven on by hunger, too.
> Streaked with brine, and swollen, he terrified them,
> so that they fled this way and that. Only
> Alkínoös' daughter stood her ground, being given
> a bold heart by Athena, and steady knees. (Book VI, p. 103)

Matisse's version clearly shows an Odysseus taken by surprise as the three pretty maids in a row calmly appear in the early sketch (which records facial expressions), staunchly aligned, fearless, and dominant against an Odysseus who appears through foreshortening to be smaller and somehow vulnerable in his nakedness despite his brute strength. Apart from the fact that the center female figure clasps the other two around the shoulders, there is no indication as to which of the women is Nausicaa, and the expressions on the faces belie any difference of attitude: Nausicaa looks neither more nor less in control than her compatriots. By the final sketch (figure 5), the women too have been stripped of their garments and are revealed in their heavy-thighed and full-busted girth, their faces wiped of any human features. The extended arm of Odysseus, which had originally been raised in an oblique form of greeting and placed at Nausicaa's sashed waist, is now placed firmly against her navel, as though she in particular were being rebuffed. . . .

In contrast, the sketches for Circe are capricious, whimsical in tone, hinting not at the darker side of her seductive power (the ability to turn men into swine) but at that which makes her so irresistible—her charm and sexual allure. In the first sketch (figure 6), Matisse delineates a recognizably human woman, complete with facial features, hair, even a suggestion that she is wearing dancing shoes (the only piece of clothing on her naked body). She is posed in mid-somersault, and the sketch suggests movement in a lithe body totally unlike the heavy women of Nausicaa or the full-thighed figures in Calypso. Matisse's Circe is delicate: small of waist, with firm, beautifully-shaped thighs and buttocks, slim ankles and small feet, displaying round breasts and shapely, slim arms. She is perhaps a dancer or an acrobat, but she is certainly a coquette, a flirt doing tricks to seduce her victim and daring him to be seduced. The smile hidden by her arms is revealed in the twinkle of her eyes. Importantly, there is a quality of vulnerability about this woman, a suggestion that her power lies in guile and unpredictability rather than in the earthy, Gea-Tellus sensuality that has characterized her counterparts: she displays less of the pendulous womanhood of Molly Bloom than the little-girl charm of Milly Bloom.

This first sketch is compelling, too, because Circe is alone, a single extended figure looped upwards against a blank background. But in the following sketches and the final lithograph, Circe has disappeared, her personality lost in a sea of upturned limbs, bent legs, and globular heads. By the final sketch (figure 7), there is no charm, no allure, no sense of playfulness inhering in her personality. The overturned body with firm, round breasts is barely distinguishable amidst a flat, cluttered entanglement of incomplete female forms. If the attempt has been to suggest various positions of female seduction, its effect has been lost, I think, drained of meaning by a distortion of the clarity of tone so evident in the opening sketch. Of the lithographs which illustrate human forms, this is the most disappointing; one wishes that Matisse had stayed with his singular Circe, and one is grateful for the decision by the Limited Editions Club to include the various sketches for each lithograph.

Matisse's image of Circe bears a much closer resemblance to Homer's description of her than to Joyce's Dublin brothel madame, Bella Cohen. Homer's Circe is described as being "*quick as a cat*" (Book X, p. 174), and indeed there is something feline in the arched figure drawn by Matisse. Joyce's Circe is by contrast "*a massive whoremistress*" (*U*, p. 527), with "*deeply carboned*" eyes, sprouting a moustache on a heavy face, "*slightly sweated and fullnosed, with orange-tainted nostril.*" Bella is presented from the outset as latently masculine, and her psychodramatic alteration from female to male (Bella to Bello) is completely within character. There is nothing here of the slim, young, seductive Circe who beguiles her lovers by her singing. The conception of Circe represents a departure for Matisse in the portrayal of women, but she seems particularly antithetical to Joyce's Circe as well, simply because she appears to be so young; although obviously not innocent, she does not display the middle-aged cynicism typifying Madame Cohen, and whereas Matisse's women are often heavy and powerful in their femaleness, they are never masculine. Homer's Circe (and Matisse's) turns men to swine by her craft, beguiling her lovers with song and wit; Joyce's Circe commands by a power that is essentially virile, as her fan-wand explains: "the missus is master" (U, p. 527).

When Matisse turns his pen toward the masculine—toward brute strength and latent power—he does so in The Blinding of Polyphemus, a drawing that bestows strength on the physically smaller man (Odysseus) and shows helplessness in the over-sized, lionesque giant (the Cyclops). Like the Nausicaa sketches, the one for Cyclops is carefully worked through a number of separate drafts which are included in the text, and the stages of development demonstrate an intense probing of violent movement and reflected pain. As figures 8 and 10 illustrate, the intensity of the violence is essentially purged by the final sketch, in part by the purified lines and the amount of white space surrounding the two figures. Both Matisse and Joyce were well-known pacifists who shied away from physical violence and confrontation. Joyce goes to some lengths in the Cyclops chapter of Ulysses to treat the incipient violence of the scene on the verbal level only and to reduce the potential danger for Bloom to a misfired biscuit-tin leveled at him from the doorway of Kiernan's pub as he escapes in a carriage. But Matisse's drawing turns to Homer's text, to the grim details laid bare by the description of the pain inflicted on the brutish Polyphemus by the searing heat of the birch spike; interestingly, it takes four men, plus Odysseus, to hoist the spear into the Cyclops' eye—whereas in both the Matisse and Joyce versions, Odysseus-Bloom (whose spear is a large cigar) acts alone:

> straight
> forward they sprinted, lifted it, and rammed it
> deep in his crater eye, and I leaned on it
> turning it as a shipwright turns a drill
> in planking, having men below to
> swing the two-handled strap that spins it in the groove.
> So with our brand we bored that great eye socket
> while blood ran out around the red hot bar.
> Eyelid and lash were seared; the pierced ball
> hissed broiling, and the roots popped. (Book IX, p. 156)

Matisse began, of course, with a conception of Polyphemus in human form and probably drew on the struggles between Hercules and Antaeus shown in a painting by Antonio Pollaiuolo in the

Uffizi.[6] Matisse's Polyphemus bears a striking resemblance to the Hercules of this painting, turned on his backside in the position of victim. The details of figure 9 show clearly Matisse's concern with the human elements in this drama of the unsuspecting victim, one foot raised in pain, or surprise, the left arm dangling at an odd angle, helpless. But by the final version, the human emphasis is no longer present; Polyphemus is faceless, and the red hot stick bores into what is now only a mass of hair, suggesting a lionesque form rather than the human. The body is no longer muscular and contracted but has developed an almost feminine roundness of line, the curved buttocks and fat thighs reminiscent of Calypso and Nausicaa. Odysseus, who had never assumed an important part in Matisse's conception of this configuration, is kept well in the background, significantly smaller than the giant Cyclops, with arms that are rectilinear in contrast to the sensuous curves of the flailing giant. As with the Circe representation, it seems that by a process of distillation, so common to Matisse's work, the final plate has lost the intensity, surprise, anger, and pain that is reflected in the earlier versions of the scene.

It seems rather obvious, when one looks at the collected illustrations, that Matisse has expressed in them a very individual conception of the Homeric/Joycean subject. In contrast to the epic proportions of Homer's poem or Joyce's novel, Matisse's lithographs are exceedingly slight, suggesting (to some) that his intention was marred by a naîveté, almost a simplemindedness, which prevented him from delineating the intellectual content of his subject or reflecting the massive proportions appropriate to the epic. Matisse's method, then, might better be put to use illustrating fragile symbolist poems (such as Mallarmé's) than in confronting a large-scale drama such as *Ulysses*. Since Matisse chose to address Homer directly and Joyce only obliquely, his insistence upon illustrating the human interest of the story, rather than the manipulation of its events by gods and goddesses, is significant. No Hermes, Zeus, or Pallas Athena appears in these drawings; the principals are Odysseus, "that man skilled in all ways of contending, / the wanderer, harried for years on end" (Book I, p. 2), and the giants and nymphs against whom he must prevail. In the single instance in which Matisse chooses to delineate a goddess, Circe, he begins with a recognizably human, girlish conception, smaller and more vulnerable than his Calypso and Nausicaa, displaying a whimsical humor un-

---

[6]Barr, p. 249 illustration is more closely related to the Lucas van Leyden.

known to Homer's Circe of "dire beauty and divine" (Book X, p. 169).

Matisse joins Joyce, then, in emphasizing the human context of *Ulysses*, stressing a treatment of his subject which is both amoral and sympathetic. Behind this conception lies the notion that the classical world is not sealed or "dead," but open to reassessment and restatement, that its subjects need not be consigned to an irrelevant past or approached with a reverent, Victorian, belief in the High Seriousness of classical themes. Significantly, too, the moralistic assumptions of a T. S. Eliot, who views modern degeneration against an arbitrary standard of excellence typified in the glory of Greece and the grandeur of Rome, is not available to Joyce and Matisse, who share an essentially amoral and humanistic view of the world. Central to the modernist construct is its insistence upon the human dimensions of its subject, even when that subject is drawn from the classical past rather than from the present; thus, the moral implications of Odysseus' struggle to return to Ithaca are subordinated to the essential humanness of his *desire* to return. In Joyce and Matisse, Odysseus is reduced in stature but broadened in the scope of his humanity: Leopold Bloom is both more and less than his epic counterpart, and Matisse's Ulysses is always presented as smaller than, and significantly vulnerable to, those whom he encounters and is struggling to escape from. It is now a commonplace of criticism that Joyce's comic vision is in its application both amoral and humorous (and therefore modernist); although Matisse never reaches the level of Joycean irony—perhaps because he is neither Irish nor Jesuit trained—he certainly displays a gentle good humor which contributes to a nonjudgmental and loving treatment of his subject, qualities that are common to Joyce's art as well. By shifting the focus toward the human level rather than elevating the epic and theocratic, these two modernists insist upon the pre-eminence of man in a world no longer controlled by capricious gods who sport with the lives of mere mortals, but a world where man is caught by coincidence and wins not through struggle but through equanimious good humor. . . .

Figure 1

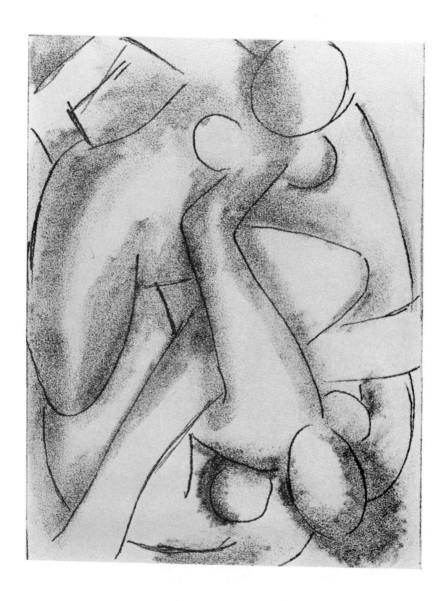

Figure 2

Figure 3

Figure 4

Figure 5

Figure 6

Figure 7

Figure 8

Figure 9

Figure 10

James Joyce and the First Generation New York School

Evan R. Firestone

The artists of the first generation New York School, most of whom are known collectively as Abstract Expressionists, were as a group generally well-read or well-informed and in touch with the literary currents of their time. Non-fiction works by Nietzsche, Freud, Jung, and James Frazer combined on their reading lists with the writings of Baudelaire, the French Symbolist poets (especially Rimbaud), Herman Melville, André Breton and Garcia Lorca, among others. Although scholars have examined the connections between this group of artists and literature rather carefully, except in the case of David Smith there has been relatively little mention of James Joyce.[1] This is surprising since Joyce is considered by many to be one of the greatest writers of fiction in the twentieth century, and a number of first generation New York School artists have acknowledged their interest in him. For example, James Brooks, speaking of his friend Bradley Walker Tomlin, said, "I think a writer who influenced most of us, and I think him pretty strongly, certainly one who influenced me more than any painter, was James Joyce."[2] Others of this generation who have indicated admiration for Joyce include Robert Motherwell, Jackson Pollock, Philip Guston, Barnett Newman, Jack Tworkov, Ad Reinhardt, and Tony Smith.

A number of characteristics of his writing appealed to American artists of the 1940s and '50s, but initially, it was Joyce's "stream of consciousness" technique that attracted them. Joyce's method of directly conveying his characters' unedited interior thoughts, begun in *A Portrait of the Artist as a Young Man*, and expanded in *Ulysses*, provided another literary equivalent of the visual automatism they were struggling to develop. In Robert Motherwell's case, his appreciation of Joyce preceded his preoccupation with the "automatic writing" of the Surrealists. His conviction that a modern artist must be experimental was in part formed by his reading and intense discussion of *Ulysses* while a student at Stanford University in the mid-1930s.[3] The implications of Joyce's writing must have further crystallized for Motherwell when he discovered Surrealist writing and art in the early '40s.

Motherwell's involvement with Joyce has been recognized in the literature by his choice of a title for *The Homely Protestant* of 1948. He has described how this title was selected:

> I could not find a title for possibly my single most important "figure" painting. Then I remembered a Surrealist custom, viz, to take a favorite book and place one's finger at random in it. In either *Ulysses* or *Finnegans Wake* (I forget which), my finger rested on the words "the homely protestant. . . ."[4]

For the record, the title is located in a list of abusive phrases on page 71 of *Finnegans Wake*.[5] Motherwell's interest in Joyce continues to this day. It has been reported that he still "regularly dips back into *Ulysses*,"[6] and in recent years titles of a number of works, for example, *The River Liffey, Stephen's Iron Crown, Stephen's Gate* and *Bloom in Dublin*, carry Joycean references. Although the titles were assigned after the works were completed (that is, Joyce was not consciously on his mind while he was working), the choice of titles underscores Motherwell's perception, which he shared with a number of others of his generation, that Joyce's writing was relevant to the art they were creating.[7]

That the "simulated" automatism of Joyce's "stream of consciousness" writing ("simulated" because Joyce's prose actually is very carefully constructed) influenced artists is evidenced by Barnett Newman's activities in the mid-1940s. According to Thomas B. Hess, "he started to write fiction, influenced by Joyce's *Ulysses*, automatic writing, getting it down as fast as he could."[8] At the same time, Newman was creating a series of rapidly executed drawings and watercolors, no doubt influenced by the biomorphic marine imagery and automatist techniques of Surrealism, but equally as Joycean in spirit. The equation between automatism and aquatic imagery, which in Surrealism pertains to the preconscious or subconscious mind, is characteristic of Joyce's thinking as well.

Several of the most extended "stream of consciousness" mono-logues in *Ulysses* occur in Chapters III and XIII, in settings at the seashore. Chapter III, the "Proteus" episode, in particular, is a model for the merger of vividly fluid marine imagery and free asso-ciational thought. At the opening of this chapter we find these lines:

> Signatures of all things I am here to read, seaspawn and seawrack. the nearing tide. that rusty boot. Snotgreen, bluesilver, rust: coloured signs.[9]

The sea, which yields from its depths unexpected objects and signs, is easily recognized as analogous to the mind. Joyce was familiar with Freud's theories, incorporated them in his writings, and conse-quently, his works have encouraged a significant amount of Freud-ian interpretation.[10]

In one strikingly visual passage towards the end of Chapter III we read the following description:

> Under the upswelling tide he saw the writhing weeds lift languidly and sway reluctant arms, hissing up their petticoats, in whispering water swaying and upturning coy silver fronds . . . (*U.* 49:35–37).

Not only does this sound like a possible description of a poured painting by Jackson Pollock, but in Joyce's next paragraph we find the source for the title of one of Pollock's breakthrough pictures of 1947, the silver, green-blue, and white *Full Fathom Five* (Fig. 1). Al-though there is no minimizing the difficulties associated with attach-ing importance to titles in Abstract-Expressionist works, especially in Pollock's case, Pollock did admire Joyce's writings, and the liter-ary context in which the title of *Full Fathom Five* is found may have iconographical significance for the painting.

Lee Krasner has recalled that Joyce was one of Pollock's favorite authors.[11] His library contained *Stephen Hero, Ulysses,* and *Finnegans Wake.*[12] Betty Parsons, Pollock's early dealer, remembered that "he often talked about Joyce."[13] His neighbor in East Hampton, the art-ist Alfonso Ossorio, observed that Pollock "read *Finnegans Wake,* and you felt that he was in tune with the idea that one word could mean many things. . . . He loved the Joyce recordings of his collected works, the music of Joyce's voice."[14] Some who knew him, Fritz Bultman and B. H. Friedman, for example, feel that although Pol-lock was attracted to Joyce, he probably did not read deeply into the works. More likely, they believe, his occasional perusals of Joyce were greatly supplemented by the recordings and by friends such as Tony Smith, who as early as the '40s was known to quote large chunks of Joyce by heart.[15]

The title for *Full Fathom Five* is located in a passage which speaks of "a loose drift of rubble," quite befitting a painting that has embedded in its surface pebbles, nails, tacks, buttons, keys, coins, matches, and other debris:

> Five fathoms out there. Full fathom five thy father lies. At one he said. Found drowned. High water at Dublin bar. Driving before it a loose drift of rubble, fanshoals of fishes, silly shells. A corpse rising saltwhite from the undertow, bobbing landward, a pace a pace a porpoise. There he is. Hook it quick. Sunk though he be beneath the watery floor. We have him. Easy now (*U*, 50:4–10)

The poured paintings of 1947 were given titles after they were completed in picture-naming sessions with Pollock, Lee Krasner, and their neighbors in East Hampton, Ralph Manheim and his wife. It is generally agreed that most of the titles were supplied by Manheim. However, as B. H. Friedman has pointed out, Pollock had final approval of the titles, and they clearly convey a sense of his artistic ambitions and concerns.[16]

Could the passages which so aptly describe the color, movement, and "drift of rubble" in *Full Fathom Five* also provide a clue to its content? Citing Lee Krasner that Pollock once told her, "I choose to veil the imagery," Charles F. Stuckey finds in Pollock's poured paintings "images hidden or 'veiled' from sight by his webs. . . ."[17] He notes, "The titles Pollock chose for some of his non-representational canvases refer to spooky presences embedded in or hidden behind angled, nearly impervious barriers. . . ."[18] In the case of *Full Fathom Five* Stuckey could not have been more correct, although the source for the title was apparently unknown to him. It is provocative to consider the possibility that Pollock's title, whether initially his or not, provides evidence of hidden imagery, in this instance represented by a corpse "sunk though he be beneath the watery floor."

Alfonso Ossorio has commented on Pollock's interest in *Finnegans Wake*, and it is with this great book, first published in 1939, that the artist's work is most instructively compared. One Joyce critic, Clive Hart, has called *Finnegans Wake* "the most outstanding example of what can be done with objet trouvé collage in literature."[19] He sees Joyce's method as "strikingly similar" to twentieth-century painting techniques: "Bits and pieces are picked up and incorporated into the texture with little modification, while the precise nature of each individual fragment is not always of great importance."[20] Borrowing a term from Claude Levi-Strauss, Margot Norris describes Joyce's "practice of using bits and pieces of heterogeneous materials without regard to their specific function" as "bricolage."[21] The parallel is obvious with Pollock's amalgamation of materials in *Full Fathom Five*, allowing an assortment of foreign objects to retain their individuality, but a great deal of Pollock's work can be understood in terms of "bricolage."

As in the case of *Finnegans Wake*, which has been described as "essentialy visual . . . [t]here never was a book more cluttered with visual symbols,"[22] Pollock's pre-1947 paintings are dense with signs and symbols. Both writer and painter create complex worlds that evoke a sense of endless symbolic interplay. Pollock, as Ossorio noted, appreciated Joyce's use of portmanteau words, the conjoining of semantically dissimilar words to suggest multiple and contradictory meanings. These constructions provide a literary analogue to the artist's symbol-making tendencies. Pollock also must have been drawn to Joyce's use of words as material, which gave them an apparent quality of abstraction and autonomy. In a formal sense, a number of pre-1947 paintings, like Joyce's text, read as "parts placed side by side without transition, parts in a variety of rhythms, shapes and tones."[23] Pollock's friend, James Brooks, observed that:

> Joyce had a non-narrative style. What you were reading was right there. You're not waiting for something to come. I hated to leave a paragraph because I didn't need to go anywhere else. But his irreverence, his strange juxtaposition of things and unexpectedness was pretty much what we were after at that time. That was in the air.[24]

The "substitutionality of parts" and the "variability and uncertainty of structural and thematic elements" are features common to Joyce's book and Pollock's pre-1947 paintings. In both "meanings are dislocated—hidden in unexpected places, multiplied and split, given over to ambiguity, plurality, and uncertainty. . . . "[25] The element of unpredictability created by fluid symbolism and continually shifting relationships in *Finnegans Wake* and Pollock's earlier paintings is finally heightened and transformed by the artist's adoption of a radical automatist technique in the poured paintings of 1947–1952.

Margot Norris sees *Finnegans Wake* as "a decentered universe" in which "The formal elements of the work . . . are not anchored to a single point of reference, that is, they do not refer back to a center."[26] Simply put, this is what modern painters call allover composition, a concept with which Pollock is inseparably linked. Clement Greenberg, Pollock's critical champion in the '40s, noted in a 1948 essay that Joyce provides a literary parallel for "all-over" painting.[27] James Brooks observed that in *Finnegans Wake*, "The plot wasn't the important thing. You are not getting from one place to

another. But the whole book was spread out over an enormous ex-
panse."[28] It is conceivable that Pollock related this aspect of Joyce to
his own work.

Aside from any influence Joyce may have had on Pollock, the fun-
damental similarities between these men had profound significance
for twentieth-century literature and art. For both, the making of art,
the process of creation rather than the result, was the meaningful
part of the effort. As is frequently said about their respective en-
deavors, "everything is in a constant state of becoming."[29] Most importantly, in exploring the relationship between the conscious and
unconscious mind, they developed new languages which under-
mined traditional notions of artistic structure.[30] Like the letter in
Finnegans Wake, the book's principal "expanding symbol [which]
quickly comes to stand for the book itself,"[31] Pollock's painting:

> . . is not a miseffectual whyacinthinous riot of blots and blurs and bars
> and balls and hoops and wriggles and juxtaposed jottings linked by
> spurts of speed: it only looks as like it . . .(*FW*, 118:28–30).

David Smith frequently alluded to Joyce's writing and its relevance
to contemporary art, and a number of his comments have been recorded in the literature. In 1965, Robert Motherwell offered this recollection of Smith:

> I have known David Smith for twenty years, ever since that afternoon
> we met by prearrangement (but unknown to each other) during the
> 1940s . . . In those days I was full of French Symbolist aesthetics, of
> Rimbaud and Mallarmé, and of André Breton, of the possibilities of
> representing reality indirectly but passionately in one's medium. I can
> still see David saying, with his characteristic bluntness and inalterable
> sense of his own identity, "I don't need them. I've read James Joyce!"
> He was right, all of it *is* in *Ulysses,* and I looked at him with a sudden
> intellectual respect that has not yet diminished as my affection for him
> has continually grown.[32]

Smith, who had a dog named Finnegan,[33] recommended "the study
of Joyce's work, such as *Finnegans Wake*, wherein the use of words
and relationships function much as in the process of the creative
artist's mind."[34] Stanley Meltzoff reported in a 1946 essay, "One of
the sculptor's main influences was the appearance of 'Work in Progress' in *transition* [sic]."[35] He compared Smith's "sculptural use of
metamorphising objects" to Joyce's "literary use of the pun," and
observed that certain of his works "are as complicated as parts of
'Finnegans Wake' and as complete as a departure. . . . "[36]

Although a number of Smith's pieces have been compared to
Joyce's writing, only *The Letter* of 1950 can be directly related to the

author's work (Fig. 2). Referring to this sculpture, Smith told Thomas Hess, "That relates the Little Red Hen that scratched in Joyce . . . the Little Red Hen that scratched the letter up."[37] The letter, as previously noted, is the central symbol in *Finnegans Wake*, "a sprawling and somewhat formless motif-complex which . . . recurs in literally hundreds of places in more or less fragmentary form."[38] It is evident that Smith strongly identified with the writer and his symbol. He observed, "I'm always scratching up letters and that's one of the nice things about Joyce. There's a part of Joyce in me all my life."[39]

Rosalind Krauss sees *The Letter* as an assimilation of Joyce's symbol by reference to Adolph Gottlieb's pictorial structure in the "Pictograph" paintings.[40] Be that as it may, I find that the content and structure of *The Letter* reflect a very direct response to Joyce's text. It is true that there are numerous fragmentary references to the letter throughout *Finnegans Wake*, but it is quoted and described at some length in Chapter V where a number of descriptions are compellingly visual. Smith's sculpture, which in Krauss' words, "reads like a set of secret glyphs for which the viewer has no key,"[41] not only conveys the inscrutability of Joyce's discussion of the letter, but can be seen as a rather faithful representation of the writer's images:

> . . . ruled barriers, along which the traced words run, march, halt, walk, stumble at doubtful points, stumble up again in comparative safety . . . with lines of litters slittering up and loads of latters slettering down . . . (*FW*, 114:7-9, 17-18).

Or again, in Joyce's description of the letter previously quoted in connection with Pollock—"a miseffectual whyacinthinous riot of blots and blurs and bars and balls and hoops"—we find a possible source for Smith's Ys ("whyacinthinous"), Os ("balls and hoops"), and the lines ("bars") that Joyce earlier called "ruled barriers."[42]

Joyce's letter, comprised of letters, came from litter scratched up by the hen in a dump. Joyce informs us, "if you are abcedminded . . . what curios of signs in this "allaphbed" (*FW*, 18:17–18), and he asks, "will this kiribis pouch filled with litterish fragments lurk dormant in the pouch . . . .?" (*FW*, 66:25–26). Smith, who could not have failed to see the dump, or "allaphbed," as a symbol of the unconscious mind, said, "I don't differentiate between writing and drawing, not since I read that part of Joyce."[43] However, *The Letter*, and *17 h's and 24 Greek Y's* of the same year, can quite literally be seen to have come from an "allaphbed" since the steel letters that Smith used were part of an assortment of junk metal he bought from a hardware dealer.[44] Like Joyce and Pollock. Smith was one of the great "bricoleurs" of the century, making "bricolage" out of a personalized, fragmented symbolism and bits and scraps of material.

Joyce the "bricoleur" is displayed in *Ulysses* and *Finnegans Wake*. His earlier novel, *A Portrait of the Artist* as a *Young Man*, although containing some elements of the later works, propounds an aesthetic antithetical to the concept of bricolage. In Chapter V, Stephen Dedalus advocates what "amounts to a theory of impersonality and autonomy . . . a theory of art for art's sake . . . [a] static contemplative art."[45] Joyce had an audience for these ideas also. In a 1953 article Thomas Hess noted that "[Ad] Reinhardt enjoys the phrasing of Joyce—young Stephen's trinity of wholeness, radiance and harmony. . . ."[46] On another occasion, Hess observed that many of Reinhardt's illustrated art satires were strongly influenced by Joyce's later writings.[47] An obvious example is found in the title of one of the better-known art jokes, "A Portend of the Artist as a Yhung Mandala," where the author's early title is conjoined with the punning word play of *Finnegans Wake*. It is worthy of note that Hess recorded Reinhardt's appreciation of Stephen Dedalus' aesthetics at the time the artist's work was evolving from relational compositions emphasizing shape, value, and color contrasts to the monochromatic pictures that culminated in the "Black Paintings". I do not mean to infer a crucial connection between Joyce and Reinhardt, only that this aspect of the writer's work may have had some influence on Reinhardt's thinking, or at the least reinforced it.

In a discussion with a friend, young Stephen translates Aquinas' "*Ad pulcritudinem tria requiruntur integritas, consonantia, claritas*" as "Three things are needed for beauty, wholeness, harmony and radiance" (*AP*, 248: 18–21), and then explains his theory of art at length:

> . . .the esthetic image is first luminously apprehended as selfbounded and selfcontained . . . You apprehend it as *one* thing. You see it as one whole. You apprehend its wholeness. That is *integritas* (*AP*, 249:5–10).
> . . . immediate perception is followed by the analysis of apprehension. Having first felt that it is *one* thing you feel now that is a *thing*. You apprehend it as complex, multiple, divisible, separable, made up of its parts and their sum, harmonious. That is *consonantia* (*AP*, 249:16–21).
>
> The instant wherein that supreme quality of beauty, the clear radiance of the esthetic image, is apprehended luminously by the mind which has been arrested by its wholeness and fascinated by its harmony is the luminous silent stasis of esthetic pleasure. . . .(*AP*, 250:12–17).

The process of perception that Joyce has Stephen describe matches the experience of many viewers of Reinhardt's "Black Paintings." The writer who has best described the gradual recognition of structure in Reinhardt's later works is Lucy Lippard. She has written:

> On entering a room with one or more black paintings, one has a first impression of only the most general nature. One sees a black square hanging on the wall . . . After a period of looking at the dull glow, one begins to perceive the nonblackness . . . the extremely muted colors begin to emerge, and with them, but lagging a little, comes the trisection [of the surface].[48]

Lippard has given us, without making the association, an excellent description of Stephen's *integritas* and *consonantia*. But what of *claritas*, radiance? Once again, Lippard writes:

> Reinhardt's development from around 1949 to 1960 traces the process of draining color from light, so that in the last works, light practically replaced color . . . Black, white and gray are called achromatic colors though black is caused by a complete absorption of color. A high degree of light absorbence is not the same as total absence of light. The light has been taken in rather than rejected, the opaque surfaces have paradoxically become transparent containers of light.[49]

Sidney Tillim observed the same phenomenon, stating that "Darkness in Reinhardt's painting is a form of light, not illumination of chiaroscuro but an aspect of form—what might be called total light."[50] Reinhardt intentionally created this effect, thinning his paint and superimposing layer upon layer of color to get "not colored light" as Reinhardt wrote to Sam Hunter, "but color that gives off light."[51]

Not only do Reinhardt's "Black Paintings" provide a visual demonstration of Stephen Dedalus' wholeness, harmony and radiance, but Joyce and Reinhardt agree on the subject of the artist's presence in a work of art. Joyce has Stephen say, "The personality of the artist . . . finally refines itself out of existence, impersonalizes itself . . . remains within or behind or beyond or above his handiwork, invisible, refined out of existence" (*AP*, 252:15–23). Reinhardt's opinion of artists expressing themselves is well known, but on one occasion he said simply, "The less an artist obtrudes himself in his painting, the purer and clearer his aims."[52]

Tony Smith was perhaps the biggest fan of Joyce's writings. Although he came into prominence as a sculptor in the 1960s, he was a friend and colleague in the '40s of Newman, Rothko, Pollock. and other artists of the first generation New York School. Irish, with a Jesuit education, and an artist, Tony Smith strongly identified with

Joyce.[53] He was always ready to quote Joyce, and frequently related his work to the writer's. He once cited *A Portrait of the Artist as a Young Man* as one source of his interest in mazes.[54] Although Stephen's family name is similar to that of Daedalus, the mythological maze-maker, *Ulysses* and especially *Finnegans Wake* would seem to offer more obvious examples of labyrinthian structures. At one point Smith speculated on inflatable sculpture which he related to Surrealism, topology, and to the writings of Joyce.[55] He was interested in all of Joyce's major works, and seems to have assimilated them in his sculpture.

In some instances, Smith's work provides a three-dimensional exposition of Stephen's ideas. A piece such as *Amaryllis* of 1965, for example, initially appears to consist of simple forms quickly grasped. However, it can not be understood from a single vantage point. Made of two truncated prisms, the sculpture's appearance and impact change with each viewpoint. Smith, with a down-to-earth illustration, succinctly paraphrases Stephen's discussion of wholeness, harmony, and radiance:

> I'm interested in the inscrutability and the mysteriousness of the thing. Something obvious on the face of it . . . is of no further interest. A Bennington earthenware jar, for instance, has subtlety of color, largeness of form, a general suggestion of substance . . . It continues to nourish us time and time again. We can't see it in a second, we continue to read it.[56]

Smith's *Wandering Rocks* (1967) derives its name from the "phantom" chapter heading of Chapter X in *Ulysses*. Any serious reader of Joyce, of which Smith was one, knows that he assigned to each episode of his novel a heading based on a Homeric reference, and these titles are employed in discussions of *Ulysses* in the Joyce literature. Since there are no wandering rocks in Homer's *Odyssey*, except by allusion, the title of Smith's sculpture is undoubtedly Joycean, as is the spirit of the work. In Chapter X, an assortment of Dubliners, named and described, come into contact, pass each other, and continue their perambulations around the city. They are, as William York Tindall says, "connected with others, but arbitrarily and by temporal coincidence alone." He observes that "human elements, like parts of fractured atoms, collide, part, go separate ways . . . Related by time and place, they lack vital relationship."[57] So it is with Smith's sculpture. Each of the five pieces is different and individually named (Smohawk, Crocus, Slide, Shaft, and Dud), yet as six-sided prisms they share a familial relationship. Viewed from numerous vantage points, with the possibility, encouraged by the sculptor, of each installation being different, Smith's sculpture communicates those elements of unpredictability, simultaneity, connectedness and disconnectedness that Joyce examined in "The Wandering Rocks" episode.

The title of Smith's *Gracehoper* (1962–72) is an explicit reference to Joyce's fable of the "Ondt and Gracehoper" in Chapter XIII of *Finnegans Wake*. According to Joyce:

> The Gracehoper was always jigging ajog, hoppy on akkant of his joyicity, (he had a partner pair of findlestilts to supplant him), or if not, he was always making ungraceful overtures. . . . He would of curse melissciously, by his fore feelhers, flexors, contractors, depressors, and extensors, lamely. . . . (*FW*, 414:22–24, 29–31).[58]

Smith's looming, lumbering sculpture is aptly named after Joyce's Gracehoper. The question is, did he have the creature in mind when he was making the piece, or for that matter, was he consciously thinking of the chapter in *Ulysses* when he was working on *Wandering Rocks*? In Smith's case, a man whose thinking was pervaded by Joyce, who committed extensive portions of Joyce to memory, and who frequently related his work to Joyce's writing, it is almost a chicken-or-egg question. It is safe to say that his sculpture reflects a significant involvement with Joyce's images and ideas.

Tony Smith frequently put sculpture together like Joyce wrote prose. For instance, *Willy* (1969) is made up of parts from several sculptures, and *P.N.* (1969) is a piece of a model from another work enlarged and turned upside down.[59] This way of working is not uncommon in twentieth-century art, but with Smith the comparison to Joyce seems inescapable. He is related to the other "bricoleurs" of his generation, who, to one degree or another, absorbed and reconstituted Joyce's methods in the creation of expressive visual objects.

A number of artists undoubtedly identified with *A Portrait of the Artist as a Young Man*. Echoes of Stephen Dedalus can be discerned in the pronouncements of members of the first generation New York School. Motherwell's statement in the '50s that the aim of Abstract Expressionism "was to forge a whole new language of painting,"[60] as Phil Patton has noted, is reminiscent of Stephen's desire to forge "the uncreated conscience of my race." Stephen's view of the artist as "a priest of the eternal imagination, transmuting the daily bread of experience into the radiant body of everlasting life" (*AP*, 260:1–3), finds a counterpart in Motherwell's claim that "abstract art is a form of mysticism . . . one's effort to wed oneself to the universe, to unify oneself through union."[61] The polemical nature of Ad Reinhardt's various writings has more than a little suggestion of Stephen's confident aesthetic discourse. As Nathan Halper, a Joyce scholar and one-time art dealer, sees it, Joyce, because of the life he led and the radical explorations he made, became "a sort of patron saint" of avant-garde artists in the '40s and '50s.[62] Certainly, for these painters and sculptors Joyce stood as a convincing example, a symbol, in fact, of the modern artist, his work and vision.

An abbreviated version of this essay similarly titled was presented as a paper in the Second Annual Symposium on Contemporary Art, Fashion Institute of Technology, New York City, April 30, 1982.

Notes

1. Joyce's name has been invoked every so often in discussions of Abstract Expressionism, but usually as simple comparison, not in terms of concrete relationships. Thomas B. Hess spoke of "the Joycean addition of ambiguity employed by De Kooning," "Is Abstraction Un-American?" *Art News*, vol. XLIX, no. 10, February, 1951, p. 41; Ethel K. Schwabacher saw Gorky's "composite structures" developing "in the direction of James Joyce's elaborate analogies," *Arshile Gorky*, New York, 1957, p. 126; and Karen Wilken, "Adolph Gottlieb: The Pictographs," *Art International*. vol. XXI/6, December, 1977, p. 28, observed that the literary equivalent of Gottlieb's pictographic images "would be the portmanteau word coinages of James Joyce, with their superimposed layers of meaning . . . .but in the cases of all three there is little evidence of a special interest in Joyce."

2. Christopher B. Crosman and Nancy E. Miller, "Speaking of Tomlin," *Art Journal*, Winter 1979/80, vol. XXXIX/2 p. 114; from an interview with Brooks and Ibram Lassaw, East Hampton, New York, September 5, 1975.

3. H.H. Arnason, "On Robert Motherwell and his Early Work." *Art International*, vol. X/1, January 20, 1966, p. 19.

4. H.H. Arnason, *Robert Motherwell*, New York, 1977, p. 103.

5. My page and line references are to The Viking Press editions of *Finnegans Wake*, first published in New York in 1939, which henceforth, as a citation in the text, will be referred to as *FW*.

6. Phil Patton, "Robert Motherwell; The Mellowing of an Angry Young Man," *Art News*, vol. 81, no. 3, March, 1982, p. 76.

7. This perception is demonstrated by the invitation to Nathan Halper, author of several articles on Joyce in the late '40s and early '50s, and later an art dealer, to speak about Joyce at The Club, the artists' club that was first established in 1949 at 39 East 8th Street, and which then moved to various addresses in the '50s. In a March 10, 1982 letter to the author, Halper recalled; "Early in the '50s, I was not as yet involved in the art world; but living in the Village, I would meet some of the painters. When they found that I had published a few articles on Joyce, I was asked to give a talk about him to The Club. Not about Joyce and painting or sculpture—but Joyce in general. It was felt that he was relevant." Joyce was also the subject of a seminar held during "Forum '49," an exhibition in Provincetown, Massachusetts in the summer of 1949 that included the work of Pollock, Baziotes, Rothko, Tomlin and Pousette-Dart, among others.

8. Thomas B. Hess, *Barnett Newman*, Museum of Modern Art, New York, 1971, p. 43. The artist's *Ulysses*, 1952, according to Hess (p. 82). "probably is Newman tipping his hat to James Joyce, one of his first heroes."

9. I am using the Random House, 1961 edition of *Ulysses*, p. 37, lines 2–4. Henceforth, as a citation in the text, this work will be referred to as *U*.

10. Dore Ashton, *The New York School: A Cultural Reckoning*, New York, 1972, p. 37, states: "Literary enthusiasts were actively linking their favorite writers with Freudian theories. James Joyce, for instance, was immediately perceived to be a stream-of-consciousness exemplar of Freud's speculations . . . Already in the bohemian circles of the immediate postwar period Freud was as potent a subject as cubism, Ezra Pound, and Joyce's *Ulysses* (then being published in installments in *The Little Review*)."

11. Francis Valentine O'Connor and Eugene Victor Thaw. *Jackson Pollock, A Catalogue Raisonné of Paintings, Drawings, and Other Work*, New Haven and London, p. 193:IV.

12. *Ibid.*

13. Francine Du Plessix and Cleve Gray, "Who Was Jackson Pollock," *Art in America*, vol. 55, no. 3, May-June, 1967, p. 55. Betty Parsons' interview was reprinted in B.H. Friedman, *Jackson Pollock: Energy Made Visible*, New York, 1972, pp. 181–182.

14. Du Plessix and Gray, p. 58.

15. Conversation with Fritz Bultman and B. H. Friedman, February 27, 1982 in New York City. Bultman and Friedman also men-

tioned Weldon Kees, the poet-painter, one of the "Irascible Eighteen," as a great transmitter and enthusiast of Joyce in the '40s and early '50s.

16. Friedman, *Jackson Pollock . . . .* p. 120. Lee Krasner has stated that some of the titles were Pollock's, although she can not recall which ones. See Judith Wolfe, "Jungian Aspects of Jackson Pollock's Imagery," *Artforum*, vol. XI, no. 3, November, 1972, pp. 72, 73 note 41.

17. Charles F. Stuckey, "Another Side of Jackson Pollock," *Art in America*, vol. 65, no. 6, November-December, 1977, pp. 84, 86.

18. *Ibid.*, p. 88.

19. Clive Hart, *Structure and Motif in Finnegans Wake*, Evanston, Illinois, 1962, p. 34.

20. *Ibid.*, pp. 34–35. Critics of Joyce on a number of occasions have compared his writing to the visual arts. Frank Budgen, a painter, friend of Joyce's, and one of his early critics, in *James Joyce and the Making of Ulysses*, Bloomington, Indiana, 1960 (reprint of 1934 edition). pp. 91–92, writes that Joyce's method of internal monologue "is more like impressionist painting. The shadows are full of colour; the whole is built up out of nuances instead of being constructed in broad masses; things are seen as immersed in a luminous fluid, colour supplies the modelling, and the total effect is arrived at through a countless number of small touches. . . ." A more recent critic, William York Tindall, *A Reader's Guide to James Joyce*, New York, 1959, p. 238, says, "To proceed from *Ulysses* to *Finnegans Wake* is like proceeding from a picture by Cezanne to a recent abstraction. In the absence of identifiable surface, we must make what we can of blots, blurs, and scratches, patiently awaiting the emergence of an order which, though there maybe, is not immediately visible."

21. Margot Norris, *The Decentered Universe of Finnegans Wake*, Baltimore and London, 1974, p. 130.

22. Hart, p. 37.

23. Tindall, p. 37. Norris, p. 131, associates the habit of mind that produces "bricolage" with the compiling of voluminous notebooks. She reports that Joyce's notebooks were "crammed with list upon list of apparently unrelated words, phrases, snatches of thought, and bits of data." Pollock, too, filled numerous notebooks, particularly in the '30s, and made countless sketches.

24. Crosman and Miller, p. 114. Many of the syllable combinations that Brooks puts together to create titles for his paintings have a Joycean flavor.

25. Norris, p. 7.

26. *Ibid*, p. 120.

27. Clement Greenberg. "The Crisis of the Easel Painting." *Art and Culture*, Boston, 1961, p. 157. Reprinted from an essay in *Partisan Review*, April, 1948, Greenberg also mentions Gertrude Stein, Ezra Pound, and Dylan Thomas as other parallels in literature.

28. Crosman and Miller, p. 114.

29. See Hart, pp. 50–51, for a discussion of process in Joyce.

30. Joyce's and Pollock's works constitute an attack on the traditional concept of structure. Norris, p. 121, discussing Joyce, notes that "This attack was not isolated, but belonged to an 'event' or 'rupture' in the history of the concept of structure, which, according to philosopher Jacques Derrida, took place in the history of thought sometime in the late nineteenth or early twentieth centuries . . . The 'rupture' . . . results in the idea of a structure in which presence is not so much absent as unlocatable."

31. Hart, p. 200.

32. Frank O'Hara, *Robert Motherwell*, Museum of Modern Art, 1965, p. 56; excerpt from Robert Motherwell, "A Major American Sculptor: David Smith," *Vogue*, February 1, 1965.

33. Rosalind E. Krauss. *Terminal Iron Works*, Cambridge, Massachusetts, 1971, p. 139, note 16. Jackson Pollock had a dog named Ahab in appreciation of Herman Melville. The bestowal on these canines of names derived from literary sources suggests the amusing possibility of a study of pet names among artists as an index of their cultural interests.

34. Garnett McCoy (ed.), *David Smith*, New York, Washington, 1973, p. 64. From a talk titled "What I Believe About the Teaching of Sculpture," Midwestern University Art Conference, Louisville, Kentucky, October 27, 1950.

35. Stanley Meltzoff, "David Smith and Social Surrealism," *Magazine of Art*, vol. 39, no. 3, March, 1946, p. 100. Portions of *Work in Progress*, the working drafts for *Finnegans Wake*, appeared in seventeen issues of the journal *transition* between 1927 and 1938.

36. *Ibid*, p. 101.

37. McCoy, p. 180. Reprinted from Thomas B. Hess, "The Secret Letter," *David Smith*, exhibition catalogue, Marlborough-Gerson Gallery, New York, 1964.

38. Hart, p. 182.

39. McCoy, p. 180.

40. Krauss, p. 136, note 16.

41. *Ibid.*, p. 84.

42. Edward Fry, *David Smith*, The Solomon R. Guggenheim Mu-

seum, New York 1969, p. 62, offers the following interpretation of *The Letter*. "The imagery in the words of his sculptural letter includes the schematic interior of a house, a running man, and a hermit crab; and Smith's reply, couched in Joycean verbal-visual puns was thus the question of why o why did he ever leave Ohio."

43. McCoy, from Hess' "The Secret Letter," p. 185.

44. Krauss, pp. 136, 139.

45. Tindall, pp. 95–96. I will be quoting The Modern Library, Random House, 1928 edition of *A Portrait of the Artist* as a *Young Man*; henceforth, as a citation in the text, it will be referred to as *AP*.

46. Thomas B. Hess, "Reinhardt: The Position and Perils of Purity," *Art News*, vol. 52, no. 8, December, 1953, p. 59. Hess adds that for Reinhardt, "even this verge toward the soul and essences of Celtic hokum." In a telephone conversation March 27, 1982, Rita Reinhardt confirmed that her husband had read and enjoyed Joyce, and she vaguely recalled discussions about Joyce, who she noted, was the subject of conversations among many artists and intellectuals in the '40s and '50s. She also said that had Hess been inaccurate in his writing, Reinhardt would have corrected any misrepresentations in print.

47. Thomas B. Hess, "The Art Comics of Ad Reinhardt," *Artforum*, vol. XII, no. 8 April, 1974, p. 47. Hess wrote, "The twin heroes of this effort [the art satires] . . . were Joyce and Beckett. The spirit of the former presides over Reinhardt's lust for cataloguing and naming everything in the world. . . . You hear Joyce in the tropes, oxymorons, onomatopoeia and alliterations, in the lilt of the language, in the dirty jokes, plays on names, scholarly, almost pedantic references."

48. Lucy R. Lippard, "Ad Reinhardt: One Work," *Art in America*, vol. 62, no. 6 November-December, 1974, pp. 96–97.

49. *Ibid.*, pp. 97–98.

50. Sidney Tillim, "Ad Reinhardt," *Arts Magazine*, vol. 33, no. 5, February, 1959, p. 54.

51. Letter to Sam Hunter, Summer, 1966, cited in Margit Rowell, *Ad Reinhardt and Color*, The Solomon R. Guggenheim Museum, New York, 1980, p. 21.

52. Ad Reinhardt, "Twelve Rules for a New Academy," *Art News*, vol. 56, no. 3. May, 1957, p. 38.

53. Smith's special attraction to Joyce was described to me by Fritz Bultman in a conversation on July 16, 1981 in Provincetown, Massachusetts. *A Portrait of the Artist* as a *Young Man*, of course, is largely involved with the Jesuit education of an aspiring artist.

54. A letter from Tony Smith, October, 1975, in "Janet Kardon Interviews Some Modern Maze-makers," *Art International*, vol. XX/4–5, April-May, 1976, p. 65.

55. Lucy R. Lippard, "Diversity in Unity: Recent Geometricizing Styles." *Art since Mid-Century: The New Internationalism*, Greenwich, Connecticut, 1971, p. 247.

56. Samuel Wagstaff, Jr., "Talking with Tony Smith," *Artforum*, vol. 5, no. 4, December, 1966, p. 18.

57. Tindall, p. 180.

58. Eleanor Green, "The Morphology of Tony Smith's Work," *Artforum*, vol. XII, no 8, April, 1974, pp. 55–56, quotes a section of this passage and parts of others (416: 8–13, 26–30) in relation to *Gracehoper* and briefly discusses the connection between Joyce and Smith.

59. Lucy R. Lippard, "Interview with Tony Smith," *Tony Smith: Recent Sculpture*, exhibition catalogue, M. Knoedler & Co., New York, 1971, pp. 9, 19.

60. Patton, p. 75.

61. Robert Motherwell, "What Abstract Art Means to Me," *Museum of Modern Art Bulletin*, vol. 18, no. 3, Spring, 1951, pp. 12–13.

62. Letter to the author, March 10, 1982. Halper feels that perhaps "Motherwell and Tony Smith were the only ones to do more than make an obligatory dip into the waters" of Joyce, but his perspective is that of a Joyce scholar.

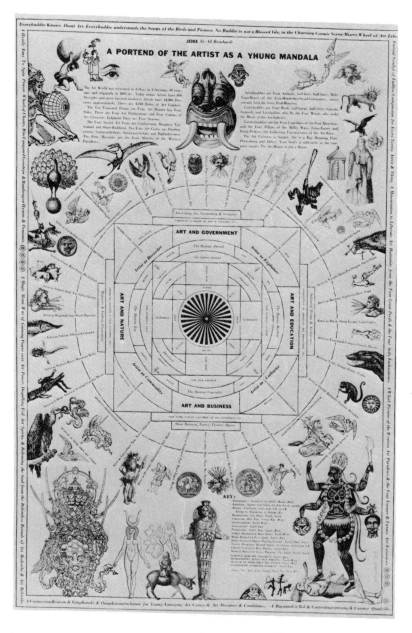

This Joycean cartoon, Ad Reinhardt's A Portend of the Artist as a Jhung Mandala, is the culmination of a series of graphic commentaries made by the artist in the 1950s. (© Anna Reinhardt. Courtesy of Pace Gallery)